www.wadsworth.com

www.wadsworth.com is the World Wide Web site for Wadsworth and is your direct source to dozens of online resources.

At *www.wadsworth.com* you can find out about supplements, demonstration software, and student resources. You can also send email to many of our authors and preview new publications and exciting new technologies.

www.wadsworth.com
Changing the way the world learns®

Mississippi Freedom Summer

John F. McClymer
Assumption College

THOMSON

WADSWORTH

Australia • Canada • Mexico • Singapore • Spain • United Kingdom • United States

THOMSON
WADSWORTH

Executive Editor: Clark Baxter
Senior Assistant Editor: Julie Yardley
Editorial Assistant: Eno Sarris
Technology Project Manager: Jennifer Ellis
Marketing Manager: Caroline Croley
Marketing Assistant: Mary Ho
Advertising Project Manager: Tami Strang
Project Manager, Editorial Production: Catherine Morris

Print/Media Buyer: Karen Hunt
Permissions Editor: Sommy Ko
Production Service: Shepherd, Inc.
Copy Editor: Michelle Livingston
Cover Designer: Preston Thomas
Cover Image: © Bettmann/CORBIS
Compositor: Shepherd, Inc.
Text and Cover Printer: Webcom

Printed in Canada

1 2 3 4 5 6 7 07 06 05 04 03

For more information about our products, contact us at:
Thomson Learning Academic Resource Center
1-800-423-0563
For permission to use material from this text, contact us by:
Phone: 1-800-730-2214
Fax: 1-800-730-2215
Web: http://www.thomsonrights.com

Library of Congress Cataloging-in-Publication Data

McClymer, John F.
  Mississippi freedom summer / John F. McClymer.—1st ed.
    p. cm.—(American stories series)
  ISBN: 0-534-62131-7
  I. Title. II. Series.

2003105926

Wadsworth/Thomson Learning
10 Davis Drive
Belmont, CA 94002-3098
USA
http://www.wadsworth.com

Asia
Thomson Learning
5 Shenton Way #01-01
UIC Building
Singapore 068808

Australia/New Zealand
Thomson Learning
102 Dodds Street
Southbank, Victoria 3006
Australia

Canada
Nelson
1120 Birchmount Road
Toronto, Ontario M1K 5G4
Canada

Europe/Middle East/Africa
Thomson Learning
High Holborn House
50/51 Bedford Row
London WC1R 4LR
United Kingdom

Latin America
Thomson Learning
Seneca, 53
Colonia Polanco
11560 Mexico D.F.
Mexico

Spain/Portugal
Paraninfo
Calle/Magallanes, 25
28015 Madrid, Spain

*For John Wholey and the
many other students who have
contributed to my education*

Contents

An army invaded Mississippi during the "Freedom Summer" of 1964. After a week of training in the North, hundreds of volunteers—white and black, many of them college students—fanned out across the state. Working with Student Non-Violent Coordinating Committee (SNCC) field-workers and local volunteers, they helped organize voting registration drives, opened schools and clinics, and attracted enormous attention from the national media. They also attracted bitter hostility from local whites. This book tells their story.

The summer of 1964 witnessed the most astounding successes of the Civil Rights movement and also the beginning of the dissolution of the political and social coalition that made those successes possible. The invasion was the most-effective campaign ever launched against segregation; it produced the most-effective cooperation ever among African Americans and white sympathizers; and it generated overwhelming political pressure on the national government finally to shoulder its responsibility to protect the rights, including voting rights, of all its citizens. These rights were supposedly guaranteed by the Fourteenth and Fifteenth Amendments, adopted nearly a century earlier. It would take the Civil Rights Act of 1964 and the Voting Rights Act of 1965 to make them realities. The invaders helped local African Americans counter the "whites-only" primary in Mississippi—a system the Supreme Court had held unconstitutional two decades earlier but which still held sway—with the creation of the Mississippi Freedom Democratic Party. The Freedom Party, composed overwhelmingly of poor blacks, over the next several years improbably succeeded in replacing the so-called regular Democratic Party in the State.

The invasion culminated in a battle in Atlantic City in August at the Democratic National Convention. Both the "regular" Mississippi Democrats and the Freedom Party sent delegations. At the behest of Lyndon Johnson, the national party offered the Freedom Party two at-large seats. It also promised to ban whites-only delegations in the future but would seat the regulars this time. It was a "compromise" that outraged civil rights activists and that white supremacists spurned.

Even as the Freedom Summer marked the climax of the Civil Rights movement, it also marked the emergence of a "Black Power" ideology within SNCC, the very organization which so brilliantly coordinated the energies of blacks and whites in the Mississippi Delta. At the very moment the Johnson Administration was passing the strongest civil rights legislation in almost a century, the Mississippi volunteers who did so much to bring that about were deciding that they could not trust the system. A New Left emerged, fueled by this distrust, at the very moment "the system" finally began to respond.

Triumphs, tragedies, and ironies abound in the story of the Freedom Summer. To understand how so much could happen in so short a time, it is necessary to appreciate what white Mississippians meant when they proudly called their state "the most southern place on earth." Mississippi was the poorest state and the most segregated. Its politicians were the most openly racist, no small distinction in the first half of the 1960s. Its state government funded a white supremacist agency, the Sovereignty Commission, charged with opposing desegregation. White Citizens Councils, comprised of leading businessmen and professionals, organized local resistance to civil rights. The Ku Klux Klan carried on the state's terrible tradition of violence against African Americans who tried to claim their rights as citizens. Yet civil rights activists believed that, if they could succeed in Mississippi, they could bring down the entire edifice of segregation across the nation, hence their willingness to risk life and limb in so dangerous and difficult a place.

SNCC began its Mississippi campaign in 1961 when Robert Moses, a schoolteacher from New York, moved into the state. Working in the Delta, and elsewhere in Mississippi, meant living in a war zone. At night, when SNCC field-workers found themselves driving along lonely two-lane roads, the set of headlights in the rearview mirror might signal an attack by "night riders." These were white supremacists carrying on the practice of the KKK to terrorize or kill blacks who "don't know their place." Walking into a courthouse on a bright morning to help someone register to vote could, and usually did, cause a hostile crowd to gather. Someone in the crowd was sure to hurl racial insults; often SNCC and other civil rights workers were pushed and punched, sometimes beaten into unconsciousness. Late some evenings cars and trucks, with their headlights off, would circle SNCC offices. Shots sometimes rang out. If scare tactics did not succeed, white racists turned to violence, including murder. In 1963, Medgar Evers, head of the Mississippi branch of the National Association for the Advancement of Colored People (NAACP), was assassinated in his driveway as he returned from work.[1]

Living with constant danger over a period of years took a tremendous toll on SNCC and other civil rights activists. Federal indifference made it worse. Federal Bureau of Investigation agents routinely ignored threats and acts of violence against civil rights workers, even though such acts violated federal law. Instead agents continued to cooperate actively with local sheriffs and deputies who were often among the most violent and dangerous white supremacists. For white and black volunteers alike Mississippi was a school in disillusionment, altogether too good a school in a state otherwise known for the low quality of its educational institutions. In it SNCC field-workers and many of their white allies learned to distrust the national government, even as they succeeded in generating much of the national pressure that led to the Civil Rights Act of 1964 and the Voting Rights Act of 1965. They also learned to distrust each other. Thus the terrible ironies. Those who most effectively demonstrated the power of a multiracial approach turned to Black Power and separation. Those who forced the system to work as it was supposed to lost their faith in the ability of people like themselves to influence it.

We continue to live with the outcomes, for good and for ill, of that summer. The story begins earlier, however, with the reelection campaign of Senator Theodore Bilbo in 1946 and the first attempt to achieve voting rights for African Americans in the state, recounted in the "Prologue."

Historians and political scientists do not routinely rate senators the way they do presidents. If they did, Theodore Bilbo might well be chosen as the worst senator in American history. Certainly he was the worst of his time. The self-proclaimed "Prince of the Peckerwoods," a local colloquialian for rednecks, a redneck, Bilbo reviled African Americans while proclaiming himself their "real" friend. But he also poured abuse upon Catholics, Jews, immigrants, Eleanor Roosevelt, the British, and

---

[1]On June 12, 1963, a sniper hid in the honeysuckle bushes near the Evers' driveway and shot Evers in the back. His two small children, awakened by the noise, saw him die. The police arrested white supremacist Byron De la Beckwith. His fingerprints were found on the murder weapon. Two white policemen provided him with an alibi, testifying they saw him in Greenwood, Mississippi, 60 miles away from the Evers home.

Byron De la Beckwith was acquitted twice in 1964 by all-white juries. Mississippi Governor Ross Barnett personally congratulated him on his acquittal. Thirty years later a jury of blacks and whites in Hinds County, Mississippi, found Beckwith guilty of murder. He was sentenced to life in prison where he died in 2001 at the age of 80.

numerous other targets. He was profane; he was corrupt. He was, colleagues on both sides of the aisle believed, a disgrace to the Senate.

In 1946 he sought reelection, a matter of winning Mississippi's whites-only Democratic primary since the Republicans would not bother to contest the race. The United States Supreme Court had recently declared whites-only primaries unconstitutional, and a group of black Mississippians, mostly veterans of World War II, decided to challenge Bilbo's election. Among the challengers were Medgar Evers and his brother, Charles. As noted above, Medgar Evers would go on to head the Mississippi chapter of the NAACP until his assassination in 1963. Charles would then succeed his brother.

Just as the Senate was about to organize a hearing on the suitability of Theodore Bilbo taking his seat as the senior senator from Mississippi in January 1947, his cancer flared up. Bilbo left Washington for a hospital in New Orleans. The Senate determined to do nothing until his health improved enough for him to attend the hearing. Instead Bilbo died. The question of election violations became moot.

Bilbo's victory had been challenged by a group of African American veterans on the grounds that he had incited whites to use violence to keep black voters away from the polls. The Supreme Court had already ruled Mississippi's whites-only primary was unconstitutional. Bilbo's often profane calls for whites to "visit" potential black voters on the night before election was, the veterans charged, a clear violation of both the Fourteenth and Fifteenth Amendments. Bilbo gloried in his membership in the Ku Klux Klan. Everyone in the state knew what a Klansman meant by a "visit" to blacks who tried to vote.

Nor was that the only strike against Bilbo. A Senate committee, investigating allegations that he had traded votes for contributions, found there was sufficient evidence to sustain the charge. Moreover, 1946 had proven a Republican year. Senator Robert A. Taft—son of the former president and chief justice, William Howard Taft—a stalwart conservative, was the new majority leader. He and the rest of the Republicans in the Senate were eager to get rid of Bilbo. So were a significant number of northern Democrats, despite their need for every vote. The reason for this bipartisan majority was simple. Its members viewed Bilbo as a disgrace to the Senate. He had answered objections to his use of anti-Semitic terms from the B'nai B'rith with an open letter addressed to "Dear Kike." He had also penned a public "Dear Dago" letter to Italian Americans. He had denounced everyone with whom he disagreed as a "niggah-loving Communist." He cited *Time* publisher Henry Luce's support for Republicans in the 1946 Senate races as "proof" of his Communist leanings and branded those, like Eleanor

Roosevelt, who worked for racial equality as not only "Communists" but also traitors to their white blood.

At the same time he boasted of how he used his political position to avoid paying taxes, of the luxurious home he had constructed, even of his ability to get any white Mississippian who was arrested in Washington out of jail. Most of his fellow senators despised him. Now his political fate was in their hands. A preliminary vote against a potential filibuster by other Deep South Democrats to block the hearing showed that the challenge to Bilbo's election would succeed. Instead his illness led first to the hearing's postponement and then to its cancellation.

Historians rarely pay much attention to cancelled events, but this is a case in which we should. Had Bilbo's cancer spread more slowly, a bipartisan majority led by Republicans would have endorsed the cause of a group of previously disenfranchised African Americans. A voting rights drive in Mississippi might well have begun in 1947, under federal scrutiny, in tandem with the special election to replace the self-proclaimed "Prince of the Peckerwoods."

Such a majority did not form. A voting rights drive in Mississippi would have to wait for another generation. And the whites-only primary continued without effective challenge until the 1960s, despite the Supreme Court's ruling against it. Instead of Republicans taking the lead, northern Democrats became the chief supporters of civil rights. Historically, the issue had belonged to the Republicans, when anyone had chosen to champion it. The Democrats were the party of the "solid South," the party of segregation and Jim Crow. True, Franklin Delano Roosevelt had yielded to the threat of an African American march on Washington during World War II to create the Fair Employment Practices Commission (FEPC), which was designed to give blacks equal employment opportunities as well as equal pay. Bilbo had led the opposition. But the FEPC was not in itself enough to make civil rights a Democratic issue. Had a Republican-led bipartisan majority invalidated Bilbo's election, the politics of civil rights over the succeeding decades would have been very different.

As it was, President Truman took the next important step by issuing an executive order integrating the military in 1948. Many inside and outside the armed forces howled in protest. As commander in chief, however, Truman did not need congressional authorization. Further, at the 1948 Democratic Convention, Minneapolis Mayor Hubert H. Humphrey led a successful effort to insert a civil rights plank into the party platform. In 1964, ironically, Lyndon Johnson would send Humphrey to the Freedom Party delegation at Atlantic City with his ill-fated compromise. In 1948, white southerners bolted the convention and formed the Dixiecrat Party with Governor Strom Thurmond of South Carolina, who would twenty years later lead white southerners into the Republican Party, as their presidential candidate. Truman also faced a defection from the party's liberal wing in the form of the Progressive Party whose candidate was former Vice President Henry Wallace. Given Republicans' confidence that their candidate, New York Governor Thomas E. Dewey, was certain to win unless he made a disastrous mistake, the GOP stood aside and let Truman and Thurmond battle it out over civil rights.[2] Truman's victory helped make the Democrats the national supporters of civil rights.

The fact that northern Democrats led the campaign in Congress for civil rights, with occasional assistance from Republicans, proved to be immensely important. Every civil rights measure threatened the Democrats' increasingly tenuous unity. That in turn meant that Republicans began to attract white southern voters. Since Democrats had long counted on a solid South in national races, these defections caused first John F. Kennedy and then Lyndon B. Johnson to seek ways to balance support for civil rights against their need for support from white southern politicians. This was the political context in which the SNCC and other groups, loosely organized at the Congress of Federated Organizations (COFO), sought to organize a voting rights campaign in Mississippi in the 1960s.

During the Eisenhower years civil rights organizations, especially the NAACP, pursued lawsuits instead of voting rights drives. Ever since its ruling that the whites-only primary election system was unconstitutional, the Supreme Court had invalidated one legal basis of segregation after another. Then in *Brown* v. *Board of Education* (1954), the Court unanimously overturned its 1896 *Plessy* ruling that "separate but equal" facilities were constitutional. In *Brown* the Court held that separate facilities were "inherently unequal." It thereby swept away the underlying legal justification for Jim Crow. A dismayed President Eisenhower said that his selection of Earl Warren as chief justice was the "biggest damfool mistake" he ever made. Even so, Eisenhower did enforce the Court's decision when, in 1957, a lower court ordered the integration of Little Rock High School. Also in 1957, following a march of hundreds of thousands upon Washington, Congress passed the first civil rights measure since Reconstruction.

---

[2]Wallace also took a strong civil rights stand, refusing to appear before segregated audiences.

Brown vindicated the NAACP's strategy of challenging segregation through the courts. But the continuation of Mississippi's whites-only primary for a generation after the Supreme Court had ruled it unconstitutional threw the limits of that strategy into bold relief. So did two highly publicized events: the murder of Emmett Till and the success of the Montgomery Bus Boycott, led by Dr. Martin Luther King, Jr.

Till's murder showed not only the brutality of white supremacy but also the immunity granted to white supremacists under state law. In August 1955 the fourteen-year-old Till, who had grown up in Chicago with his widowed mother, paid a visit to relatives in the Mississippi Delta. Seeking to impress some new friends, Till boasted of his white girl friend. Mississippi blacks could not imagine such a thing. To prove it, Till took a dare. He walked into a store where Carolyn Bryant, a young, attractive, and married white woman, was working and asked her for a date. She chased him from the store with a pistol. Till, in a gesture of adolescent bravado, responded with a "wolf-whistle."[3] Several nights later Caroline Bryant's husband Roy and his half-brother J. W. Milam dragged Till out of his family's home. They beat him brutally. Then Milam shot him in the head. He and Bryant next tied a seventy-pound cotton gin fan around Till's neck with barbed wire and dropped his body into the Tallahatchie River.

Till's mother insisted on an open casket. Thousands of mourners filed by. Newspapers and magazines ran pictures of Till, usually pairing a graduation portrait of him smiling in a new suit with one of his battered corpse. The case became front-page news across the country.

Finding the murderers was not difficult. Till's uncle identified the two men who came to his house that night. They admitted that themselves. And they admitted beating Till. They did deny the shooting. But the murder weapon belonged to Milam. It took the jury a little over an hour to acquit them both. This kept intact a record. No white person had ever been convicted for murdering an African American in the Delta.

Also in 1955, in Montgomery, Alabama, Rosa Parks, a longtime NAACP member, refused to give up her seat to a white person and move to the back of the bus, the "colored section." Her arrest led to a mass meeting of the city's blacks in Holt Street Baptist Church where the boycott began. Later, headquarters for the boycott were moved to

---

[3]Some suggest that Till did not whistle, that he had a speech impediment which caused him to make a whistling sound when excited.

Martin Luther King, Jr.'s Dexter Avenue Church. African Americans refused to ride the buses until they were desegregated. The struggle lasted until 1956, when a federal court ruled that making blacks sit in the back of the bus was unconstitutional. This victory did not lead to the immediate integration of bus lines elsewhere. Instead its principal impact was upon the black community, particularly its college-age members. Nonviolent direct action could work. Despite the Till murder, blacks in the Deep South were not powerless. They *could* do something.

There was, however, no coherent national strategy to pursue nonviolent civil disobedience in the late 1950s. One reason was that different people attached different meanings to nonviolence. For King, it was a moral force. Inspired by Mahatma Gandhi's leadership of the Indian campaign for independence, King argued that nonviolence forced the oppressor to confront his own evil. It also forced others to ponder the morality of segregation and racism. Most importantly, it forced white Americans to decide whether they actually believed in the principles they claimed were the basis of their democracy. Others thought of nonviolence as a tactic. Given the monopoly of force enjoyed by the white power structure in the South, it would be foolish to resort to violence. Further, it would alienate whites outside of the South who might otherwise support their struggle. Initially, this divergence could be papered over since, in the short term, both views endorsed the use of nonviolent protest.

Another reason was organizational. Montgomery had been a local initiative. King sought to follow it up with the creation of the Southern Christian Leadership Council (SCLC); but building an organization took time. Then came another local initiative.

In Greensboro in 1960 several students at the all-black North Carolina Agricultural and Technical University decided to integrate the lunch counter of the local Woolworth's. Woolworth's was a national chain of retail stores selling a wide range of inexpensive products. Like other big retailers, it followed local customs with respect to race. In the North its stores were integrated. In the South, anyone could shop in Woolworth's but only whites could eat at its lunch counters. The North Carolina A & T students were determined to challenge this. Their tactic came from the trade union movement, the sit-down strike. They sat down at the counter and refused to move until they were served. This attracted a noisy and angry crowd of whites. The store manager called the police. The students resisted nonviolently. After their arrest, classmates took their place.

Woolworth's was a well-chosen target. It depended upon black customers (as had the Montgomery City Lines, Inc.), not only in Greensboro but especially throughout the North. A boycott would cost the chain dearly. Further, its senior management did not have the same sense of loyalty to Jim Crow that bus company officials had. The sit-in gave the company a major public relations problem that it decided to solve by giving in to the students' demands.

Greensboro not only reinforced the lessons of Montgomery. It demonstrated that a new generation of African Americans, many of them college students, were determined to assert their rights. How best to tap their energy and dedication became the question. Black students elsewhere in the South started their own sit-ins. They chose their own local targets, mapped out their own strategies. The need for coordination was plain.

Dr. King had asked Ella Baker, a longtime civil rights activist, to come from New York City to Atlanta to help him organize the Southern Christian Leadership Conference. He and she then organized a conference at Shaw University in Raleigh, North Carolina, Baker's alma mater, for college-age people looking to work for civil rights. SNCC emerged from this meeting. SNCC would organize volunteers and coordinate activities with the NAACP, the Congress of Racial Equality (CORE), and Dr. King's Southern Christian Leadership Conference. The idea was to avoid overlap and confusion, on the one hand, and to provide coherent direction on the other. In practice, coordination proved elusive. SNCC often went its own way. In part, this was because it reflected Baker's ideas. She was uncomfortable with the way the SCLC was evolving into a vehicle for King's leadership. She felt that the emphasis should be upon grassroots organization. Leadership, she thought, should grow out of community activities. Baker's own style of leadership was to stay in the background and to encourage others. SNCC workers came to revere "Aunt Ella," or "Miss Baker," as they invariably addressed her. And they employed her notion that decisions should arise from consensus, not from the decisions of powerful leaders.

SNCC volunteers took on the most difficult, and the most dangerous, of all the civil rights initiatives—voter registration in the Deep South. A small group of activists could stage a sit-in or organize a freedom ride all by themselves. Voter registration meant persuading hundreds and then thousands of individuals to challenge segregation. This was risky. Blacks who had the reputation for making waves, for being uppity, were often fired from jobs, denied leases on farms, refused credit, and, in many cases, beaten or killed.

SNCC field-workers had to convince people to run these risks even though everyone knew that, in the vast majority of cases, the white registrar of voters would refuse the application. Registrars had a variety of devices at their disposal for barring African Americans. Some states had literacy tests which unschooled whites routinely passed and blacks with advanced degrees routinely failed. Other states had used poll taxes, a practice that had disenfranchised substantial numbers of poor whites as well. Still others used a "grandfather clause." Only those whose grandfather had been eligible to vote could register. Mississippi required prospective registrants to write out an arbitrarily chosen portion of the state constitution and then write an essay explaining it. Theodore Bilbo explained how it worked in a 1946 stump speech:

> The poll tax won't keep 'em from voting. What keeps 'em from
> voting is Section 244 of the Constitution of 1890 that Senator George
> wrote. It says that a man to register must be able to read and explain
> the Constitution or explain the Constitution when read to him. . . .
> And then Senator George wrote a Constitution that damn few white
> men and no niggahs at all can explain.[4]

A trip to the registrar's office, in short, had almost always proved a fool's errand.

The NAACP challenged these provisions in federal court. Progress proved steady but slow as state legislatures replaced registration obstacles thrown out by the courts, such as grandfather clauses and poll taxes, with new ones. Further, federal courts could not offer protection against threats or violence. The Till murder and countless other unpunished murders showed state or local officials would not lift a finger to help. Indeed country sheriffs and deputies often actively assisted white supremacist groups in campaigns of terror. In Mississippi matters were worse still. An official Sovereignty Commission, funded by the legislature, actively worked against civil rights for blacks. It collected information on activists, pressured local officials to take measures against "troublemakers," and even investigated the racial status of individuals who were suspected of "passing" as whites.

Only the federal government could help. Would it? As of 1961, the FBI had done nothing. The Kennedy administration publicly

---

[4]"Bilbo," by Harry Henderson and Sam Shaw, *Colliers*, July 6, 1946, excerpted on page 15.

proclaimed its support for the goals of the civil rights movement even as it lobbied Dr. King and others to avoid sit-ins and other "confrontational" strategies. It urged them to concentrate upon legal challenges. Ironically, it was just such a challenge that most clearly demonstrated the administration's reluctance to take a stand. It also forced action in spite of that reluctance.

In 1962 a federal district court ordered the University of Mississippi to admit James Meredith. He, like the Evers brothers and others who had challenged Bilbo in 1946, was a veteran. Like them, he felt that the country he had served in uniform owed him equal treatment under the law. The court agreed. Mississippi Governor Ross Barnett vowed to prevent Meredith from registering. For the first time since the challenge to Bilbo, a showdown between Mississippi white supremacists and the federal government was in the offing.

Precisely because the bipartisan majority of 1947 had never formed, the Kennedy administration found itself torn between its public commitment to civil rights and its need for southern white votes. What would it do? The answer was to strike a backstage bargain with Governor Barnett. He could "stand in the schoolhouse door," as the phrase then went, and breathe defiance. That would make him a hero to Mississippi whites. Then he could stand aside, in the face of federal force. That would enable Meredith to register and the administration to carry out its obligation to "execute the laws."

Could Kennedy and Barnett trust each other enough to make such a deal work? Each was caught in the coils of a dilemma. Kennedy had urged civil rights activists to concentrate upon court cases. Here was such a case. If he did not enforce the decision, he would have no credibility with African Americans at all. On the other side, no Democrat could imagine winning a national election without carrying a substantial portion of the South. No matter what happened with respect to voter registration drives, in 1964 the voters in the South would be overwhelmingly white.

Barnett's quandary was the mirror image of Kennedy's. Ever since the *Brown* decision, candidates in Mississippi, as in the rest of the Deep South, outdid each other in promising to protect Jim Crow. If Barnett did not "stand in the schoolhouse door," his political career would be in ruins. Yet, if he defied a federal court order, he would wind up in prison for contempt.

Both men, in sum, were looking for a way to stage manage the confrontation. They secretly agreed that Barnett would initially block Meredith. He would make a rousing speech. Then a Justice

Department official, backed by federal marshals, would hand him a court order. Faced with the prospect of overwhelming federal force, the governor would yield. They even agreed on the number of marshals and their weapons.

The plan was too clever by half. It assumed that Barnett had the same degree of control over what happened locally as Kennedy did over the federal response. This was not so. Kennedy could order an exact number of marshals to go to Ole Miss. He could specify they only carry small arms. Barnett could not orchestrate local reactions. He did not even dare to inform officials in his own administration of the agreement with Kennedy. They accordingly assumed that their job was to resist "federal intrusion." In addition, Barnett continued to call upon white Mississippians to rally around the cause of segregation. As a politician, he felt he had no choice. But he also had no way of controlling how many would decide to go to the university. Nor could he control what they would do once they got there.

Adding to the danger was the presence on the scene of General Edmund Walker who had been recently relieved of his command in Europe because of suspicions of mental instability.[5] Walker, a favorite among the white conservatives, declared he would offer his military skills to those going to the university to stand up for "states' rights."

What ensued was a tragedy that almost turned into a bloodbath. Federal agents secretly moved Meredith onto the campus. Thousands of angry students and thousands of militant white supremacists gathered around the building housing him. They threw stones, lit fires, threatened to bulldoze the structure. The marshals fired tear gas, but the mob did not disband. The marshals almost ran out of the gas. If they had, the mob would have stormed the building and seized Meredith. Faced with this potential disaster, Kennedy called out the military. United States Air Force troops occupied the University of Mississippi. They prevented further violence. James Meredith registered and attended classes.

Kennedy and Barnett blamed each other for the riot, loss of life, and destruction of property. African American civil rights activists blamed them both. Barnett was a somewhat more presentable Bilbo.

---

[5]Walker's alleged mental instability provoked a change in U.S. policy regarding nuclear weapons. Prior to the Walker case, field commanders had authority to use tactical nuclear weapons. Concern that another field commander might also prove unstable and perhaps start a nuclear conflagration led to a decision to revoke that authority. Film director Stanley Kurbrick used the case as fodder for his "Doctor Strangelove or How I Learned to Stop Worrying and Love the Bomb." In the film, Air Force General Jack D. Ripper launched an attack upon the Soviet Union on his own.

They had expected nothing from him. Kennedy's reluctance to use force until tragedy had already struck confirmed their worst suspicions. The administration would act only when forced.

Here was the challenge facing SNCC as its first field-workers went to Mississippi. It had to win the confidence of the black community, which entailed convincing people with good reason to be skeptical that it was possible to challenge Jim Crow in the "most southern place on earth." SNCC workers were young and comparatively inexperienced. Many were not from the state. They had little money and little in the way of political connections. Meanwhile white supremacists were organized across the state in White Citizens Councils and in the Klan. The state's Sovereignty Commission provided funding and intelligence. County sheriffs and deputies kept an eye out for organizers, "outside agitators," as they were called. You had to be very brave to work for or with SNCC.

Leading the effort was Robert Parris Moses who preferred to be called Bob. A graduate of Hamilton College with a degree in mathematics and of Harvard University with a master's in philosophy, Moses was soft spoken, not an orator on the model of Dr. King. He had no taste for the dramatic gesture. Like Ella Baker, he believed that community organization was paramount and that leadership should emerge from the local communities. He was, in addition, intelligent, resilient, patient, and courageous. Many of those who worked with him would later say that he was the finest person they had ever met. This is, to a considerable extent, his story. He did nothing single-handedly, as he himself endlessly pointed out. But he was, to borrow a phrase often used of George Washington, "the indispensable man." It was on his integrity that everyone else relied.

Moses spent 1961 and 1962 learning first hand about Mississippi. He was beaten, arrested, jailed. He made local contacts. He established a reputation as someone who would stick, who would not quit no matter how bad things got. In 1963, working with Allard Lowenstein, a brilliant lawyer and activist, he organized a symbolic election. With volunteers from northern law schools, most of them white, SNCC set up an alternative to the white primary in Mississippi. Tens of thousands of blacks voted, even though their votes did not count in the "regular" election results. The high level of participation gave the lie to white supremacist claims that "good" blacks did not actually want the vote. It also attracted a fair amount of media attention nationally.

Building upon this success, however limited, Moses developed a strategy for 1964. Once again SNCC would appeal to northern students, most of them white, to come to Mississippi to help register voters. White Mississippians would treat them the way they invariably treated those they considered a threat to their way of life. They would use insult, intimidation, and violence. But, they would be insulting, threatening, and harming affluent white students from the North as well as poor blacks from Mississippi. The Till and Evers murders aside, the media paid little attention to violence against African Americans. But attacks upon young, middle-class white students would be news. Moses called for a biracial campaign to organize Mississippi blacks into a new Democratic party.

Many within SNCC opposed the plan. They argued that white volunteers would push local blacks, and themselves, into the shadows. Whites would prove arrogant, insensitive, and bossy. Besides, blacks needed to learn to rely upon themselves. Moses agreed that many of their concerns were justified. There would be difficulties if white college students, often from very affluent backgrounds, flooded into Mississippi. Some, perhaps most, would prove arrogant. They would assume that they knew more about the campaign than black SNCC workers who had spent months or years in the field. They would get the lion's share of attention. Moses was like Ella Baker in several respects. One was his willingness to listen. Another was his reluctance to push himself into the forefront. And, like Baker, he possessed such moral authority that others listened to every word he uttered.

There were, he continued, powerful reasons for including the white volunteers, despite the very legitimate concerns. Some were strategic. They needed to find ways to pressure the Johnson administration to take action. Getting the national media to cover events in Mississippi would generate that pressure. But the media would cover the story because of the white volunteers. That was just a fact. Other reasons flowed from the nature of their struggle. The goal was a multiracial society. They were about to decide whether they themselves could, or would, function in a multiracial organization. If they decided in the negative, they were giving up on the goal.

In the end, Moses' argument prevailed. SNCC adopted his strategy. His plan succeeded more brilliantly than he could have hoped. It also had consequences he feared and sought to prevent.

PROLOGUE: THE CHALLENGE TO SENATOR THEODORE BILBO, "THE PRINCE OF THE PECKERWOODS"

What did white Mississippians mean when they proudly affirmed that their state was "the most southern place on earth"? One way of approaching this question is by examining Theodore Bilbo's 1946 reelection campaign for the U.S. Senate. As noted in the "Introduction," most of Bilbo's colleagues regarded him as a disgrace and an embarrassment. He was corrupt, vulgar, and a hate-mongering demagogue. He was also, as he liked to boast, "the Prince of the Peckerwoods," the hero of the poor whites in the state. The word *peckerwood* was a local variation on *woodpecker*, the rednecked bird, and came to refer to "rednecks," the poor whites who worked in the Delta sun.

The following article appeared in *Collier's*, a popular magazine of the day. Its authors sought to explain to those not from Mississippi Bilbo's hold over poor whites in the state. The authors, that is, assumed that their readers could not imagine voting for such a person themselves. So they printed and analyzed large portions of one of Bilbo's stump speeches. They also detailed the audiences' reactions. In the process, they revealed much about how racism influenced state politics. Bilbo would die the next year; the racism he enflamed would not.

"BILBO"

Harry Henderson and Sam Shaw

The hot Mississippi sun beats down on a crowd of 1,500 grizzled farmers and townsfolk. Some squat on their hunkers, pick aimlessly at the grass. Others stand with powerful sun-reddened arms across their chests or with hands thrust deep in their jeans. In front of a flat-bed truck which has become a platform by the addition of the Stars and Stripes, there are a few benches and folding chairs for old, cane-carrying men and the finest ladies of the town, with parasols. Uptown, most stores have closed. Here and there some folks seek the shade of the trees on the courthouse lawn. A handful of older men enjoy the

Source: "Bilbo," *Collier's,* July 6, 1946 by Harry Henderson and Sam Shaw.

Buck Bilbo Rides Again

"Buck Bilbo Rides Again," 1942. Image from *Dr. Seuss Went to War* (Mandeville Special Collections Library, UC San Diego).

refreshing coolness of a seat on the stone steps of the courthouse. Standing off, here and there on the outskirts of the crowd, sometimes half hiding behind the parked cars, are Negroes, some of them old and gray and some of them ex-G.I.s wearing mud-spattered remnants of Uncle Sam's uniform.

Everyone is listening. They are listening to a short, potbellied little man of sixty-nine years—a "runt," he calls himself. He is dressed in a natty suit, sporting a florid necktie emblazoned with a diamond horseshoe. The microphone which he speaks into carries his hoarse, rasping voice a quarter of a mile away through two loud-speakers mounted atop a secondhand hearse painted white. Listen:

"Ah am in the prime of mah life. Ah am young in mind and body. Last yeah Ah went up to Mayo clinic and had 'em cut me open. You oughta see mah scar. . . . And afterwards the doctor said mah organs were perfect. 'You'll live to be a hundred, Bilbo—if someone don't shoot you,' "

The crowd roars. This is Bilbo, Theodore J. Bilbo, senior United States Senator from Mississippi, the best-known man in the state, and right now he's looking for a job—the same one he has. He's fighting in the Democratic primary and if he wins a majority of the votes, he's elected.

The crowd knows Bilbo. For thirty-three years he has been the wildest, most turbulent figure in their public life—and the most entertaining. He is a first-rate comedian with better timing than Bob Hope and better gags than Senator Claghorn, and that's no joke son. It's a big thing in country where you have to drive twenty miles to see a three-year-old B movie.

The people know a survey by a national magazine found him regarded as the "worst man" in the Senate and that Senator Robert A. Taft has called him a disgrace to the Senate. If they don't, Bilbo tells them. As for the magazine, that's just "a damn' niggah-loving, Northern social equality magazine," and as for Taft, he just wants to be President, "a mockingbird just out of its shell, all mouth and no bird at all."

To most of the country Bilbo is known for his violent racial prejudice, his filibustering against the FEPC, his opposition to the antilynch bill, his offensive language in the dignified Senate chamber, his inflammatory attacks on legislation aimed at reducing racial and religious discrimination, and for his letters addressed "Dear Dago," and "Dear Kike." The people of Mississippi know he has blackened the name of their state, made them, as they put it, the laughing stock of the country. They are embarrassed by his language, by the name he has won for all of them. But listen:

"Ah have been smeared from coast to coast by the damn' niggah-loving, social equality press and magazines and radio. . . .

"These boys hyeah," meaning us, "Ah know them. They'ah nice boys. Ah sit down with them. Ah talk to them. Ah travel with them. They'ah nice fellows. They'ah just doing their job. They don't have anything to do with what is written in the magazines." He pauses, "If they did, Ah'd lick 'em afore they got outa Mississippi."

A CRUELING CAMPAIGN SCHEDULE

He's a martyr in Mississippi, speaking for two hours three times a day, racing almost 100 miles between speeches in a big 1946 sedan, chewing and smoking a ten-cent cigar. Listen:

"In 1934 when Ah went to Washington, Ah made mah great decision. There were two roads open to me. Oh yes, Ah could have taken the easiest road, the road of least resistance. Yes, Ah could have enjoyed the best drinks and the choicest food. Yes, Ah would have been known as the great senator from Mississippi. Oh yes. Ah would have enjoyed laudatory and complimentary articles in the press. Yes, Ah would have gone down to a grave banked with flowahs while sweet and melodious words of eulogy were uttered ovah me. . . .

"But Ah'd have been a traitor. Ah'd have been a traitor to the South, a traitor to mah people, a traitor to mah ideals, a traitor to mah white blood. . . . Ah'll get to that latah. . . ."

The crowd is solemn. They believe him, are touched by the picture he draws. He has always claimed to be a martyr to them. In 1910 he called a man a "cross between a hyena and a mongrel and born in a niggah graveyard at midnight." The man beat him up, and Bilbo, the martyr, swathed in bandages, was elected lieutenant governor. In 1911 he took a bribe of $645, then a few days later claimed he had taken it in order to expose bribery. He missed impeachment by one vote, but was character-ized by the state legislature as "unfit to sit with honest and upright men in any respectable legislative body." Bilbo the Martyr took that for his text and was elected governor. Sent to jail for contempt of court for fail-ing to appear as a witness in a seduction case, he announced his candidacy for governor, again a martyr, and emerged from the jail to open his campaign on a platform built just outside. He was again elected. . . .

. . . He was elected to the Senate in 1934, promising to "raise more hell than Huey Long."

Bilbo was the eighth child of a hard-working Baptist farm couple who lived at Juniper Grove, Pearl River County. When he was fifteen he made up his mind to a "life of public service," which is what he calls what he does. He spent the next fifteen years preparing—studying at the University of Nashville and Vanderbilt while news-butchering on trains.

"Ah've never been defeated," he cries, "but Ah've been delayed a few times." He was delayed literally at the post, for in his first bid for "public service," the circuit clerkship of his home county, his neighbors picked his opponent. But a few years later, in 1907, he was elected to the State Senate by touring the district playing Baptist hymns on a melodeon. He has been delayed few other times. In 1920 he was rejected in a Congressional race and in 1923 he was rejected in a bid for the governorship. . . .

But Bilbo goes on. He fought for the Tennessee-Tombigbee River canalization and now northeastern Mississippi "will blossom like a rose." And he's important in Washington. Listen: "Ah'm the rankin' membah of the District of Columbia Committee. That makes me mayor of the city of Washington, ex-officio mayor of the capital of the country. . . . That's a big job. . . . That's important information. If you ever come to Washington and get in trouble, get thrown in jail, whya, call me up. Ah'll get you out."

He reads, angrily, explosively, a letter from the Senate disbursing office stating that they withheld from his salary for taxes over $1,000 each year since the withholding tax became law. Listen:

"So you can see what a damn' lie that is," His scowls fade, become a grin. " 'Course, Ah was entitled to some deductions, every man is . . . that took off some." The crowd roars with laughter. He begins reciting deductions. "Fire insurance, you're entitled to deduct that. Ah believe in fire insurance. Ah got everything insured. My fire insurance amounts to $1,400 a year. . . . And then, you're allowed to deduct for charity. . . . Ah been educating a Baptist minister over hyeah at Fort Worth these past fouah years. Ah deduct for him. . . . Ah didn't have time to preach myself, so Ah just got me someone and sent him out to do it for me. . . . And then there's interest, You can deduct that. Ah'm a pore man. Ah used to owe a lot of money. Ah don't owe but $35,000 now. So you see when Ah got to interest, whaya, that just sorta wipes me out." The crowd is laughing so hard nobody seems to notice Bilbo has virtually admitted his opponent's charge. If they do, they don't care. This is Bilbo, looking for a job. Listen:

"There are four running against me. A regular quartet. . . . all singing the same song. 'Away with Bilbo.'

"Now Ross Collins, he used to be mah friend. In 1910–11 Ah introduced him to Mississippi politics. Yes, you'll have to blame me for him too. Ah took him in my surrey and hauled him all over this state and gave him forty-five minutes of every speaking engagement Ah had.

"But now Ross Collins is runnin' up and down the state saying 'Bilbo oughta be re-tahed,' No man in this state knows more about being re-tahed than Ross Collins. . . . He's been re-tahed more times than any man in Mississippi. . . . Why, in 1910 when three men got on the train at Starkville to assassinate me, Ross Collins was sitting beside me. But when he saw those men coming at me with their drawn guns, whaya, he re-tahed. . . .

"He re-tahed to that little room of public convenience you'll find in every railroad car in the country. . . . and nobody but his laundry-man knows how scared he was!"

This is Bilbo, senior senator from Mississippi, and the crowd is laughing its head off, gasping for breath, snuffling and chuckling, clapping and slapping its knees. This is 1946, but in 1911, shortly after the incident, Bilbo told the story this way:

"Mr. Collins had been forced to stand in the corner of the coach at the point of a gun. . . . Mr. Collins was unarmed, as he never carried a pistol in his life and was absolutely helpless to render me any assistance, for an overt act on his part would have precipitated a shooting. . . . which would have resulted in the death of us both.". . .

"And then there's Peachtree Harper." The farmers all laugh. Harper is an aging Jackson florist who years ago sold peach trees to farmers all over Mississippi. "The ole fool. He's more to be pitied than condemned. . . . Somebody told him he wasn't campaigning right. You got to light right into old Bilbo, they said.

" 'Well,' said the ole fool, 'what should Ah say?' "

" 'Call him a ladies' man,' they told him. And do you know what that damn' fool did? He got up at Tupelo and said, 'Solomon with his 300 wives and his 700 women couldn't hold a light to Bilbo. . . . They oughta be ashamed telling an old man to say things like that." The crowd cackles and giggles, remembering Bilbo's jail term in connection with the seduction case and the sensational divorce charges by his wife in 1938, that throughout his career he was "all mixed up with low, lewd women of the streets.". . .

Then suddenly the hoarseness has disappeared and you know he could continue, as he warns the crowd, "foah thirty days." He flails the air with his right arm and beats his chest, puts a weary hand to a brow that is as wide as a prairie, and tears at his collar and tie. But he is in no hurry. If the crowd laughs at a quick, thrown-away line about "that damn' fool, Eleanor," he picks it up and expands it into a whole skit, complete with mincing little steps and a falsetto imitation of the widow of the late president.

In towns where there are Army camps near by the ground in front of the platform is filled with G.I.s. They are from California, South Dakota, Pennsylvania, Ohio, Missouri, and they are busy as beavers writing down everything he says, writing it down to send to their unbelieving folks back home. Sometimes Bilbo's inflammatory racial prejudice, his demagoguery are more than they can take and they stalk out angrily, frightened and sick. . . .

This is Bilbo, senior United States Senator from Mississippi, looking for a job. He feeds upon opposition, quoting "Northern" papers and "niggah" papers to prove he is the flower of the South. Time and again, he builds up tremendous tension in the audience, then explodes it with an aside, a gag, insinuation, or invective. His voice drops as he speaks of his large, beautiful house outside Poplarville, one of the minor scandals of Mississippi. Listen as he whispers:

"Sure, Ah have a beautiful home. Ah call it the Dream House, the House by the Side of the Road Where the Race of Men Go By. It's the finest home in Mississippi. Ah got twenty-seven rooms. One time Ah slept thirty-two people there, two in a bed. Ah built it as a memorial to mah mother and father. Come and see me. Stay all night. . . . Don't all come at once, though."

Listen:

"These enemies of mine in New York, Pennsylvania, Chicago, New Jersey. . . . The Commonists and the C.I.O., headed by this furriner Sidney Hillman from Russia, whya, they've made the boast they are coming down hyeah with a million dollahs just to beat Bilbo. . . . Now it's wrong to take that money. It's wicked. . . . But, if you need it, take it. Take it home and wash it off, then buy the wife a dress, buy the kids something, give the family a treat, give some to the preacher, and then vote for Bilbo!"

The crowd screams with delight. Bilbo ducks his head to hide a smile.

But he's quiet about the money for his own campaign. He has it and that's enough, son. It is not much of a secret in Mississippi that most of it is coming from contractors whom he helped to get war construction jobs.

The money for his opponents' campaigns is really secret. It does not amount to much and it is mostly from local businessmen who think being the laughingstock of the country doesn't help business. But nobody contributes openly. "We want to stay in business," one Hattiesburg businessman explained. "He'd make not buying in our store part of his campaign."

Bilbo plays upon the sympathies, the problems, the desires, the humor, the fears of the crowd with the consummate skill of a concert pianist tackling Beethoven. An opponent has charged Bilbo has reported only $72 income tax to the federal government since 1913. He expands this to cover his entire public life, he angrily denounces it as a lie, "broadcast to the four corners of the earth by that scoundrel, Walter Winchell."

. . . The farmers shuffle their feet and shift their 'baccy to the other cheek and the townspeople glance anxiously at one another as Bilbo launches into his main tirade against the Negro people. All through his speech Bilbo has been building up to this with insinuations, wisecracks and insults, whetting prejudices, reviving myths, reminding them that 52 per cent of Mississippi's people are Negroes. Up front a Bilbo county chairman launches a rebel yell. Listen:

"Ah believe in white superiority, white domination and the integrity of mah white blood. Whaya, we have behind us fouah thousand yeahs of culture, learning, education and wisdom. . . . And the niggah—I got nothing against the niggah. Ah'm his best friend—but the pore devil is only a hundred and fifty yeahs removed from the jungle and eatin' his own kind."

The crowd gasps. They have heard this kind of talk all their lives, they are accustomed to it, they have believed it, they believe it now. But always in private. They have never heard it as an open political program. Then the Bilbo men up front send up the rebel yell and the shock is over. They applaud and whistle and cheer. It is like a plunge into cold water. Listen:

"Whaya, I read a book written by fouahteen niggah leaders and every one of them wanted the same thing: social equality, intermarriage and interbreeding. . . . Ah read all them niggah papers. That's what they all want."

He goes on, painting a ridiculous picture of Negro political power in Northern states, claiming they hold the balance of power in the Democratic Party and control it. . . .

"That's why Harry Truman does what he does. That's why he's had to come out for FEPC and the antilynch bill and the anti-poll tax. He's a Southerner. His grandfather fed the Confederate Army. His mother's an unreconstructed rebel. He thinks like us. Ah know 'cause Ah've talked to him by the hour. But he wants to be President. He's gotta cater to the niggah vote."

On and on the tirade goes, so much of it vile, profane and inflammatory that no newspaper in the North or South would publish it *in toto*.

Shouting and screaming, grinningly proclaiming himself the Negroes' best friend, tearing his collar open wide, he defies the Negroes of Mississippi to register and vote. Listen:

"The poll tax won't keep 'em from voting. What keeps 'em from voting is Section 244 of the Constitution of 1890 that Senator George wrote. It says that a man to register must be able to read and explain the Constitution or explain the Constitution when read to him. . . . And then Senator George wrote a Constitution that damn' few white men and no niggahs at all can explain." He grins and the crowd rocks with laughter.

He continues, talking white supremacy, the integrity of his white blood, white domination, white ingenuity, white culture, white government. . . . Listen:

"Whaya, the niggahs are having meetings all over the state. We don't know what they're up to! They've had meetings in every county, meetings behind locked doors. Two policemen up at Jackson broke in on one of their meetings and do you know what they found? Northern niggahs teaching them how to register and how to vote." The crowd gasps. Bilbo is talking to win now. He does not have to get many votes to win. Mississippi's population totals only little more than two million.

Over half are Negroes—effectively barred from the polls; only 2,000 are registered in the state, by Bilbo's figure. And the poll tax—which must have been paid for the last *two* years, amounting to $4—keeps another 100,000 white voters away. The result is that only 145,914 votes were cast in the last election. Of these Bilbo had 85,000. Only 1,400 votes were cast in the city of Natchez (population 15,000) in the last senatorial election; 829 for Bilbo, 629 for his opponent.

The vote probably will run higher this year because the returned G.I.s, white and black, have been exempted from the poll tax requirement. They number 200,000. Roughly 80,000 are Negroes. Some of the white vets are rabid Bilbo men, but many, remembering the razz they took for him all over America, think him a disgrace.

The Negroes won't talk—but Bilbo will. . . . He hammers out hoary tales of Reconstruction days. In World War II, the Negro soldiers ran, he screams. He is winding up. Listen:

"Mississippi is white. We got the right to keep it that way and Ah care not what Tom Clark and Hugo Black say. . . . Ah'm callin' on every red-blooded American who believes in the superiority and integrity of the white race to get out and see that no niggah votes. . . . And the best time to do it is the night before!"

The crowd screams and yells. Here and there a man shakes his head sadly. The few Negroes on the fringe of the crowd react differently; the old ones grin and nod uneasily and the ex-G.I.s stare sullenly.

In Jackson we asked him what he meant when he said, "the best time to do it is the night before."

"Oh-oh, watch out," said his manager, Birney Friend.

But he grinned. "That's a Southern expression, boys, you wouldn't understand that. . . . Ah won't say another word."

As he finishes speaking, the crowd is cheering, breaking, surging forward. He is soaking wet. A little chap named Rabbit Daniels with a big cigar rushes up and puts a trench coat on him so he won't catch cold. People jam close, grab his hand, old ladies pat him on the back. He is winded, trying hard to remember names, faces, old friends, but Rabbit is pushing him through the crowd to the car. The door closes and the car begins to move. People are still clustered by it, one or two trot alongside. In the old "cheese and cracker" campaign days he tried to shake hands with everybody. That's out now. The new impression is power, speed, determination. The big car roars out onto the highway. The next town is 85 miles away.

People still stand about in clusters, on the courthouse steps, by the Confederate monument. One farmer says to another, "Ole Bilbo sho did lay it on the line," and they all nod. They admire his skill as an orator, the way he held the crowd for over two hours. "Yep," says one with a grin, "ole Bilbo got all the cows in the barn and he sho milked them."

At Meridian, a chamber of commerce member walked over to us. "Please," he said anxiously, "don't say anything bad about Mississippi. You can say anything you want about Bilbo. He's a disgrace to us. He helps keep industry out of the state. But don't say anything bad about Mississippi. These are nice people, good people, they mean well."

"Can we quote you?" we asked.

"Don't quote me," he said, "I've got a business here. Just don't say anything bad about Mississippi."

Beginnings

One of the most striking character traits of Robert Moses, the SNCC organizer who coordinated the voter registration campaign in Mississippi, was his commitment to honesty, with himself and with those whom he brought into the struggle. This integrity is a major reason why he commanded such respect, and why, as Mississippi field-worker Anne Moody noted, others in the movement nicknamed him "Jesus." Historian and activist Staunton Lynd called him "probably the most respected, even revered, leader in the experience of the American New Left." This speech at Stanford, given just two months before the beginning of the Freedom Summer, helps explain the extraordinary respect Moses commanded. In it, Moses gave a historical sketch of SNCC's work in Mississippi. He explained the dangers he and others faced, the national attention their work was starting to attract, and the plans he and the other SNCC field-workers had for the summer. The second portion of this speech is printed later in this collection.

Moses' account of the early days in Mississippi is characteristically understated, particularly with reference to himself. It is best read in conjunction with a talk he gave in late 1962. This first appeared in the January 1970 issue of *Liberation*, a journal of the "New Left." The editors decided not to tidy up grammar or syntax as a means of preserving the authenticity of Moses' talk. Neither Staunton Lynd, who wrote the introduction, nor Howard Zinn, who used the original tape recording of the talk for his *SNCC: The New Abolitionists*, could determine exactly when or under what circumstances Moses spoke. Despite this, the talk is an important source. It not only provides a sense of the dangers and hardships Moses and other activists faced, but also describes the amazing courage and determination of the people they sought to help, and it affords a rare glimpse into the personality of Moses himself.

Robert Moses

When we first went to Mississippi, we didn't know what we could do. And we went there more or less with the attitude to try and find out what was possible, that is to see what could be done. We didn't have any resources really and we weren't sure how we should go about or what it was that we should do. The first, I guess, real sense of what we had to do came with some of the contact that we had, particularly with rural farmers because perhaps for the first time certainly in my life I met some people who were—seemed extremely simple in their conception of life but very direct in terms of what they wanted and what they needed and in terms of certain elemental ideas about justice and feelings about people. And if we have any anchor at all—I mean if— if there's any base from which we operate—if there's any reasons why we don't really go crazy—why we don't have more problems than we do have—if there's any reason why we can skip around from the bottom of Mississippi to the top of the skyscrapers in Manhattan and still maintain some kind of internal sense of balance, I think a lot of it has to do with those people and the fact that they have their own sense of balance which is somehow independent of what goes on around the rest of the country because they're not affected by it. Most of them say they don't have telephones. They don't have newspapers. They have very little contact with the outside world. They do have radios. They

---

[1]The speech was transcribed by Peter Bratt for the Voices of Freedom Web site at Stanford University. I have corrected several obvious errors in the transcription, for example, *streams* to *extremes*, which is clearly what Moses said.

Source: Speech by Robert Moses at Stanford University, April 24, 1964.

do have televisions, so they have some contact. But yet, in many ways, they've managed to maintain something which is fundamental and which gives I think many a worker's real strength when he's working down in the rural areas of Mississippi. . . .

. . . There was, in the South, with the kids who were acting in the sit-in movement, some idea that somebody was doing something about some key problem in the state, in the country. And it was in direct response to that challenge that the kids, the sit-in people, gave that myself and other people began to move down south. Now, when we first got into Mississippi we were really on our own and very much alone.

I just will recount one instance; I took two people down to Liberty to register about four weeks or more after I had been working in that county. I met with a group of white people who proceeded to attack us and they singled myself out and I was—my head was tattooed to several stitches. The Justice Department's reaction to that was they didn't have a really clear-cut case because we were walking through the streets on our way to the courthouse. The news of that never got out and around the country and in many ways that's just as well. And we really realized in what was brought home to us . . . that for the time being we were out there fighting by ourselves. There was no help either from the federal government in any real sense. The FBI agent who came around to do the investigation, although we called them that same night, showed up four-two [*sic*] weeks later for the first time and then proceeded to try and convince me that I really hadn't been beaten but had fell. And he tried to convince me that I fell three times and that the wounds in three different places were from those three different falls. And his concern and really the concern that we've had time and time again since then from southern FBI agents was at that time to—to try and picture, color the story to the tune of their concern so that the picture that went back to Washington was one which would in any case favor them. Now, we operate that way for about a year in 1961 through 1962 more or less on our own—really a small band of people—four or five people—but we did discover several things—that it was possible to pick up in the Negro community young people and get them to work. It was possible to find in most every community in which you worked one or two people who would be willing to take a stand—who would be willing to identify with you—who would provide some kind of foothold in that community and allow you a chance to work and to organize. It was possible to move around the state and begin to get the feeling within the state of the dimensions of the problem, just how immense the problem was, just how deep it was rooted, just how long a struggle it would be, just how limited we were in our resources.

Now along about 1962 in the summer, we began to get the first bit of help from the outside. And it came in the form of political help. It was at this time that President Kennedy and the people in the White House decided to push voter registration and to help with the drive with the court cases of the Justice Department in terms of much needed funds which were to be used for people to help in organizing voter registration drives. So then there began to develop a small fund of money based really out of New York City that was available for people to work in voter registration in the South. So whereas up to then, we were really living in catch as catch can day by day in many cases off the community depending on whether we were able to find friends and people who would house us and feed us.

From the summer of 1962 on through the summer of 1963 we began to get a little more support. And it was during that time that we began to develop what became known as the Council of Federated Organizations and really began to see that it was possible in Mississippi to locate in isolated rural communities and in some towns, groups of people who could be put in touch with each other—who would be able to work with each other who might form the basis for some kind of organization within the state and might form the basis ultimately for some kind of political organization to tackle Mississippi's establishment. Because by that time it was clear that the problems in Mississippi in terms of—where to be focused on political problems that what we had to do was somehow begin to tackle the political establishment in Mississippi—that the white citizens councils, the governor, the state legislature, the judiciary were all part of one monolithic system and that in order to find any kind of gaps in it we were gonna have to hit right at its heart.

"MISSISSIPPI: 1961–1962"

Robert Moses

My name is Robert Moses and I'm field secretary for the Student Nonviolent Coordinating Committee. I first came South July, 1960 on a field trip for SNCC, went through Alabama, Mississippi and

Source: "Mississippi 1961–1962" by Robert Moses from *Liberation*, January 1970.

Louisiana gathering people to go to the October conference. That was the first time that I met Amsy Moore. At that time we sat down and planned the voter registration drive for Mississippi. I returned in the summer of 1961 to start that drive. We were to start in Cleveland, Mississippi in the delta. However, we couldn't; we didn't have any equipment; we didn't even have a place at that time to meet. So we went down to McComb at the invitation of C. C. Bryan who was the local head of the NAACP. And we began setting up a voter registration drive in McComb, Mississippi.

What did we do? Well, for two weeks I did nothing but drive around the town talking to the business leaders, the ministers, the people in the town, asking them if they would support ten students who had come in to work on a voter registration drive. We got a commitment from them to support students for the month of August and to pay for their room and board and some of their transportation while they were there. The drive began August 1, and lasted, as it turned out, through December, not just through the month of August. We began in McComb canvassing for about a two week period. This means that we went around house-to-house, door-to-door in the hot sun everyday because the most important thing was to convince the local townspeople that we meant business, that is, that we were serious, that we were not only young, but that we were people who were responsible. What do you tell somebody when you go to their door? Well, first you tell them who you are, what you're trying to do, that you're working on voter registration. You have a form that you try to get them to fill out. Now the technique that we found best usable, I think, was to present the form to them and say, "Have you ever tried to fill out this form? Would you like to sit down now and try to fill it out?" And then, psychologically as they were in the process of filling out the voter registration form, one of the questions asked them to do something while they were at the registrar's office, so that psychologically they have to complete a gap and imagine themselves at the registrar's office. As you know, in Mississippi, currently you have to fill out a form which has about 21 questions on it, and in addition to routine questions, it has a question where you write and then interpret some section of the constitution of Mississippi and finally a section where you write and describe the duties and obligations of a citizen in Mississippi.

Now we did this for about two weeks and finally began to get results. That is, people began to go down to Magnolia, Mississippi which is the county seat of Pike County and attempt to register. In the meantime, quite naturally, people from Amite and Walthall County, which are the two adjacent counties to Pike county, came over asking us if we wouldn't accompany them in schools in their counties so they could go down and try to register also. And this point should be made quite clear, because many people have been critical of going into such tough counties so early in the game. The position is simply this: that farmers came over and were very anxious to try and register and you couldn't very well turn them down; one, just from the human point of view, they had greater needs than those people in Pike County where we were working and, secondly, from the psychological point of view where the whole problem in Mississippi is pervaded with fear. The problem is that you can't be in the position of turning down the tough areas because the people then, I think, would simply lose confidence in you; so, we accepted this. We worked out a plan first whereby some of the students, John Hardy and two other students who had just come off the Freedom Rides, went into Walthall County to begin work. That was about the middle of August.

At about the same time, I accompanied about three people down to Liberty in Amite County to begin our first registration attempt there. One was a very old man, and then two ladies, middle-aged. We left early morning of August 15, it was a Tuesday, we arrived at the courthouse at about 10 o'clock. The registrar came out, I waited by the side for the man or one of the ladies to say something to the registrar. He asked them what did they want, what were they here for in a very rough tone of voice. They didn't say anything, they were literally paralyzed with fear. So, after a while, I spoke up and said that they would like to come to register to vote. So, he asked, "Well, who are you? What do you have to do with them? Are you here to register?" So I told him who I was and that we were conducting a school in McComb and that these people had attended the school and they wanted an opportunity to register. Well, he said that I'd have to wait "cuz there was someone there filling out the form." Well, there was a young white lady there with her husband and she was sitting down completing the registration form. When she finished, then our people started to register one at a time. In the meantime, a procession of people began moving in and out of the registration office. The sheriff, a couple of his deputies, people from the tax office, people who do the drivers' license, looking in, staring, moving back out, muttering. A highway patrolman finally came in and sat down in the office. And we stayed that way in sort of uneasy tension all morning. The first person who filled out the form took a long time to do it and it was noontime before he was finished. When we came back, I was not permitted to sit in the office, but was told to sit on the front porch, which I did. We finally finished the whole process at about 4:30; all of the three people had had a chance to register, at least to fill out the form. This was victory, because they had been down a few times before and had not had a chance to even fill out the forms.

On the way home we were followed by the highway patrolman who had spent the day in the registrar's office, Officer Carlyle. He tailed us about ten miles, about 25 or 30 feet behind us, all the way back towards McComb. At one point we pulled off, and he passed us, circled around us and we pulled off as he was passing us in the opposite direction, and then he turned around and followed us again. Finally he flagged us down and I got out of the car to ask him what the trouble was because the people in the car were very, very frightened. He asked me who I was, what my business was, and told me that I was interfering in what he was doing. I said I simply wanted to find out what the problem was and what we were being stopped for. He told me to get back in the car. As I did so, I jotted his name down. He then opened the car door, shoved me in and said, "Get in the car, nigger," slamming the door after me. He then told us to follow him and took us over to McComb where I was told that I was placed under arrest. He called up the prosecuting attorney; he came down, and then he and the highway patrolman sat down and looked through the law books to find a charge. They first charged me with interfering with an officer in the process of arresting somebody. Then he found out that the only person arrested was myself and they changed the charge to interfering with an officer in the discharge of his duties. The county attorney asked me if I was ready for trial and I said, could I make a phone call. He said yeah, so I picked up the phone and called Washington, D.C. and the Justice Department, because I had been in communication with some members of the Justice Department and particularly John Doar and had received letters delineating those sections of the Civil Rights act of 1957 and 1960 which guaranteed protection to those people who are trying to register and anyone who is aiding people who are trying to register. And he also indicated that if we had any trouble we were to call Washington or the nearest office of the FBI. So I called them, collect; the people in the office were rather astonished that the call went through and then they began to get fidgety. Well, as to the call, I explained to Mr. Doar exactly what happened in their presence and told him that I thought the people were being intimidated simply because they had gone down to register.

Well, we had the trial right after that. I was found guilty of this charge of interfering with an officer, and the judge and the county prosecutor went out, consulted, and came back and I was given a suspended sentence, 90 days suspended sentence, and fined $5 for the cost of court. I refused to pay the $5 cost of court and argued that I shouldn't be given anything at all and should be set free since I was obviously not guilty. I was taken to jail then, and this was my first introduction to Mississippi jails. I spent a couple days in jail and was finally bailed out when the bondsman came through, supplied by the NAACP. We decided at that point to appeal the case, though later the appeal was dropped. Well, that was our first introduction to Amite county.

Immediately after that we rode out to Steptoe's house, who was the local president of the NAACP, in the southern part of the county, and made plans to set up a school on his farm. We did and for the last two weeks in August we proceeded to teach people, farmers in the southern part of Amite County at the little church there, coming two, three, sometimes five at a time. We were severely handicapped because we didn't have any transportation. And the farms there were fairly far apart, so we had to wait on the people at the Church. While we were out there next week another team went down to Liberty to register, and they didn't have any difficulty at all. This was Aug. 22. In fact, the boys that went down with them were able to stay in the registrar's office and the people were able to complete their registration without difficulty. They sent word of this back out to us at Steptoe's and we were somewhat encouraged by this.

After that, we planned to make another registration attempt on the 29th of August, which was again a Tuesday. We didn't figure we would have much trouble, although there had been rumors sort of floating around out there at Steptoe's that there might be trouble if people made another registration attempt down there at Liberty. This was the day then that Curtis Dawson and Preacher Knox and I were to go down and try to register. This was the day that Curtis Dawson drove to Steptoe's, picked me up and drove down to Liberty and we were to meet Knox at the courthouse lawn, and instead we were to walk through the town and on the way back were accosted by Billy Jack Caston and some other boys. I was severely beaten. I remember very sharply that I didn't want to go immediately back into McComb because my shirt was very bloody and I figured that if we went back in we would probably be fighting everybody. So, instead, we went back out to Steptoe's where we washed down before we came back into McComb.

Well, that very same day, they had had the first sit-in in McComb, so when we got back everybody was excited and a mass meeting was planned for that very night. And Hollis and Curtis had sat in the Woolworth lunch counter in McComb and the town was in a big uproar. We had a mass meeting that night and made plans for two things: one, the kids made plans to continue their sit-in activity, and two, we made plans to go back down to Liberty to try to register some more. We felt it was extremely important that we try and go back to town immediately so the people in that county wouldn't feel that we had been frightened off by the beating and before they could get a chance there to rally their forces.

Accordingly on Thursday, August 31, there was more activity in Liberty and McComb. In McComb, there were more sit-ins, in Liberty, another registration attempt coupled with an attempt by us to find the person who had done the beating and have his trial. Well, it turned out that we did find him, that they did have his trial, that they had a six-man Justice of the Peace jury, that in a twinkling of an eye the courthouse was packed. That is, the trial was scheduled that day and in two hours it began and in those two hours farmers came in from all parts of the county bearing their guns, sitting in the courthouse. We were advised not to sit in the courthouse except while we testified, otherwise we were in the back room. After we testified, the sheriff came back and told us that he didn't think it was safe for us to remain there while the jury gave its decision. Accordingly, he escorted us to the county line. We read in the papers the next day that Billy Jack Caston had been acquitted. . . .

To top it all off, the next week John Hardy was arrested and put in jail in Walthall County. He had been working there for two weeks and they had been taking people down, and finally one day he had taken some people down to the registrar's office, had walked in, they had been refused the right to register, and he had asked the registrar why. The registrar recognized him, took the gun out of his drawer and smacked John on the side of his head with a pistol. John staggered out onto the street and was walking down the street when he was accosted by the sheriff who arrested him and charged him with disturbing the peace. John wound up in the Magnolia jail in Pike County because it was too hot for him in Walthall County, and they had to transfer him immediately. He was in the cell next to the sit-in kids. That was the first time I had gone down and had a chance to see them all in jail down there. It was pretty hot down there and they told me that they were not allowed to take baths, that the food was pretty bad and their spirits, however, were good, except that they were obviously losing weight and one of them was very anxious to come home. Well, the Justice Department entered immediately on John Hardy's case. Took place I think on Sept. 7. Two days later they had filed a suit in the District Federal Court in Jackson, asking for an injunction to stop the trial which was to take place the next day, I think, in Walthall County. Judge Cox, who was the first appointee of President Eisenhower and a long friend of Senator Eastland, an obvious patronage or an obvious result of the senatorial privilege in appointing judicial appointments to the Federal Courts, refused to give them a favorable hearing. I suppose that it was a victory that he heard it at all that evening and that they were able then to fly on to Montgomery that night, I think it was a Thursday night, and wake up Judge Reeves in Montgomery, Alabama at 12 o'clock at night and ask him to give a temporary injunction and overrule Judge Cox.

Well, in the meantime, we had to go back to Walthall County, John Hardy and myself, to face this trial the next morning. We didn't know whether the Justice Department would be able to get a stay or not. I remember that morning that we were both rather quiet and a little shook at the thought of going back into Walthall County to face this trial. We got there early in the morning, and there were people gathering and gathered as soon as we appeared. They sent us up into the buzzard's roost, a little sort of sloping shelf-like extension at the back of the courtroom at Tylertown which is the county seat of Walthall County. Then all the old farmers and the young ones and the thugs and all-man male chorus gathered downstairs to see if the trial was going to take place. While we were sitting there, the county prosecuting attorney came and announced that the Justice Dept. had obtained a stay from Judge Reeves in Alabama and that the trial would be continued from term of court to term of court and that until that time John Hardy was free and not bound to stay in jail. So we left, at least we tried to leave. The people were rather thick in the corridors as we were leaving and were grabbing hold of John by the shirt-sleeve and making nasty remarks at him as we left. We finally got through into the car and there, of all things, the car door was stuck, so we couldn't get it open. Finally, a local policeman came and told us that we had better hurry up and get out of there because he could only hold up the people back of us for so long. We backed out into the mob and then got on out of town being very careful to stay under the speed limit. We finally got back into McComb. Well, that was about it. A couple of days before John Hardy was arrested, we had gone back into Amite County to Liberty. This time I was not beaten, but Travis Britt was. I think that was on the 5th of September, and I stood by and watched Travis get pummeled by an old man, tall, reedy and thin, very, very, very mean with a lot of hatred in him. Luckily, he wasn't very strong and he didn't do too much damage to Travis who suffered an eye bruise and some head knocks. At that particular occasion, Travis and I had been sitting out front of the courthouse and then decided to move around back because the people began to gather out front. Finally, everybody, about 15 people, gathered around back and began questioning Travis and myself. My only reaction to this in all these instances is simply to shut up, to be silent. I get very, very depressed. So people were talking with Travis and he was answering them some. They were asking him where was he from and how come a nigger from New York City could think that he could come down and teach people down here how to register to vote and have all those problems up there in New York City, problems of white girls going with nigger boys and all such like that. Finally they began to beat on Travis, and I started going towards the sheriff's office and was cut off. Finally went back and tried to get Travis away from this fellow who was beating on him. We did this. And we walked over to a truck nearby and got in it and went on back to McComb. . . .

And then, finally, the boom lowered, on September 31: Herbert Lee was killed in Amite County. We had spent the previous week in Amite County with lawyers from the Justice Department investigating and taking affidavits from all the people who had been down to register. The Sunday before Lee was killed, I was down at Steptoe's with John Doar from the Justice Department and he asked Steptoe was there any danger in that area, who was causing the trouble and who were the people in danger. Steptoe told him that E. H. Hearst who lived across from him had been threatening people and that specifically he, Steptoe, Herbert Lee and George Reese were in danger of losing their lives. We went out, but didn't see Lee that afternoon. At night John Doar and the other lawyers from the Justice Department left. The following morning about 12 noon, Doc Anderson came by the Voter Registration office and said a man had been shot in Amite County—that he had brought him over to McComb and he was lying on the table in the funeral home in McComb, and he asked me if I might have known him. I went down to take a look at the body and it was Herbert Lee; There was a bullet hole in the left side of his head just above the ear. He had on his farm clothes and I was told that he had been shot that morning. Well, wasn't much to do; we waited until nightfall and then went out into Amite County and for the next four or five nights we rode the roads, from the time it got dark until light, about three or four in the morning.

Our first job was to try to track down those people, those Negroes, who had been at the shooting and to try to get their stories, and there were three such people who had been at the shooting, who had seen the whole incident and essentially they told the same story. Essentially, the story was this: they were standing at the cotton gin early in the morning and they saw Herbert Lee drive up in his truck with a load of cotton, E. H. Hearst following behind him in an empty truck. Hearst got out of his truck and came to the cab on the driver's side of Lee's truck and began arguing with Lee. He began gesticulating towards Lee and pulled out a gun which he had under his shirt and began threatening Lee with it. One of the people that was close by said that Hearst was telling Lee, "I'm not fooling around this time, I really mean business," and that Lee told him, "Put the gun down. I won't talk to you unless you put the gun down." Hearst put the gun back under his coat and then Lee slid out on the other side, on the offside of the cab. As he got out, Hearst ran around the front of the cab, took his gun out again, pointed it at Lee and shot him. This was the story that three Negro witnesses told us on three separate nights as we went out in Amite County, tracking them down, knocking on their doors, waking them up in the middle of the night. They also told us another story: two of them admitted that they had been pressured by the local authorities, the sheriffs and the deputy sheriffs, and some of the white people in town, that there had been a fight, that Lee had had a tire tool, that he had tried to hit Hearst with the tire tool, and that Hearst had shot Lee in self-defense. They said that this story was not true, but that they had been forced to tell it for fear of their own lives. Lee, in any case, was a small man, about 5'4", weighing about 150 lbs. Hearst was a large man, about 6'2", upwards of 200 lbs. I understand. It is inconceivable that he could have been so threatened by Lee with a tire tool, that he would have had to shoot him. The fact was, as I believe, as one of the witnesses who was standing directly behind Lee stated, was that Lee never raised a hand to hit him and that Hearst simply ran around the front of his car and shot him. Doctor Anderson, who received the body later in McComb, said that there were no powder burns on Lee's head and that it was not possible, as Hearst claimed, that the gun went off accidently as he hit Lee on the side of the head. Lee's body lay on the ground that morning for two hours, uncovered, until they finally got a funeral home in McComb to take it in. No one in Liberty would touch it. They had a coroner's jury that very same afternoon. Hearst was acquitted. He never spent a moment in jail. In fact, the sheriff had whisked him away very shortly after the crime was committed. I remember reading very bitterly in the papers the next morning, a little short article on the front page of the *McComb Enterprise Journal*, said that the Negro had been shot in self-defense as he was trying to attack E. H. Hearst. That was it. You might have thought he had been a bum. There was not mention that Lee was a farmer, that he had a family, that he had nine kids, beautiful kids, that he had been a farmer all his life in Amite County and that he had been a very substantial citizen. It was as if he had been drunk or something and had gotten into [a] fight and gotten shot. That wasn't the end of the case; we tried to track down and see if we could prove or attach it to the voter registration drive. Now we knew in our hearts and minds that Hearst was attacking Lee because of the voter registration drive, and I suppose that we all felt guilty and felt responsible, because it's one thing to get beat up and it's another thing to be responsible, or to participate in some way in a killing. We found out only that Hearst had been waiting for Lee on the road at a State Senator's house the morning of the killing, that when Lee came by Hearst said, "Oh, there goes Lee. I have something to see him about" And he got into a truck and drove off. Wasn't even driving his own truck, was driving Billy Jack Caston's truck, yet the shooting was done with his own gun, which probably means that he was carrying it on his person, which we also know is contrary to his accustomed use. People saw them passing on the highway first close behind Lee and then the people saw the actual killing. But, all the material of the Citizens Councils meetings that had taken place in Liberty where people had come from counties 200 miles away to discuss the voter registration drive, the plans that had been made at the meetings, the plans to stop the drive, were not available and try as we might we couldn't get people who even lived in town to breathe a word about any of the things which the white people invariably tell Negroes when things are about to happen.

There was in the end, about a month later, one of the witnesses "came over to McComb to tell us that they were going to have the grand jury hearing, that he had told a lie at the coroner's jury, that he wanted to know that if he told the truth . . . at the grand jury hearing, would it be possible to provide him with protection. We called the Justice Department and talked to responsible officials in that department. They told us that there was no way possible to provide protection for a witness at such a hearing and that probably, in any case, it didn't matter what he testified and that Hearst would be found innocent. So this man went back and told the story that he told the coroner's jury to the grand jury and they did obviously fail to indict Hearst.

For this man, that wasn't the end of his troubles, and about six or eight months later, his jaw was broken by the deputy sheriff who knew that he had told the FBI that he had been forced to tell a lie to the grand jury and to the coroner's jury, because the deputy sheriff told him exactly what he had told the FBI. It's for reasons like these that we believe the local FBI is sometimes in collusion with the local sheriffs and chiefs of police and that Negro witnesses aren't safe in telling inside information to local agents of the FBI. Well, I supposed that we would have been very, very, very beat down except that we didn't have the time. . . .

REVOLUTION IN MISSISSIPPI

Tom Hayden

Along with the almost entirely black Student Non-Violent Coordinating Committee (SNCC), the mostly white Students for a Democratic Society (SDS) helped organize a renewed activism among college students in the early 1960s. Both groups would later become part of a self-proclaimed New Left. As of 1962, however, when this report on the SNCC drive in Mississippi was written, both SNCC and SDS were still part of the liberal wing of American politics. Tom Hayden was one of the organizers of SDS and one of its most visible and articulate leaders. His account of Mississippi complements Moses' in several respects. Most importantly, he highlights Moses' own role, something Moses always sought to downplay.

Hayden's admiring account was one of the ways in which potential recruits for the Freedom Summer first learned of SNCC's campaign in Mississippi. Young men and women who hoped to do something meaningful with their lives, to "make a difference," began to see in Bob Moses and other field-workers a role model and in the Mississippi campaign an opportunity to participate in a noble cause.

> We are smuggling this note from the drunk tank of the county jail in Magnolia, Mississippi. Twelve of us are here, sprawled out along the concrete bunker; Curtis Hayes, Hollis Watkins, Ike Lewis, and Robert Talbert, four veterans of the bunker, are sitting up talking— mostly about girls; Charles McDew ("Tell the story") is curled into the concrete and the wall; Harold Robinson, Stephen Ashley, James Wells, Lee Chester Vick, Leotus Eubanks, and Ivory Diggs

Source: *Revolution in Mississippi* by Tom Hayden, published by Students for a Democratic Society, 1962.

lay cramped on the cold bunker; I'm sitting with smuggled pen
and paper, thinking a little, writing a little; Myrtis Bennett and
Janie Campbell are across the way wedded to a different icy
cubicle.

Later on Hollis will lead out with a clear tenor into a freedom
song; Talbert and Lewis will supply jokes; and McDew will discourse
on the history of the black man and the Jew. McDew—a black by
birth, a Jew by choice and a revolutionary by necessity—has taken on
the deep hates and deep loves which America, and the world, reserves
for those who dare to stand in a strong sun and cast a sharp shadow.

In the words of Judge Brumfield, who sentenced us, we are "cold
calculators" who design to disrupt the racial harmony (harmonious
since 1619) of McComb into racial strife and rioting; we, he said,
are the leaders who are causing young children to be led like sheep
to the pen to be slaughtered (in a legal manner). "Robert" he was
addressing me, "haven't some of the people from your school been
able to go down and register without violence here in Pike county?"
I thought to myself that Southerners are most exposed when they
boast.

It's mealtime now: we have rice and gravy in a flat pan, dry bread
and a "big town cake"; we lack eating and drinking utensils. Water
comes from a faucet and goes into a hole.

This is Mississippi, the middle of the iceberg. Hollis is leading off
with his tenor, "Michael, row the boat ashore, Alleluia; Christian
brothers don't be slow, Alleluia; Mississippi's next to go, Alleluia"
This is a tremor in the middle of the iceberg—from a stone that the
builders rejected.

Bob Moses
Nov. 1, 1961

WHY MCCOMB?

To understand the choice of McComb for a pilot project, we must
trace the actions of Robert Moses during 1960–1961. During the
spring of 1960, Moses, a teacher, spent his evenings working in the
New York office of the Southern Christian Leadership Conference. In
July 1960, Moses went to work for SNCC in Atlanta.

Moses was sent on a field trip, specifically to get people from
Deep South areas to attend SNCC's fall meeting. Stopping in
Cleveland, Mississippi, Moses became acquainted with Aimsie
Moore, a militant Negro leader, who convinced him of the potential
efficacy of an all-out campaign to register Negro voters.

The adult Negro population of a remote, rural Mississippi county
far removed from industrial society do not even possess means of

communication among themselves, much less means of communication with the outside world. This situation precluded the non-violent direct action characteristic of the sit-ins. But Moses and Moore saw the possibility of getting out on those dirt roads and into those old broken homes, talking the language and living the life of the oppressed people there, and persuading them to face the trials of registration. That trial passed, a Negro community with an actual voice in local, if not regional, politics, might be built, thereby acquiring the possibility for educational and social reforms. Most of all, a spirit that is vital to the eventual destruction of segregation might replace the spiritual apathy which now characterizes the Negro community.

Moses began drafting a proposal for SNCC to begin a voter registration project in the delta region, where two-thirds of the over-21 population is Negro. It took nearly a year, but this summer Moses was back in Mississippi, SNCC had completed its organizational reshuffling, and the project was ready to begin.

At this point accident again influenced events. The national Negro magazine *Jet* printed a brief note about the proposed Mississippi project. It was read by C. C. Bryant, head of the NAACP chapter in Pike County where McComb is located. Bryant wrote to Moses, indicating the desirability of such a project in the Pike County area. Moses was having difficulty obtaining anything better than deteriorated buildings in which to establish his Voter Registration School in the delta. He went to see Bryant in McComb, found conditions more suitable for immediate action, and decided to establish the project there and in the adjoining counties, Walthall and Amite.

THE PROJECT BEGINS

SNCC, in its attempt to ignite a mass non-violent movement, designated the formidable and sovereign state of Mississippi as the site of its pilot project. Moses moved to McComb, a city of 13,000. He found a number of local adults, high school students, and non-student youth eager to assist him. They provided contacts, housing, some transportation, and (particularly the students) began canvassing the surrounding area, determining the numbers of registered and unregistered voters, informing the citizens of the SNCC program and inviting them to participate. By the end of the first week, John Hardy, Nashville, and Reggie Robinson, Baltimore, had arrived as SNCC field representatives to help in the project.

On August 7, 1961, the SNCC Voter Registration School opened in Burglundtown in a combination cinder block-and-paintless wood frame two-story structure which houses a grocery below and a Masonic meeting hall above. A typical voter registration (or citizenship) class involved a study of the Mississippi State Constitution, filling out of sample application forms, description of the typical habits of the Southern registrar—whose discretionary powers are enormous—and primarily attempted the morale building, encouragement and consequent group identification which might inspire the exploited to attempt registration.

On the first day of the school, four persons went down to the registrar's office in nearby Magnolia, the county seat of Pike; three of them registered successfully. Three went down on August 9th; two were registered. Nine went down on August 10th; one was registered. By this time, articles in the local press, the (McComb) *Enterprise-Journal,* had increased awareness of the project, stirring a few Negroes from Walthall and Amite to come to the McComb classes. However, the thrust of the movement was somewhat blunted on the evening of August 10th when one of the Negroes who had attempted to register was shot at by a white. (It is now clear that the shooting had nothing to do with the attempted registration that day. However, in the minds of the Negro community, for whom the vote is intimately connected with intimidation and violence, the association was made between the two events.) Attendance at the Voter Registration School quickly diminished.

Moses and the others began to rebuild. People were talked to; nights were spent in the most remote areas; days were spent canvassing all around. Then on August 15th, the first of a still continuing series of "incidents" occurred. On that day, Moses drove to Liberty (yes, it is ironic), the county seat of Amite, with three Negroes (Ernest Isaac, Bertha Lee Hughes and Matilda Schoby) who wished to register. Moses was asked to leave the registrar's office while the three attempted to fill out the registration forms. The three claim that while they were so engaged the registrar assisted a white female in answering several of the questions. Upon completing the test, the applicants were told by the registrar that their attempts were inadequate. The registrar then placed the papers in his desk and asked the three not to return for at least six months, at which time presumably they might try further. (I have been told by a reliable Federal source that the tests were not of a quality character.)

Leaving Liberty, driving toward McComb, the group was followed by a highway patrolman, Marshall Carwyle Bates of Liberty, who flagged them over to the side of the road. Bates asked the driver, Isaac, to step out of his car and get inside of the police car in the rear. Isaac complied. Then Moses left the car and walked back to the police car to inquire about the nature of the pull-over. Bates ordered Moses back to the car and shoved him. Thereupon, Moses began to write the Marshall's name on a pad of paper, and was shoved into the car. Moses, incidentally, was referred to as the "nigger who's come to tell the niggers how to register." Finally, the contingent of four Negroes was ordered to drive to the Justice of the Peace's office in McComb, where Moses was eventually charged with impeding an officer in the discharge of his duties, fined $50 and given a suspended sentence. Moses phoned the Justice Department, collect, from the station, which alerted the police to his significance. (The local paper called collect the next day, was refused by the Justice Department, and asked editorially why Moses was so privileged.) The fine was paid by the NAACP in order to appeal the case, and Moses did go to jail for a period of two days, during which he did not eat.

On the same day several other SNCC persons entered Pike County: Gwendolyn Green, Washington; Travis Britt, New York; William Mitchell, Atlanta; Ruby Doris Smith, Atlanta; James Travis, Jackson; and MacArthur Cotton, Jackson. Responsibilities were divided and the canvassing increased.

REGISTRATION, SIT-INS, AND VIOLENCE

During this same time there had been requests from Negroes in Walthall county to set up a school there. A site for the school and living quarters were offered. John Hardy was selected to go to the area. Along with several others, he established the school on August 18th. About 30 persons attended the first session. Eighty percent of the Negroes in Walthall are farmers, and 60 percent own their own land. The heavy schedule imposed on the farmers at this time of year required that classes be scheduled so as not to conflict with the workday schedule. School was held at the Mt. Moriah Baptist Church and at private homes. Moses came into Amite several days later and remained for nearly a week, teaching and visiting "out the dirt roads." On August 22nd, four Negroes tried to register in Liberty; none succeeded; no incident occurred. By this time, however, dramatic events were occurring in Pike County.

On August 18th, Marion Barry from Nashville, a SNCC field representative particularly concerned with initiating direct action, arrived in McComb. Those students too young to vote, many of whom had canvassed regularly, were eager to participate actively. The Pike County Non-Violent Movement was formed; workshops in the theory and practice of non-violence were held. On August 26th two of the youths, Elmer Hayes and Hollis Watkins (both 18), sat-in at the lunch counter of the local Woolworth's, the first direct action incident in the history of the county. The two were arrested and remained in jail 30 days. The charge: breach of peace. Their arrest set the stage for a mass meeting in McComb on August 29th. The Reverend James Bevel, of Jackson, spoke to a crowd of nearly 200. The paper of the following day carried the story lead, in large type, and the local columnist warned the citizens that the Negroes were not engaged in a mere passing fad, but were serious in intention.

On August 30th, a sit-in occurred at the lunch counter of the local bus station. Isaac Lewis, 20, Robert Talbert, 19, and Brenda Lewis, 16, were arrested on charges of breach of peace and failure to move on. They remained in jail for 28 days. By now, a current of protest had been generated throughout the counties. Subsequent events intensified the feeling. On August 29th, Bob Moses took two persons to the registrar's office in Liberty. They were met by Billy Jack Caston (cousin of the sheriff and son-in-law of State Representative Eugene Hurst) who was accompanied by another cousin and the son of the sheriff. (Should this seem peculiar, read Faulkner.) Caston smashed Moses across the head and dropped him to the street. The other Negroes were not harmed. Moses' cuts required eight stitches. Moses filed assault and battery charges against Caston, perhaps the first time in the history of Amite that a Negro has legally contested the right of a white man to mutilate him at fancy. Approximately 150 whites attended the trial on August 31st. Among other questions, Caston's attorney asked Moses if he had participated in the riots in San Francisco or Japan; Moses replied that he had not. Upon the suggestion of law officials, Moses left the trial, at which he was the plaintiff, before the "not guilty" verdict in order to escape mass assault.

Meanwhile in Walthall, the first attempt to register Negroes since the Justice Department suit of the Spring of 1961 was made. Five persons went to Tylertown, the county seat, with John Hardy. As all businesses close at noon on Thursdays, only two of the five had time to take the test. One was a teacher, the other a senior political science major at Jackson State College (Negro). Both failed. On the same day Hardy, in an interview with the editor of the *Tylertown Times*, made a remark which was interpreted as an endorsement of atheism. This was to "mark" Hardy, if he had not already been marked. On the following evening a mass "encouragement" meeting was held in rural Tylertown; about 80 attended. Again, a mass meeting was held on September 4th to emphasize the significance of the vote and of citizenship.

On September 5th, three Negroes waited two hours in Tylertown, then were informed that the registrar had to attend a meeting and would not be able to register them. The following day another Negro appeared at the registrar's office, and was told to return at a time more convenient for the registrar.

Back in Liberty (Amite county seat), on August 31st, Travis Britt had appeared at the registrar's office with several Negroes. He was told by the registrar to get out of the office. As he stood outside, Bob Moses approached with two witnesses of his August 29th beating to prepare affadavits against Caston. Suddenly two shots were fired outside. Two of the three Negroes attempting to register interrupted their work to rush out, thinking Moses and Britt were in jeopardy. A crowd of whites had gathered as had police, but the source of the shooting was unclear. At any rate, the office was scheduled to close at noon, which prevented the three from finishing the test. They report that they had been told by the registrar that they could return whenever ready. No incidents occurred outside when they all left, although the white group remained.

On September 5th, fear became terror throughout the region as a result of the beating of Travis Britt in Liberty. He and Moses accompanied four Negroes to the registrar's office. Let Britt's words tell the story: "There was a clerk directly across the hall who came rushing out while we were waiting, and ordered us to leave the hallway. He said he didn't want a bunch of people congregating in the hall. So we left and walked around the building to the court house, near the registrar's window. By the time we reached the back of the building a group of white men had filed into the hall, in about the same spot we'd been 'congregating' in. They were talking belligerently. Finally one of the white men came to the end of the hall as if looking for someone. He asked us if we knew Mr. Brown. We said no. He said, You boys must not be from around here. We said he was correct. This conversation was interrupted by another white man who approached Bob Moses and started preaching to him: how he should be ashamed coming down here from New York stirring up trouble, causing poor innocent people to lose their homes and jobs, and how he (Bob) was lower than dirt on the ground for doing such a thing, and how he should get down on his knees and ask God forgiveness for every sin of his lifetime. Bob asked him why the people should lose their homes just because they wanted to register and vote. The white gentleman did not answer the question, but continued to preach. He said that the Negro men were raping the white women up North, and that he didn't want and wouldn't allow such a thing to start down here in Mississippi. He went on to say that the Negro in New York was not allowed to own homes or establish businesses so why didn't we go the hell back home and straighten out New York instead of trying to straighten out Mississippi. At this point Bob turned away and sat on the stoop of the court house porch, and the man talking to him took a squatting position. Nobody was saying anything. I reached in my pocket and took out a cigarette. A tall white man, about middle-aged, wearing a khaki shirt and pants stepped up to me and asked 'Boy, what's your business?' at which point I knew I was in trouble. (Recall: Moses had already been beaten earlier, had filed charges, had called Washington, and was much less 'open game' than Britt at this point. T.H.) The clerk from the hallway came to the back door leading to the courthouse with a smile on his face and called to the white man, 'Wait a minute; wait a minute!' At this point, the white man, whom they called Bryant, hit me in my right eye. Then I saw this clerk motion his head as if to call the rest of the whites. They came and all circled around me, and this fellow that was called Bryant hit me on my jaw, then on my chin. Then he slammed me down; instead of falling, I stumbled onto the court house lawn. The crowd (about 15, I think) followed, making comments. He was holding me so tight around the collar; I put my hands on the collar to ease the choking. The clerk hollered 'Why don't you hit him back?' This set off a reaction of punches from this fellow they called Bryant; I counted fifteen; he just kept hitting and shouting, 'Yes, why don't you hit me, nigger? Yes, why don't you hit me, nigger?' I was beaten into a semi-conscious state. My vision was blurred by the punch in the eye. I heard Bob tell me to cover my head to avoid any further blows to the face. I told Bryant if he was through beating me, I was ready to go. The clerk said, yes, I should go. Then this guy they called Bryant yelled, 'Brothers, shall we kill him here?' I was extremely frightened by the sincere way he said it. No one in the crowd answered the question, and Bryant (I found out his last name was Jones) released me. Moses then took me by the arm and took me to the street, walking cautiously to avoid any further kicks or blows. The Negro fellow that had been taking the registration test gave up in the excitement, and we saw him in his truck. The white men advised him to get the hell out of town, saying they were surprised that he was associating with our kind." Charges were not pressed.

On September 7th, John Hardy accompanied two persons to the registrar's office at Tylertown. The two were informed by the registrar that he didn't want to have anything to do with them because he was already involved in a suit with the Federal government. Says Hardy: "I entered the office to ask why. The registrar, John Woods, had seen me on one other occasion, the 30th. After telling him my name, he came out very insultingly and boisterously questioning my motives and reasons for being in Mississippi and said I had no right to mess in the niggers' business and why didn't I go back where I came from. He reached into his desk drawer and ordered me out at gunpoint. As I turned to leave he struck me over the head with the pistol. I left his office and walked about a block. I decided to go to the sheriff's office to report the assault and possibly make charges. But this was not necessary because the sheriff found me. He told me to come with him or he would beat me 'within an inch of your life.' After being put in jail (the charge was resisting arrest and inciting a riot, and later disorderly conduct) I was interrogated at length by a city attorney and later by the district attorney. About 7:30 I was taken to Magnolia jail for 'your own protection.' I was in jail until the following night." . . .

On September 20th, the Justice Department, filing its complaint before U.S. District Judge Harold Cox in Meridian, Mississippi, asked for court orders forbidding intimidation or coercion of Negroes seeking to vote in Walthall and appealed for prevention of the Hardy trial.

On September 21st, Judge Cox declined to stop the state court trial. Among his remarks, as quoted by the Associated Press: "It is difficult to conceive how the United States can possibly be irreparably damaged by this criminal case down in Walthall County, Mississippi." "While it must be presumed that John Hardy is guilty of everything with which he is charged, it must likewise be presumed that justice will be done in the trial of the case." "This incident occurred September 7th and the government waited until September 20th to ask for instant relief. It looks like the government has a self-made emergency." "(It would be improper) for me to permit a clash of the sovereignty of the state and Federal governments on such a case."

The Federal government announced it would next appeal to the 5th Circuit Court of Appeals, in Montgomery, Alabama. On October 4th, Assistant Attorney General Burke Marshall argued before the Montgomery Court that Walthall is a place of "near lawlessness." He accused Mississippi of a "trumped-up charge" in the Hardy case, which was "an attempt to intimidate them to prevent them from registering to vote." A Mississippi assistant attorney general, Edward Cates, responded (according to A.P.) that the Federal government is seeking to "condemn a whole state without evidence," that Federal lawyers have presented no proof that Negroes in Walthall are afraid to try to register following Hardy's arrest. . . .

CULMINATING IN DEATH

A little over two weeks after the Hardy beating, Mississippi terrorism reached a peak in the killing of a 52-year-old Negro, Herbert Lee. (The following information has been obtained from several private sources.) Lee was a member of the Amite NAACP. When SNCC came to Mississippi, Lee became an active, dedicated worker, assisting Moses in meeting people and arranging get-togethers. He lived on a farm just outside of Liberty, near the Louisiana line. On the morning of September 25th, he arose early, prepared to go to Liberty to gin cotton. As Lee drove his truck into Liberty, he was followed by Mississippi State Representative Eugene Hurst. Hurst and Lee had known each other for quite some time. Lee's brother, Frank, had apparently once purchased some of Hurst's land in Louisiana. In 1956 Hurst helped Lee get a cut in the cost of some land which Lee wanted to purchase. (The reduction was from $9,000 to $7,000.) Lee in turn promised Hurst a "tip" of some $500 upon completion of Lee's payments on his land. On September 25th, Lee had paid more than $6,500 on the land and was carrying a total of $287 in his pocket.

There had reportedly been a recent economic crackdown in the whole area. The white community was circulating a list of names of those Negroes seriously involved in the voter registration or NAACP "movements"; many were being cut off from basic commodities. Mr. Steptoe, the NAACP head in Amite, received a letter, for instance, telling him to pay off his debts. . . . Such was the situation that morning in Liberty, Mississippi. When Lee stopped his truck that morning, Hurst, who is the father-in-law of Billy Jack Caston, did the same. Hurst got out of his truck, and approached Lee, carrying a .38 in his hand. Lee remained in the cab of his truck. An argument ensued, partly about debts owed, partly about the .38, and partly about a tire tool Lee was alleged to be holding in the cab. Apparently the two challenged each other to put down their respective weapons. Hurst put his gun inside his belt. Lee edged across the seat, attempting to get out on the far side of the truck, which caused Hurst to run around the front of the truck. There Hurst is alleged to have said, "You didn't use the tire tool when you had it, and you're not going to use it now." Two motions followed, both by Hurst. The second motion was a downward thrust of the arm, a shot, and Lee was on his stomach with a .38 bullet in his brain. Hurst left the scene. Lee was left on the ground fully two hours before he was taken to the Negro coroner in McComb. A tire tool was near his body. A coroner's jury, after hearing whites but no Negro witnesses, ruled that the killing was in self-defense, and thereby a justifiable homicide. Hurst was never booked, charged, or tried. . . .

A week later a little scrawled but mimeographed sign went out:

Bulletin
Mass Meeting for Voter Registration
Oct. 2nd, Tuesday
Guest Speaker
Rev. Charles Jones
From Charlotte, N. C.
Masonic Hall 630 Warren
7:30
Collection will be taken for the
wife and ten children of
Mr. Herbert Lee.

The Pike County Non-Violent Movement, perhaps the youngest and most challenged in the South, was resuming operation. The five sit-inners had returned from jail. On October 3rd, the mass meeting was held. Parents attended and spoke. People stressed that the corrupt government which permitted Lee's death could only be eliminated if Negroes registered. A total of $81 was collected for Lee's wife and ten children. . . .

"HOW A SECRET DEAL PREVENTED A MASSACRE AT OLE MISS"

George B. Leonard, T. George Harris, and Christopher S. Wren

SNCC's voting rights campaign in Mississippi had attracted little national attention over its first two years. Tom Hayden's account, for example, appeared in an SDS publication with a relatively small circulation. Instead it was James Meredith's efforts to enroll at the University of Mississippi that captured the headlines. Meredith, like the Evers brothers and others who challenged Theodore Bilbo's victory in 1946, was a veteran. Like them his demand was for equal treatment under the law. In September 1962 the Federal District Court in New Orleans ordered officials at the university to allow Meredith to enroll. Led by Governor Ross Barnett, they refused. This

Source: "How a Secret Deal Prevented a Massacre at Ole Miss," by George B. Leonard, T. George Harris, and Christopher S. Wren, *Look*, Dec. 31, 1962.

set the stage for a showdown between the federal government and the state of Mississippi. On September 26th the court ordered Barnett to appear two days later to "show cause, if he has any, . . . why he should not be adjudged in contempt of orders issued by this court." Barnett faced fines of up to $10,000 a day plus the prospect of jail until he purged himself of contempt by obeying the court order.

Barnett was caught in a trap of his own design. He had made himself the responsible party for university policy as a way of winning white support. He needed a way to obey the court's order without losing that support. The Kennedy administration was also caught in a trap of its own design. It had consistently urged civil rights organizations to avoid confrontational tactics like sit-ins and to concentrate upon legal challenges to segregation. Here was a legal challenge threatening to blow up into a confrontation that might lead to mass violence and the use of federal troops against Mississippi whites. Kennedy, who had chosen Lyndon Johnson as his vice president in large part to hold on to white southern votes, faced a political dilemma that was the mirror image of Barnett's. Not surprisingly, the administration and the governor worked behind the scenes to strike a deal. This account from *Look,* a popular weekly magazine, was the first full telling of the tale of these negotiations.

Between noon and midnight of September 30, 1962, this nation came within one man's nod of a state-sized civil war. The riot that exploded at the University of Mississippi in Oxford brought death to two men and injuries to hundreds. But it was a pep rally compared with what almost happened.

A group of Mississippi leaders had been secretly planning to form a wall of unarmed bodies that would not yield until knocked down and trod upon by Federals. Many segregationists were prepared to go to jail. Many were ready to fight with fists, rocks and clubs. Some resolved to stand until shot down. Others planned to defy the orders of their leaders and conceal pistols on their persons.

"In retrospect, I'm thankful that 5,000 to 10,000—maybe 15,000 to 20,000—fellow Mississippians didn't go there and get killed," said Dr. M. Ney Williams, 40, a director of the Citizens' Council and adviser to Gov. Ross Barnett in the crisis. This earnest segregationist may have overstated, but he is one of a small group who knew the situation's real potential. No one who understood Mississippi's "wall-of-flesh" strategy estimates that less than "hundreds" would have been killed had the plan been carried out.

What the segregationists did not know is this: While Barnett was encouraging their efforts, he was—throughout the four days before the riot—secretly suggesting schemes to Attorney General Robert Kennedy that would allow Negro James Meredith to enter Ole Miss.

This strange story has never been told. To uncover the facts behind the Battle of Ole Miss, three LOOK editors spent weeks interviewing more than 105 individuals in Jackson and Oxford, Miss., Atlanta, Ga., and Washington, D.C. From this search, LOOK has pieced together a chronicle of courage and cross-purposes, of passion and patience, of a massacre barely avoided.

The untold story begins after Mississippi's legal fight to keep Meredith out of Ole Miss had failed. By Thursday, September 27, Governor Barnett was legally on the defensive. He was under orders from the 5th U.S. Circuit Court, meeting the next day in New Orleans, to show cause why he should not be held in contempt of court. Three times already, he had blocked Meredith's attempts to enroll. Barnett knew that if he did not let the Negro into Ole Miss he probably would be held in contempt—and face a huge fine and possibly jail.

Other pressures were bearing down on Ross Barnett, an ambitious man who wanted to be loved by all. He was, of course, getting pressure from Robert Kennedy through a series of personal phone calls. But an unexpected pressure was building up in Mississippi. The state's permanent leadership—the bankers, educators, lawyers and businessmen whose power is not limited to a governor's term—had begun meeting in homes and offices, phoning one another for sobering talks. Now, on the 27th, Thursday morning, the grapevine and the telephone brought Barnett a word of caution, in contrast to the usual counsel of defiance. We back your principles, Governor, the permanent leaders said in essence, but we hope your actions will not harm Ole Miss.

Was it too late for reason to prevail? The signs were bad. By noon, a great force had gathered at Ole Miss. Barnett and Lt. Gov. Paul Johnson were there. Near the university's East Gate, some 250 state troopers and county sheriffs were lined up, surrounded and infiltrated by a restless crowd of more than 2,000 students and others. All were waiting for James Meredith and whatever U.S. marshals he might have with him. Here was Mississippi's "wall of flesh."

In this dangerous impasse, Robert Kennedy awaited a call from Ross Barnett, who, through a representative earlier that day, had suggested a way out. The call did not come. Now, at 2:50 p.m., Washington time, Kennedy took the initiative and put a call through to Barnett.

"Hello," said Kennedy.

"Hello, General. How are you?" Barnett said hospitably.

The two got right down to the business of the Governor's plan. Both understood its purpose: to allow Barnett to be overwhelmed by the Federals while crying "Never" for the segregationists' benefit.

The plan called for Barnett and Johnson to stand at the university's gate, backed up by unarmed state patrolmen. Kennedy would have Chief U.S. Marshal James McShane and 25 to 30 marshals bring Meredith to the gate. Barnett would refuse to let Meredith in. At this point, McShane would draw his gun, and the other marshals would slap their hands on their holsters. Barnett would then step aside and allow Meredith to register. The Mississippi highway patrol would maintain law and order.

In his talk with Kennedy, the Governor worried about how the scene would look to "a big crowd." If only one man drew his gun, Barnett felt that he could not back down. So Kennedy reluctantly agreed to have all the marshals draw their guns. Under Federal guns, Ross Barnett could surrender to prevent bloodshed.

Kennedy knew his own duty—to uphold the courts and to do everything in his power to avoid bloodshed. He did not wish to use Federal troops against, as he put it, "my fellow Americans." And, for the sake of a long-term solution, he wanted to leave law enforcement in state and local hands.

The plan, however bizarre, would accomplish these purposes. The Attorney General set about making plans to send Meredith and an escort of marshals down to Oxford from their base at the Naval Air Station near Memphis, Tenn.

But an hour later, Barnett called back and asked for a postponement until Saturday the 29th. He seemed shaky and unsure of his control over his people. He put Lieutenant Governor Johnson on. Johnson spoke worriedly of "intense citizens," sheriffs and deputies not directly under state control. It might take time to "move them." Everything was held in suspense until Barnett phoned again. Be there at 5 p.m., Mississippi time, he told Kennedy. It was then 2:20 at Oxford. Barnett repeatedly promised there would be no violence.

Thirteen green U.S. border-patrol sedans glided down Highway 55, the new expressway running south from Memphis. Twelve contained a total of more than two dozen marshals. They had unloaded pistols and had been briefed on their role in the coming charade. The other car was driven by border patrolman Charles Chamblee of New Orleans. With him in the front seat was Chief Marshal McShane, his rugged face tight and determined.

In back, James Meredith, cool as always, sat next to John Doar, 40, of the U.S. Department of Justice. Meredith wore the armor of the new Negro's determination to ignore personal risk. The NAACP had selected him for legal backing from among eleven students ready to apply to Ole Miss. Looking at Meredith, Doar thought here is a man who can stand almost any amount of pressure.

As the convoy rolled on, Robert Kennedy phoned Ross Barnett. Kennedy wanted specific assurances that Barnett would maintain order after Meredith got on campus. Barnett's answers were disturbing. He spoke generally of keeping order "all over the state. . . . We always do that." It was then 3:35 p.m. in Oxford.

At that point, Kennedy could not possibly realize the Governor's dilemma. Barnett had set forces in motion he could not control. The brigade at the gate didn't know that he was negotiating surrender with "the enemy." Their job, as many saw it, was to stop the Federal marshals even at the cost of their lives. But they were confused las to how they would fight. Barnett feared the "hotheads" would call the turn.

Judge Russell D. Moore, III, a blocky ex-marine in command at Oxford for the Governor, had originally disarmed all highway patrolmen and sheriffs. "We didn't want any of our officers to be incited into drawing a pistol and shooting someone," he said later. In its purest form, Mississippi strategy called for passive resistance. But Moore got word that the Federals were bringing in "the goon squad," equipped with billies and gas. So he broke out helmets, night sticks and gas masks for the highway patrol, and let his sheriffs carry blackjacks, keep their gas guns handy and bring in police dogs. Moore later said he was confident that the disciplined patrolmen would have accepted an order to give way if the Federals had drawn guns.

Oxford Sheriff Joe Ford knew, however, that the visiting sheriffs would be harder to control. "If the marshals had come with their guns drawn, they might have got by the patrol," he said later, "but when they got to the sheriffs, they would have had to use them." Then, too, at least one deputy carried a hidden pistol. "We're not going to just stand up here," another said, "and let that nigger in." Both troopers and sheriffs had their regular weapons locked in car trunks—near at hand. No matter what Barnett said, the crowd's emotion would have set off violence. "It would," Moore said later, "have been a donnybrook."

At 4:35 p.m., Oxford time, Barnett phoned Kennedy again. The Governor was, he said, worried. He was nervous. He felt unable to control the crowd. The way things were going, he thought a hundred people were liable to be killed, and that would "ruin all of us." It would, he said, be embarrassing to him.

"I don't know if it would be *embarrassing*," Kennedy said. "That would not be the feeling." He hurriedly ended the conversation and ordered the convoy to turn back. It was then just 30 miles from Oxford.

The next day, Friday, September 28, in New Orleans, the Circuit Court gave Barnett until 11 a.m. Tuesday to purge himself of contempt of court. This meant, among other things, allowing Meredith to register. Otherwise, Barnett would be fined $10,000 a day and jailed.

The Governor had his deadline. But Robert Kennedy had a worse one. Getting Meredith into Ole Miss would be difficult, perhaps dangerous. But arresting the Governor of Mississippi in his state capitol! This would not only be regrettable, but immeasurably more dangerous. Kennedy imagined the mob around the capitol building— troopers, sheriffs, "hotheads" and racists from all over. Two days before, ex-General Edwin Walker had spoken over a Shreveport (La.) radio station, calling for 10,000 volunteers from every state to come to the aid of Ross Barnett. Robert Kennedy knew he would have to do everything in his power to get Meredith into Ole Miss by 11 a.m. Tuesday.

That Friday afternoon, he met with five military leaders headed by Gen. Maxwell Taylor, Chairman of the Joint Chiefs, who, like most of the others, had worked on the Little Rock paratroop operation under President Eisenhower. They considered using—if necessary— two battalions of MP's, a battle group from the 2nd Infantry Division at Fort Benning, Ga., and logistic support.

Saturday, September 29. A lovely early-autumn day in Washington. Robert Kennedy was in his office by 10 a.m., surrounded by the small group of Justice Department officials who, informally, had become the "Mississippi task force." They included wiry, brilliant Burke Marshall, 40, head of the Civil Rights Division; Deputy Attorney General Nicholas de B. Katzenbach, 40, a big-boned law scholar; and Edwin Guthman, 43, Kennedy's assistant for public information.

At 11:50, the Attorney General got a call from the Governor's mansion. He was not expecting any change in the situation, and none was forthcoming. Kennedy put down the phone and looked grimly at the men around him.

"We'd better get moving," he said, "with the military."

He picked up the phone and, at 12:15, reached President Kennedy at the White House. The President told him to come over. Before leaving, Robert Kennedy shook his head. "Maybe we waited too long."

"No," Guthman replied. "The result would have been the same, and the record is clear that we've done everything to avoid this step."

Kennedy nodded. His face was somber and sad.

At the White House, the President, with his brother and Marshall, got to work on his television address (tentatively set for Sunday night), on military planning, and drafted a proclamation federalizing the Mississippi National Guard. Meanwhile, Governor Barnett was on the phone again. He had a new twist. He proposed that, on Monday morning, he, Johnson, the troopers and sheriffs stand defiantly at the entrance to Ole Miss. While they waited, Meredith would be sneaked into Jackson, where facilities would be set up to register him. A "surprised" Barnett would complain bitterly of Federal trickery. But on Tuesday, he would allow Meredith to come to Ole Miss. He promised the President that the highway patrol would maintain law and order.

All Saturday afternoon, the men in Washington considered the proposal. In a 7 p.m. telephone call, the President himself and Governor Barnett agreed to this plan. The Governor assured him that Meredith would be safely on the campus by Tuesday morning. So the President held back his proclamation and canceled the TV time set aside for his speech.

Robert Kennedy and Burke Marshall returned to the Justice Department. Kennedy went home around 10. Just after he left, the phone rang. It was Barnett. "Well, here we go again," Ed Guthman thought wearily as he heard Nick Katzenbach tell the operator he could reach the Attorney General at home.

Guthman was right. The Governor called off the plan. Robert Kennedy's anger rose; this seemed a clear breach of an agreement between the Governor and the President of the United States. But the two men ended the conversation amiably, with the understanding that the Federals would arrive with Meredith at Oxford Monday morning—in force. The Governor said he would call again Sunday morning, at 11, Washington time.

There is a special loneliness in the White House late on a night of crisis. John F. Kennedy sat at the long table in the Indian Treaty Room, hunched over a piece of paper. Assistant Attorney General Norbert A. Schlei sat next to him. They were alone. The President took a pen and signed the proclamation federalizing the Mississippi National Guard. Before writing the date, he hesitated. "Is it past midnight?" he asked. Schlei checked his watch. "It's just 20 seconds past 12."

At Jackson's municipal stadium, about an hour earlier, Ross Barnett stood at the peak of his glory. It was half time in the night football game between Ole Miss and Kentucky. The Rebels led 7 to 0. Some 41,000 spectators sensed the electricity in the air. Hundreds of Confederate flags waved defiantly.

Ross Barnett stood on the field, buoyed by the high-pitched clamor, smiling because he felt the warmth and love of 41,000 people. He paused before a microphone. The crowd fell silent. Barnett's face was sculptured by the stadium lights. The silence heightened. Barnett raised one arm, his fist clenched in command and defiance.

It was one of those rare moments of historical suspense that were to occur several times in the next 27 hours. A variation of only two or three words in what he said would have radically altered the flow of events. A few measured words of reason would have deflected tragedy. One phrase such as "repel the invaders" would have caused much worse tragedy on the following day.

The crowd waited. "I love Mississippi," Barnett said. The crowd did not roar; it screamed. "I love her people." Another scream. His voice was resonant, throbbing with emotion. "I love our customs." The scream was almost hysterical. Every Mississippian knew what "our customs" meant. Barnett never went beyond this point. He heightened the people's hysteria, but did not tell them what to do.

In the second half, a reporter came to Governor Barnett's box. He had word that the President had federalized the Mississippi National Guard, and asked if the Governor would care to comment. The Governor said no. Events, he knew, were closing in from both directions. . . .

. . . A Jetstar from Washington touched down at the Oxford airport. The Justice Department task force, Nick Katzenbach in charge, stepped out. Katzenbach telephoned the Attorney General. The operation was still on.

Between the airport and the campus, the convoy of marshals led by Katzenbach met the state-patrol head, Col. T. B. Birdsong. Katzenbach and Chief Marshal McShane got out to exchange pleasantries. Much of the Government's hope for that night lay with the elderly colonel's steadfastness and ability.

The convoy—seven olive-drab trucks—rolled on. A marshal with a smile as broad as his shoulders rode the running board of the third truck. Clarence Albert (Al) Butler, 33, was one of four group leaders. With practiced eyes, he judged the mood and intent of the crowd that lined both sides of the road.

"You'll be sorry," a young man shouted. Butler smiled. "Nigger lover," another yelled. Butler smiled. Compared with other mobs he had seen, this one did not seem so bad. Some people even applauded. Maybe it was sarcastic, but they applauded.

Ahead, Butler spied a boy of about five wearing a cowboy hat. Butler, not liking the look of fear on the child's face, waved and called, "Hi, Cowboy." Cowboy laughed and waved back.

Highway patrolmen stood guard at the Sorority Row entrance to the university. Obeying Birdsong's orders, they let the marshals through. The trucks rolled past stately white sorority houses, then swung around a grove that sloped gently up to the classic white-columned Lyceum.

This was the university's administration building, the marshals' first objective. The only sign of life was an occasional squirrel gathering acorns in streaks of sun and shadow on the grass of the grove. Butler was dazzled by the beauty and stillness of the place.

At 4:15 p.m., the marshals dismounted and formed a cordon around the Lyceum. Butler's group of 48 held the area directly in the front, facing the grove. Butler paced up and down in the street before his men. A crowd gathered. Within a half hour, Butler estimated the number at around 500, almost all students. The first shots fired were verbal, and Butler was a main target.

"Marshal, where is your wife tonight? Home with a nigger?"

Butler's broad grin quickly earned him the name "Smiley."

"You have a nigger mistress, Smiley. You have nigger children."

Nick Katzenbach quickly set up a phone line from the Lyceum to Robert Kennedy's office in Washington and another to the White House. He told the Attorney General that Meredith could now come onto the campus, preferably via plane to the airport, then by car from there.

The airport. It was like a bad dream. The waiting Katzenbach looked up at the twilight sky to see three almost identical light planes circling. Which was Meredith's? The first, a blue and white Cessna 310, landed. Katzenbach and Guthman ran toward it. Not their man. They turned and ran to the next plane. It was Meredith. With the help of Birdsong, they drove him onto the campus without incident and took him to his room in Baxter Hall.

Unknown to Katzenbach and Guthman, the blue and white plane they had approached contained three of the Governor's group: Moore, McLaurin and Newman. They were to meet Yarbrough on campus. These men, upon first flying into the Oxford airport traffic pattern, had stared in shock at the military planes and trucks on the ground. "It's completely occupied," State Senator John McLaurin said. He thought, "Bobby and Jack jumped the gun." He did not know that Governor Barnett had made a deal with Robert Kennedy.

The Governor's men debated taking off again. Fear rose when Katzenbach and Guthman ran out to their plane, peered in the window— and turned away in disappointment. Moore expected, he said, "search and seizure."

"We got through the Federal lines untouched," McLaurin reported when he recounted the day's events.

The three met Yarbrough at the Alumni House at 6:30 and phoned Governor Barnett. They reported the early invasion, but, McLaurin later said, "apparently he knew about it already."

When they got word that Meredith was safely on campus, Robert Kennedy and Burke Marshall drove to the White House. The President's office was crowded with TV equipment and technicians. The speech had been delayed to 10 p.m., Washington time, to be sure Meredith was first safely on the campus. Robert Kennedy and Marshall met the President and several of his assistants in the Cabinet Room.

All agreed on the content and tone of the proposed address to the nation. Robert Kennedy suggested adding an appeal to the students of Ole Miss. The reports coming over the phone from the Lyceum were still fairly reassuring.

Standing in front of the Lyceum, however, Marshal Al Butler was beginning to worry. Just as darkness fell, he was hit on the left leg with a poorly made Molotov cocktail, a soda bottle filled with lighter fluid. The fuse went out when the bottle smashed on the pavement. A few minutes later, an empty bottle hit his left arm.

The crowd swelled to 1,000, then to over 2,000. Students flipped lighted cigarettes onto the canvas tops of the Army trucks parked in front of the Lyceum. One truck was set aflame by a burning piece of paper. The driver put out the fire.

The Mississippi state troopers stood, widely spaced, between the marshals and the mob. When Butler asked the troopers to move the crowd back, they did. But members of the mob began slipping through the line of Mississippi lawmen.

The verbiage thrown at the marshals now reached the limits of obscenity. Butler was particularly shocked to hear foul epithets from the lips of pretty young girls in the crowd. Butler kept smiling. He would be thankful, he thought, if words were all he had to contend with. Nor did he particularly mind the spittle aimed at him, or the coins thrown by jeering mob members.

"Here, Marshal, pick these up. . . . Smiley will pick 'em up."

The mob edged forward. Pieces of pipe, brick and cinder block, along with the usual bottles, crashed against the steps of the Lyceum and occasionally bruised or cut a marshal. Shortly after seven, Butler and another group leader, Don Forsht, asked permission to use tear gas.

"Hold it off for a while," Chief Marshal McShane said, "and maybe things will ease up."

Down in Jackson before 7 p.m., Ross Barnett finished a surrender statement and had it read over the phone for Robert Kennedy's approval: "My heart still says 'Never,' but my calm judgment abhors the bloodshed that will follow. . . . Mississippi will continue to fight the Meredith case and all similar cases through the courts. . . ."

Gloom spread through the Governor's mansion. Most of the men there, unaware of Barnett's negotiations with the Kennedys, had spent the day making plans for a Monday confrontation with the Federals. Among others, the inner circle included George Godwin, Jackson advertising man who handled the Governor's press releases during the crisis; Dr. M. Ney Williams of the Citizens' Council; William Simmons, racist intellectual and the Council's full-time staff brain; and Fred Beard, TV station manager who was arranging television facilities for Monday. Beard had worked out the words he hoped Barnett would deliver Monday at the Ole Miss gate: "We do not submit to the illegality of your take-over. We are a peaceable people. We will not take up arms against the Federal Government. If you move over us, you will move over us by pushing us aside."

Barnett's surrender statement on the radio chilled the Citizens' Council members, still patiently forming a wall of flesh around the mansion. In the Council office, Executive Director Louis Hollis, 62, could not believe the radio report. He ran across the street to the mansion and burst in upon Barnett. "Governor, everybody thinks you've surrendered," he cried, tears in his eyes. "Everybody in the office is crying. You've got to tell them you haven't surrendered."

Oxford. Inside the Lyceum, Nick Katzenbach was desperately trying to reestablish the highway-patrol roadblocks withdrawn from the entrances to the university at 6:30. Colonel Birdsong courteously refused Katzenbach's pleas. He said he had only about 25 patrol cars, with two men each. The men were unarmed and couldn't do much good. "How about the deputy sheriffs?" Katzenbach suggested. Birdsong said he had no control over them. The Colonel offered to send "some" men to the gates, if Katzenbach would dispatch a larger number of marshals to accompany them. Katzenbach said he couldn't spare them.

While this debate seesawed, "outsiders" already were streaming in through the unguarded gates. This small stream was to become a flood before midnight. Some of the newcomers were Mississippians who had heard of the marshals' arrival. Others were agitators from as far away as Los Angeles. Many of them had figured on a Monday or Tuesday battle, but now moved directly into action.

Senator Yarbrough, a man of awesome presence, led his group to the Lyceum. "Who's in charge?" they demanded. John Doar took them to Katzenbach, McShane and Guthman. South met North.

The man in between was Colonel Birdsong. He pleaded with Katzenbach to tell Yarbrough that he had not given the marshals police protection. "I've been telling these people that all I've done is escort you onto the campus," Birdsong said. "Will you please clarify this?"

Yarbrough stepped up to Katzenbach. "You've occupied it, and now you can just have it," he said bluntly, insisting that what happened from then on was the responsibility of the Federal Government. "I want to avoid bloodshed," Yarbrough said, "and to do so, we must withdraw the highway patrol."

"I have the same interest, that is, to provide law and order," responded Katzenbach, eager to avoid a clash. "But while Federal marshals are here, this in no way displaces the state authority. All law-enforcement officers must cooperate to maintain law and order. I want to be very clear about the fact that I think the withdrawal of the state troopers will not avoid violence, but is the one decisive thing that will lead to violence."

Yarbrough said that was not his judgment, and bluntly insisted he would withdraw the patrol. It was just a question of when. Soon, the argument turned on whether he would pull them out at eight or nine.

At 7:40, Robert Kennedy came on the open line. He ordered Katzenbach to inform Yarbrough that, if he didn't keep the patrol on hand, the President, then about to go on television, would tell the whole world what had happened. Yarbrough, unaware of the Governor's deals, was unimpressed. Kennedy reached the Governor's mansion in Jackson on another phone. Minutes later, Yarbrough got a call from Jackson. He answered in glum monosyllables, turned to Katzenbach and said that he would not pull out the state patrol.

At Katzenbach's urging, the Senator went out to talk to the crowd. They thought him a marshal and booed. "I don't like this any more than you do," he said. "I'm Senator George Yarbrough, and I represent the Governor. I'm on your side. I live just 40 miles from here at Red Banks." The crowd quieted down. "We don't want any violence. Get back off the street and, if you will, go back to your dormitories."

"We want Ross!" yelled the crowd.

"All right," Yarbrough responded. "If y'all get off this street, I'll go see if I can get the Governor to come up here." As he turned back to the Lyceum, he noticed that the highway patrolmen "began to get more earnest than they had been before." The troopers, he later said, were moving the crowd back across the street toward the trees.

Inside, Yarbrough told Doar he would phone Barnett to come and quiet the students. "But first," he said, "I want assurances that the Governor will not be arrested." Doar called Kennedy, handed the receiver to Yarbrough. "I don't think it's best," said Kennedy, "for the Governor to come up there now." Even if Barnett's presence did quiet the students, it would also draw hundreds more into the fight.

Chief Marshal McShane looked at the mob and sensed danger. He thought the state troopers were unable or unwilling to move the crowd back. Some troopers seemed mixed with the crowd as far back as the fourth or fifth rank. About the time Yarbrough reentered the Lyceum, McShane saw a two-foot length of pipe arch over the crowd and strike a marshal's helmet. He shouted "Gas!"—the order for gas masks. As the marshals put on their masks, the crowd fell back for a moment.

Just then, a bottle hit Al Butler on the arm. A milky liquid sprayed on his hand, then ran under his sleeve. Hours later, Butler realized that acid was searing his flesh.

"Fire!"

McShane's command was almost lost in the roar of the mob. The marshals near the center of the line fired first. Ragged salvos followed from right, then left. The cartridges in the marshals' guns emitted a blast of raw tear gas over a range of 35 feet. Wax wadding in the cartridges struck several people, who thought they had been hit by projectiles. Several gas canisters thrown by hand also hit people, including state troopers who were directly in the line of fire.

It was 7:58 p.m. in Oxford. The Battle of Ole Miss was on.

Nick Katzenbach rushed to the phone and asked for the Attorney General. "Bob," Katzenbach said, "I'm very sorry to report that we've had to fire tear gas. I'm very unhappy about it, but we had no choice."

Robert Kennedy, in the Cabinet Room, took the news with deep regret. "I think I should really go tell the President about it," he said. "He's just going on the air."

Kennedy rushed toward the President's office to give him the news. But it was too late. The TV cameras already were in action.

Angry state troopers straggled back crying and retching from the gas. Two had been hit by canisters; one, Welby Brunt, almost died. Yarbrough squelched a rumor that Birdsong had been killed.

When some patrolmen went for their guns, Yarbrough knew it was "getting ready to get rough." He ordered the guns locked back in the trunks. Though he sympathized with the troopers, he knew better than to allow gunplay to start. He resented having to keep the patrolmen in the gassed area. At his Alumni House headquarters, he phoned the Governor's mansion and agreed that he, McLaurin, Newman and Moore should pull out. (They reported back to Jackson about 11 p.m.)

They kept coming back. Even after barrages of tear gas, the crowd surged back, throwing stones, bricks, chunks of concrete. Marshals with long riot experience had not seen a mob like this. McShane's men did not realize that, as the more reasonable students withdrew, they were replaced by outsiders, fresh and ready for a new charge.

Reporter Fred Powledge of the Atlanta *Journal* was trapped in an automobile between the marshals and the mob. Powledge had been slugged earlier. The crowd was on the prowl for reporters.

Now, crouched down in the car, he tried to figure what to do next. If he ran toward the marshals, they would think he was attacking them, and he would be plugged with tear gas. But if he went toward the mob, he would be a dead rat in a gang of cats.

He slumped lower in the seat and switched on the car radio. The President was speaking, addressing himself to the students of Ole Miss:

"The eyes of the nation and all the world are upon you and upon all of us. And the honor of your university—and state—are in the balance. . . ."

Pomp! Pomp! Pomp! Three tear-gas guns went off.

". . . I am certain the great majority of the students will uphold that honor. . . ."

A volley of stones whistled over the car.

". . . There is, in short, no reason why the books on this case cannot now be quickly and quietly closed in the manner directed by the court. . . ."

A cloud of tear gas floated over the car. Powledge, in spite of his own predicament, felt sorry for the President.

The feeling was short-lived. He heard a voice behind him: "Let's get that son of a bitch in the car." There seemed to be no escape. Just then, three marshals rushed toward him. The first jumped up in the air and fired over the top of the car. Powledge saw "a beautiful burst of smoke" billowing over his attackers. Someone yelled, "Kennedy is a son of a bitch." The crowd fell back.

Paul Guihard and Sammy Schulman were approaching Oxford when the President ended his speech. "Oh, hell," Guihard said, "the story's all over, but we might as well go up and clean it up."

The ride from Jackson had been a strange one. The road was crowded with cars bearing Confederate flags and Barnett bumper stickers; most headed north. Neither Guihard nor Schulman realized their significance. Guihard, in a mellow mood, started talking about his past life—his desire to become an actor, his early newspapering days, his ambitions as a playwright. As a modern writer, Guihard might have scoffed at the idea of a man reviewing his life just before death.

At Oxford, the pair found that the story was far from over. They heard battle sounds as they parked their car near the far end of the grove. Friendly students told them to hide their cameras, since "some bums up there are smashing them."

"I'll see what's doing," Guihard told Schulman, "and see you back here at the car in an hour then."

At that moment, the mob suddenly rushed toward them, away from the marshals. Guihard walked straight into the crowd. Some ten minutes later, he stood near a girls' dormitory, diagonally across the grove. An assassin stood close behind him and fired a .38 pistol. The bullet pierced Paul Guihard's back and entered his heart. . . .

"We want a leader! We want a leader!"

A crowd of students and outsiders milled about the Confederate statue at the foot of the grove, 170 yards from the Lyceum. Small bands rushed in several directions. Some ran to get bricks from the construction site of the new science building. One rolled a wheelbarrow load. But no one seemed able to take charge and lead the attacks.

At 9 p.m., a great cheer went up. The state troopers were pulling out. A long line of patrol cars curved around the grove and past the Confederate monument. Fred Powledge started his car and fell in line behind the last patrol car. He decided that, if anyone tried to stop him, he would run over him slowly. One rioter leaned toward the car to see who was trying to escape. Powledge shifted into low, nudged the rioter with his fender. The man fell back. Powledge was free.

"We have a leader," the crowd exulted. A tall, erect figure stood near the monument. His dark suit made him almost invisible up to the neck, but his white Western hat gave off a ghostly glow in the gloom.

"General Walker's here!" People raced to spread the news. The ex-General mounted the base of the monument. The crowd fell silent.

"I want to compliment you all on the protest you make tonight," he said. "You have a right to protest under the Constitution." This night, he said, was the long way around to Cuba. He told the crowd they had been sold out by the man who brought the marshals onto the campus, Colonel Birdsong.

Father Duncan Gray, Jr., rector of St. Peter's Episcopal Church in Oxford, tried to climb onto the monument to rebut Walker. He was pulled down and propelled to the edge of the mob. A huge sheriff shepherded him to safety. Walker climbed off the monument and, surrounded by the crowd, walked slowly toward the Lyceum.

Radio, TV and telephone carried the riot news back to the executive mansion in Jackson. By 9 o'clock, the Governor's militant advisers saw a new hope. Maybe the rioters could drive the marshals out. Outside reinforcements, the advisers guessed, might tip the balance.

Some prayed for guidance. Some demanded that Barnett act. He could issue a call to battle. He could announce that he was on his way to Oxford. Any such move, they knew, would summon thousands of angry, armed Mississippians to the campus. A great many might be killed? They would die in a just war, and their bloody shirts would warn the country of the onrushing Kennedy dictatorship. Some of Barnett's men were ready to rush to Oxford and sacrifice their own lives.

Against the fervor for bloodshed, one man fought with equal fervor for reason. He was brilliant, red-haired Thomas Watkins, 52, corporation lawyer and for years a friend of Barnett. He was the man among the Governor's advisers most trusted by the state's business leadership, and through him, many had sent their cautions against destructive tactics. Now, he served the whole state. Passionately, he argued reason's case before a wavering judge—Ross Barnett.

Watkins won. Again, a massacre was barely averted.

"Your men are pulling out," Nick Katzenbach told Colonel Birdsong in the Lyceum. "Get them back."

"Your information must be wrong," Birdsong said. "They are not leaving." His men had been badly gassed, he said, and it was hard to control them.

"If they want to get away from the gas," Katzenbach said, "let them go down to the entrances and set up roadblocks."

"They can't do that. And now that they've been gassed, I'm not sure that they are willing to." Birdsong seemed honestly surprised that the troopers had left. Most of the patrol cars regrouped just off campus; others waited at strategic spots.

For the next few hours, the patrolmen held a series of debates over their car radios. Several troopers said the mob should be controlled. Others replied sarcastically that the students should demonstrate. One patrol car 20 miles out reported intercepting a convoy or 20 to 30 cars, with about four men in each, headed for Oxford to help the students. Some troopers favored stopping the convoy; others were opposed. The convoy was not stopped. Some patrol cars reported "a large number of civilians" entering the campus on foot from cars abandoned on Route 6. One trooper radioed in that a chartered bus with some 50 armed men aboard was heading for the campus via Route 6.

When President Kennedy heard that the state patrol had pulled out, he phoned Governor Barnett to get the men back. The Governor agreed. Later, Burke Marshall told Tom Watkins that the patrol was not returning.

"I can't believe it," Watkins said.

"They're not there, Tom."

"We'll get them back."

Worse shocks were to hit the White House. *The marshals were running out of tear gas.* Katzenbach told Robert Kennedy that only five or ten minutes' supply was left. And Marshal Graham E. Same of Indianapolis had been shot in the neck. His condition was critical.

At about this time, the battle came to a halt briefly. Father Wofford Smith, Episcopal chaplain of the university, rushed up to the marshals waving a white handkerchief. Father Smith had heard that the marshals had wounded a student with a shotgun. Inside the Lyceum, he found that the marshals had no shotguns.

The scene there horrified him. Wounded marshals lay on the floor all up and down the hall. As the chaplain stood there half dazed, he got an urgent call to go outside. Some of the students were asking for a peace conference. Father Smith tells the story:

"A marshal led me out the front door of the Lyceum and down the front steps. I walked in front waving a handkerchief and shouting as loudly as I could to the crowd, which, at this point, was a great mob. They threw rocks, glass and cursed violently and shouted, and the marshal took a flashlight and walked beside me out into the street, shining the light on my clerical collar. And the mob momentarily ceased its activities of throwing things and formed a line running north and south near the front of the circle. I called out, 'You said you wanted to talk. I'm here to talk.' And the marshal kept shouting, 'Here's your priest. He will talk to you.' And the marshals also shouted to them to stay back and let one man come forward. At this point, a young student, apparently a freshman, because his head had been shaved, stepped forward. I asked him, 'Son, what is your name?' He said, 'I'd rather not say.' I said, 'I don't blame you. You people said you wanted to talk. We must talk this situation out. This situation has reached proportions that I'm sure you don't wish as a student of this university.' And I pled with him not to bring any more shame upon the school. He said that he could not help but agree, although this was the only way that they had to display their disapproval with the fact that the Court and the marshals had forced the enrollment of a Negro in the school. He said he did not feel that he was in a position to negotiate because he was only a freshman, at which point the marshal shouted out through the crowd, 'Send us a senior.' A boy walked forward to our group and identified himself as a senior. I asked

him if he played football. He said yes. Then I knew that he was one of the boys on the team, having recognized him from the night before, down in Jackson. He said that he was there to demonstrate and to protest. Then I asked him if he would cooperate and break this up. He said that this was the only way they had to demonstrate, and I said, 'Well, why are you attacking these men at this point?' He said, 'Because we want to get Meredith,' and I said, 'To my knowledge, Meredith is not in this building.' I told him they had no right to attack these innocent marshals, that they were policemen just like the policemen in any hometown. The senior did say that he would talk to the mob, which he did."

The senior faced the mob, arms outspread.

"Here's the deal," he shouted. "Here's the deal. The marshals will quit using tear gas if we'll stop throwing rocks and bricks."

Silence, then a loud voice from deep within the mob: "Give us the nigger and we'll quit."

Someone let fly with a brick. This was followed by a broadside of stones, bricks and bottles. The marshals fired a barrage of tear gas. The battle was on again.

Tear gas fast was running out. But U.S. border patrolman Charles Chamblee was en route from the airport with fresh supplies. He drove a green border-patrol car and led a rented van full of tear gas. The two vehicles came onto the campus at breakneck speed, crashing through roadblocks set by the rioters.

"Truck! Truck! Truck!" the mob shouted along the road curving up to the Lyceum. From both sides, stones and bricks crashed against the van. It made it. Twice more that night, Chamblee ran the gauntlet. Stopped once by state troopers, he used his club to beat them out of the way. Every time the marshals were almost out of gas, Chamblee miraculously appeared, his battered van filled with fresh supplies.

Ex-General Walker had been one of those scrambling back from the tear-gas barrage that ended the peace conference. Now, he stood near the rear of the mob, stock still, hands at his sides, tie askew. Rioters rushed up to him, asking his advice and moral support. Walker answered in an even voice, his eyes fixed straight ahead.

"Sir, that minister with the marshals—he wasn't for us, was he?"

"No, he was against us. They all are. They're all selling us out."

Some of the students had tears in their eyes—not just from the tear gas. They likened themselves to the Hungarian Freedom Fighters. They believed they were fighting tyranny. For weeks, they had known only one side of the controversy. They had courage.

The rioters burned their first car, a professor's station wagon, as a fiery roadblock. The entire north side of the grove was bathed in an eerie light. The crowd fell silent. The lull was a godsend to the marshals, who again were almost out of tear gas.

As the rioters stood there holding bricks and stones, the horn of the burning automobile started blowing. For ten minutes, it wailed, as if the car were crying out in agony. Shivering, many dropped their bricks and began drifting away. By midnight, most students had returned to dormitories or fraternity houses, shaken by what they had done.

The outsiders took over the fight. Hidden snipers increased their fire. One lay in a flower bed on the northeast border of the grove and emptied his .22 rifle at the Lyceum. Miraculously, no marshals were killed. At least five cars were burning at one time. Some 200 more Mississippi guardsmen made a heroic entry through roadblocks, brick barrages, gunfire, plus—this time—a wall of flaming gasoline. But they, like Captain Falkner's group, were not equipped or trained for riot control and had little effect.

Several hundred yards to the southeast, Ray Gunter, 23, an Oxford juke-box repairman, watched the fight. Quietly, he slumped forward, a .38 bullet in his forehead. He died on the way to the hospital.

Nick Katzenbach spent more and more time on the phone, asking, "Where's the Army?" Repeatedly, he was told the troops were "twenty minutes away." The big delay actually was a multitude of small delays. The great Army wheels were slow to start.

In the White House, the President, the Attorney General and Burke Marshall moved from telephone to telephone, from the President's office to the Cabinet Room. They felt frustration, along with concern and horror. Angrily, the President told the Army to get moving.

Lieutenant Bowman's helicopter seemed to creep through the night sky. It was 12:30 a.m., Monday, before Bowman reached Oxford; the last helicopter did not touch down until after one. There were more delays in the confusion and dark. Maj. Gen. Charles E. Billingslea was on hand to supervise the Army forces. President Kennedy reached him by radio at 1:35 and relayed word to move "forthwith."

At 2:04, four gray Navy buses stopped just inside the Sorority Row entrance of the campus. Donnie Bowman led his men, grim and tight-lipped, out of the first and second buses. The marshals there told the MP's the buses could never make it through the mob. The men would have to march in. A small knot of onlookers ominously heckled the soldiers: "You'll get hurt up there." A state patrolman turned his powerful flashlight into the eyes of one of Bowman's five Negro soldiers and said, "What you doing down here, nigger?"

The soldiers fixed bayonets on their loaded rifles. About every fifth man carried a loaded riot shotgun. The MP's slipped on gas masks and moved into wedge formation. In silence, they began the half-mile march to the Lyceum, past the dimly lit sorority houses and ghostly trees. The only sound was the shuffle of boots and the grunt of breath through gas masks.

From nowhere, a volley of bricks and rocks hit them. *Ambush.* Molotov cocktails exploded just in front of them. The soldiers marched through the flames. A Molotov cocktail shattered against an MP's helmet, but failed to ignite. Gasoline trickled down his face and shirt. Several men were knocked down. Others picked them up and dragged them on. "Take it, men, just take it," said Lt. Col. John Flanagan, the commander of the 503rd MP Battalion.

Bowman couldn't believe it. He was being assaulted by fellow Americans, fellow Southerners. He swung his platoon around the overturned, flaming hulks of several cars. As the soldiers—still in formation, bayonets at ready—hove into sight, the marshals cheered.

Bullets began to splatter against the Lyceum. Anyone appearing at a window drew fire. The marshals crouched behind the trucks in front of the Lyceum. Some asked permission to return fire with their pistols. The request was phoned to the White House. Permission denied.

Strangely, only a few rioters attacked Baxter Hall, which was far more vulnerable than the Lyceum. Only 24 marshals guarded it, and its only sure communication with the Lyceum was the radio in a border-patrol car parked outside. But the marshals at Baxter had secret permission to use pistols as a last resort. Meredith was there.

Katzenbach held off asking for troops as long as he could. Before 10 p.m., as the gunfire became intense, he told Robert Kennedy they had better get the Army. Then, Katzenbach phoned the National Guard armory in Oxford and asked Capt. Murray Faulkner, nephew of the late novelist William Faulkner, to bring his men to the Lyceum.

Al Butler gasped for breath. "Mr. Katzenbach," he said, "that's not a riot out there anymore. It's an armed insurrection."

At 10:45, Butler saw the lights of four jeeps and three trucks coming up toward the grove. It was Faulkner, running a gantlet of brickbats, Molotov cocktails and roadblocks. His 55 Mississippi guardsmen tried unsuccessfully to fend off the volleys of bricks and bottles. A Molotov cocktail hit Faulkner's jeep, but did not go off. Faulkner raised his left arm to shield his face; a brick struck the arm, breaking two bones. By the time they reached the Lyceum, 13 guardsmen were wounded. Six vehicles had broken windshields. One jeep collected six bullet holes.

Those guardsmen who could stand joined the marshals on the left front of the Lyceum. Untrained in riot control, with no ammunition, no tear gas and only 15 bayonets, they had to take everything the mob could deliver. Earlier, most of the guardsmen had sympathized with the rioters. In ten minutes, sympathy vanished.

Five minutes before Faulkner's men arrived, the rioters had brought a stolen fire truck up into the grove and had tried to shoot water at the marshals. A tear-gas foray beat the mob back, and a marshal fired four bullets into the hose to reduce the water pressure.

At 10:53, Al Butler heard a motor start up somewhere beyond the lower end of the grove. He heard the clank of treads. A wild Rebel yell soared up. Butler waited to see what horror was on its way.

He saw it coming out of the smoke and haze—a bulldozer, accompanied by almost the entire mob, headed straight for the Lyceum. Butler waved a signal. The marshals charged, firing all the way. An overwhelming cloud of gas enveloped the machine, and rioters fell back, cursing and vomiting. Two marshals leaped up on the bulldozer and pulled the driver off.

Butler started to disable the bulldozer, but left it to meet an attack on the right flank. Another rioter mounted the machine, aimed it toward the marshals and jumped off. It struck a tree. Finally, Marshal Carl Ryan of Indianapolis moved the machine close to the Federal line and turned it about to face the rioters with its lights on.

Butler had hardly returned to the front of the Lyceum when he heard another wild Rebel yell. The fire truck came roaring up through the grove and swung left in a dizzy circle. On the truck's second pass, Butler grubbed the handrail and swung aboard. It veered left and sent him rolling head over heels for some 20 yards. On the third pass, two marshals shot the truck's tires. They grabbed the driver, a thin young man dressed in a white sailor suit, and dragged him away.

Down in Jackson, Governor Barnett strove to prove he had not surrendered. "I will never yield a single inch in my determination to win the fight we are all engaged in," he declared in his last press release that night. "I call on all Mississippians to keep the faith and courage. We will never surrender." But he had sent Lieutenant Governor Johnson to Oxford, as a less inflammatory substitute for himself. Johnson quickly ordered the highway patrol back in action. He stationed them on roadblocks, where, by his estimate, they stopped 600 or 800 cars loaded with armed riders. "If we hadn't done that," he believes, "there wouldn't have been a marshal left that night." . . .

"A DRAFTEE'S DIARY FROM THE MISSISSIPPI FRONT"

Charles Vanderburgh

The riot at Ole Miss marked a turning point. For the first time since Reconstruction, the U.S. Army occupied a portion of Old South as troops took over the Ole Miss campus.[1] The bloody showdown neither Governor Barnett nor President Kennedy had wanted had occurred. Further, their botched attempt to stage a mock confrontation itself became news, as in the *Look* article here reprinted. Kennedy's willingness to strike a deal with white supremacists provided further evidence to civil rights activists that they could not trust the administration, even as the use of federal troops proved to white southerners that they could not rely upon the national Democratic Party leadership. Each drew the appropriate lessons. Civil rights leaders like Bob Moses realized that they would need to force the administration's hand. White supremacists determined that they could trust only those who adopted their own militant position. The voice of "moderation" became the voice of treason in their ears.

Charles Vanderburgh was one of the soldiers given the thankless task of restoring order. His account, based upon a diary he kept, details the chaos of the riot and the disbelief he and his fellow soldiers felt as they found themselves with fixed bayonets facing American citizens.

30 Sep 62 We got to bed, fully dressed with our rifles for companions, only to be awakened at one a.m. DEFCON 1—War. Fine. We still didn't believe it until we arrived at the field and saw an endless line of big four-engined turbo-prop transports trailing off out of sight in the mist. It takes a lot of planes to carry 600 men and 140 vehicles. The Air Force loaded us, competently. The pilot instructed us on emergency procedure. Any questions? Yeah, where the hell are we going? Pilot amazed by our ignorance. Navy Memphis [Tennessee]. And where is that? About twenty miles from Mississippi. We are given a mimeographed handout. In Army language it says that we don't have to like what we are doing and we are not to talk to anyone about it, especially reporters.

---

[1]U.S. troops enforced the desegregation order of the federal court in Little Rock in 1957.

Source: "A Drafter's Diary from the Mississippi Front," by Charles Vanderburgh, from *Harper's*, February 1964.

About dawn the first plane touched down at Memphis. The rest arrived all morning, unloaded quickly, and immediately took off for Texas to get the 720th MPs. The 503rd MPs and Airborne units were arriving from Bragg. Helicopter units came in from Alabama. We hear that the 2nd Division is on the road from Benning. About noon a Marine helicopter squadron flew in from Lejune. The Marines have to get in on everything.

Very, very tired. An hour ago there was a Protestant service held in the gym. The chaplain gave a complete hundred-year-old service— "Onward Christian Soldiers," "The Battle Hymn of the Republic," Biblical injunctions against rebellion, "all men are brothers in Christ," "render unto Caesar," and prayers for the soon to be dead and wounded. In the corner a man is reading Cash's *Mind of the South*. Time to sleep.

2 Oct 62 Finally some rest. The bulk of the battalion has been withdrawn into reserve at the Confederate Cemetery south of the Ole Miss campus. I had been awakened about 10 Sunday night by the toe of my CO's boot to see the rest of the battalion packing up and to notice that the far end of the gym was empty. Where's the 503rd? Gone. We fell in outside. A flurry of rumors. We heard the most awful tales of goings-on in Mississippi. In ranks, the CO passed through us and tapped men to fall out to the rear. After a few were so chosen, I noted that they were all Negroes. All of our Negro men were left behind in Memphis—10 per cent of the ranks, a third of all NCOs, a first sergeant, the adjutant, the personnel officer, and two out of three company commanders. There were tears in some of the men's eyes. That is, among the USs (draftees); the lifers (professionals) were glad to be getting out of something. We, the only Yankee outfit there, were the only unit to do this segregating. The 503rd and everyone else took every man they had.

A lieutenant came down the line. "They're not playing fun and games down there. The bastards have killed three men already." We mounted up and moved out. The CO stood in the road and watched us go. A Navy truck led us through Memphis, and Tennessee State Troopers on motorcycles escorted us to the state line. A huge sign greeted us, "Welcome to Mississippi—Land of Beautiful Women." What a ride that was! Flat out all the way. Pitch black. Not a sign of life. As if we had fallen into a pit. Only when we pulled off the interstate route to run into the Ole Miss campus did the rebels appear. Little knots of people avoided our headlights as we rounded turns. Rocks and bottles came at us from the dark. Lumbering down the road from the opposite direction came a massive old hearse. I don't know if it was planned or not but it certainly was effective. As we approached the edge of the campus the column was held up. I was sent forward to investigate.

A squad of the Mississippi "Safety Patrol" was blocking the road, saying that their orders were to keep everyone off the campus. As they talked two busloads of hard-faced characters passed. The lieutenant insisted that we might be of some use on campus. Barnett's Cossacks didn't agree. The radio operator perched high on a jeep leveled his shotgun casually. A squad of MPs with bayonets fixed moved forward. "You better not stick me with that thing, boy!" He stuck him. He moved. The Troopers looked perturbed. They put their hands on their holsters. We unlimbered our rifles. All a bluff, in the normal U.S. Army confusion, for we had switched weapons all day Sunday and wound up carrying M-1 rifles and ammo for .45 pistols. The Safety Patrol thought that they could better watch developments from back of the road. We dropped a few men to watch them and moved on. We could smell the tear gas from where we were. The noise was fantastic. Shots and loud shouting. Planes and helicopters above. Strange lights and explosions. Held up at the edge of the campus. Confusion. The 503rd vehicles being withdrawn. They are pretty battered—not a whole windshield in the lot. So we fold and cover ours. Better an MP get a brick in the face than have some of the taxpayers' glass broken.

What exactly happened is still in doubt. Story is that the company of the 503rd that was rushed down by helicopter wasted time circling about futilely before landing at the Municipal Airport two miles from campus and had to walk in. They arrived exhausted to face a barrage of bottles and bricks. Part of their motorized column got lost and the rest trickled onto campus without plan. Much the same happened to us. I don't believe we ever did get any orders. What little was done seemed to be ad lib.

The sorority girls had a warm welcome for us as we crawled up their Row pushing back stragglers. The curses that came from these Southern Belles! Bottles from Delta Gamma and books from the Tri-Delts. This hospitality only partly prepared us for the heart of the action—the Lyceum. This pseudo-Charlottesville-Greek-revival building, the target of the attacks, faces down a long, slightly sloping open space called the Grove. This vast area was totally covered with debris. The roadway just in front of the Lyceum, about six inches deep, was filled with gas shells, rocks, pipes, concrete rubble, and the now familiar bottles and bricks. On the Grove itself were a fire engine and a bulldozer the rioters had tried to crush the U.S. Marshals with.

All around the area were burnt-out vehicles. College windows shattered. Fires all over.

The U.S. Marshals looked sadly comical in their wrinkled suits with steel pots and vests for gas shells. Funny—until you see their eyes. They have been under continuous attack now for six hours with no way to strike back but for the tear gas. They are exhausted and angry. Many are wounded—hit by missiles and shot at by snipers while carrying out the law of the United States. Occasionally a captured rebel is brought up and thrown inside. The local National Guardsmen are also tired. I was surprised to see them here. Surprised the government would trust them and doubly surprised that they are loyal. They too have suffered badly. Cavalry, untrained in riot control, they can only stand and strengthen the line against their own people. I don't imagine that they were too happy about coming up here, but there is no doubt now which side they are on. I wonder though, how they will show their faces at home after supporting the Yankee.

The gas is terrible. It is impossible to move about without a mask. It wasn't the arrival of the Army, but the late hour and the accumulation of tear gas that broke the riot. The 503rd arrived piecemeal and never had the opportunity to set up a real riot-control formation. I hear Bravo Company managed to get up a semblance of a line on the edge of campus but the rioters were too few and it degenerated into individual MPs going after lone rebels. There were still small groups of rebels at the far end of the Grove with smaller groups of MPs pursuing them. A rioter is faster on his feet than a heavily laden MP. In a truck there is a form covered by a blanket: only a pair of combat boots shows. Death and fatigue. I crawl into a bush by the Fine Arts Building and sleep—rifle, helmet, gas mask, and all.

Two hours' sleep at most. Up again at dawn [on Monday], we are hastily thrown together, mounted, and rushed toward the town. At least no gas off campus. The rioters are still active out here. First close-up view of them in daylight. Side-burned white trash and students screaming. . . . Past the shanty that passes for the separate-but-equal Negro library, we enter the town of Oxford, dismount by Phil Stone's law office, and wait. The courthouse square is full of local people screaming the familiar words and hurling the familiar missiles at soldiers. Truckloads of Coke bottles are in the far end of the square, with more arriving. After much talk and staff meetings we are finally given the chance to handle the thing properly. The only way to break up a mob is with MPs, shoulder to shoulder with helmet and masks, advancing at the half-step with bayonets thrust well out in front of them. The mob falls back, is divided, gassed, and pushed back again, until it breaks up once more into individuals. Regulations say that you have to warn the crowd first, "read the Proclamation." The CO got as far as, "By the authority of the President of the United States . . ." when a Coke bottle shot by his ear and smashed on his radio operator's knee. "Gas 'em!" went out over the loudspeaker.

We were well supplied with gas. We threw cans of it at the mob. Also baseball grenades—just the right size and weight for Americans to get range and accuracy. There were many broken heads from well-aimed pegs. The rioters tried unsuccessfully to pick them up to throw back trouble. Each platoon is equipped with a gas disperser, a flame-thrower-like device that lays down a cloud of tear gas. The mob is constantly reinforced. 2nd Division MPs arrived. Things became confused again. Ideally, a riot-control formation should move like a chorus line or baroque infantry—in unison to a learned drill under the voice of one man. But no one can be heard through a gas mask over the roar of the crowd. One of the mob yelled a typical remark, "Your wife's home s . . . a black ape, you nigger-lover!" at the wrong man, an Irishman from New Rochelle with a pregnant wife at home. He gives chase up an alley. Our helmets and masks protected us from most of the missiles. A few cut heads and bruised shoulders were our only casualties. 2nd Division took over the town and we were withdrawn to campus. We hear they arrested ex-General Walker later in the morning.

The brass have arrived. I expect they are already taking the credit. What little there is belongs to the Marshals. Without proper equipment or training, they withstood the attacks of the mobs. XVIII Airborne Corps has taken over and set up their HQ at the stadium. Right away the staff are frowning at our unshaved faces and dirty boots. I'm sitting in my jeep waiting for the old man, adjusting my helmet strap when the General comes by and says in a skittish voice, "Put it on or take it off, soldier." I wonder how a man directing 30,000 men against the first armed insurrection against the United States in one hundred years can find time for such trivia. Helmet straps and boot polish are the proper concern of lifers.

Things are quieting down a bit. Marshals lounge around the Lyceum. They are as surprised at being here as we are. Some of them are Border Patrol, some screws at federal pens, and the rest had done nothing more exciting than serve writs in Brooklyn. How they can bear the gas is beyond me. I guess they are used to it by now. I hate to think of how much they put down. The whole campus reeks with it. Students hurry to class with handkerchiefs pressed to their faces, only their eyes showing tears and hatred for the invaders.

"MIND ON FREEDOM"

Even as the riot at Ole Miss and the continuing occupation of the campus by U.S. Army troops dominated the national media coverage of civil rights in Mississippi, the patient, time-consuming, and dangerous work of voter registration went on. In April 1963 *Newsweek* noticed. It described the voter registration campaign Bob Moses had organized in Greenwood, Mississippi. The story was grouped with other items in the "National Affairs" section and occupied much of two columns, on pages 25 and 26. It detailed violence, ranging from night riders firing into the SNCC office to the use of a police dog. It told of the arrest of the leaders, of the refusal of local officials to permit African Americans to register, of the determination of local blacks to continue the struggle. The article, unsigned, maintained a matter-of-fact tone. This sort of thing happened routinely all over the South in 1963, especially in Mississippi.

In the first golden glow of spring, Greenwood, Miss., looked like anything but a battleground. The redbud trees blazed along the town streets. At city hall, Mayor Charles Sampson marked the season by sticking an orchid into a 7-Up bottle on his desk. And all around Leflore County, bare-armed Negroes crisscrossed the fields on tractors, breaking the black Delta soil for still another cotton crop.

But Greenwood had become a theater of war, a likely successor to Little Rock and Albany, Ga., and Oxford, Miss., as landmarks in the Negro's long, painful revolt against discrimination. The issue was the right to vote—a right shared by 92.5 per cent of the county's 10,274 eligible whites and only 1.9 per cent of the 13,567 eligible Negroes. If they seemed to be pursuing an abstraction, the Negroes—and their allies in Washington—had come to regard the vote as the key to the bread-and-butter rewards of equality. And they had picked tough, intransigent Leflore County for the facedown—the "testing ground for democracy."

All last week, as they had for seven months, registration canvassers drove the dirt roads after dark, looking for prospects. All week, in increasing numbers, Negroes rallied in their brick and clapboard churches, fortified themselves with speeches and prayers and freedom songs, and marched downtown to register. All week, Leflore fought back, and the strands of tension drew taut.

Night Riders: First, on Sunday night, a fire broke out in the cramped campaign office on McLaurin Street. Tuesday, after dark, night riders trailed 19-year-old George Greene and two fellow canvassers to the Greene home and fired two shotgun blasts. One narrowly missed Greene; the other stitched a dozen holes over a bedroom mantel. Was Greene frightened? "You're gonna die anyway," he shrugged, "so it might as well be for the cause of freedom."

The fire was the second in a month, the shooting the third. But the next morning, 100 Negroes marching from church to city hall to protest met a new adversary: a police dog.

A policeman—one of a dozen lined up outside the buff-brick city hall—held the German shepherd on a long leather leash. Mayor Sampson, a beefy, cigar-puffing member of the segregationist Citizens Council, warned: "I'll give you two minutes to get out. . . . If you don't, we are going to turn the dog loose."

The Negroes stood fast, and the police moved in, shoving them back. Lunging into the crowd, the dog knocked one Negro down and ripped open one leg of campaign director Robert Moses' trousers. Police arrested two leaders at the scene on disorderly conduct charges, tailed the others back to church, and prodded nine more into patrol cars. (By the weekend, eight were convicted and given the maximum penalties—four months in jail and $200 fines.) With knots of sullen whites clustered around the courthouse square, the street was barricaded and the registration office closed. But when it reopened that afternoon, 100 Negroes were there, filing inside to fill out registration forms.

The dog was back next morning as the Rev. D. L. Tucker led 42 Negroes double-file from the courthouse back to church. They had gone two blocks when police cars pulled up. "All right," the dog handler yelled, "break it up and go on, or I'm going to turn him loose." As the Negroes rounded the corner, the dog bounded at Tucker. The minister fell, clutching his bitten left ankle. Two marchers crossed hands to make a seat for him and carried him off. "Sic 'em, dog!" onlookers shouted. "Let him git the niggers!"

Still the ritual procession downtown went on. Leflore was tough, and the vote workers had precious little to show: two new Negro voters on the rolls. But the harder Leflore fought, the more Negroes turned out for the nightly church rallies—and joined the daily pilgrimage to the courthouse.

'I'm Not Going Home': "The days are over when they can shoot people and burn them out, and they are gonna learn it," Bob Moses told 1,000 cheering Negroes at one church meeting. And the dog? "That dog is going to have to bite every Negro in Leflore County before we quit," the Rev. James Bevel told 2,000 more. Was the road long? "Every time a Negro stands in line and says, 'I'm tired but I'm not going home,' the walls of segregation begin to tremble," Bevel cried.

"Amen," the Negroes chanted back, and they sang: "Woke up this morning with my mind on freedom, hallelujah!"

But the Negroes needed more than songs and slogans, and their leaders knew it. The channels of communication were shut down; Mayor Sampson predictably blamed "outside agitators" for the trouble in Greenwood, and he had his own prescription: "We'll just have to load up the jail." So the Negroes looked for help elsewhere—in Washington. All week they chafed as a Justice Department fact-finding team of FBI men and lawyers prowled Greenwood. Finally, Attorney General Robert F. Kennedy sent an aide to seek a Federal court order requiring local officials to end "intimidation" of Negroes, free the eight prisoners—and call off the dog.

COMING OF AGE IN MISSISSIPPI: AN AUTOBIOGRAPHY

Anne Moody

Usually the campaign in Mississippi went on without much publicity. Scores, and then hundreds, of local volunteers joined with SNCC in the slow work of persuading African Americans to attempt to register to vote. One of these was Anne Moody. Moody had grown up in poverty in rural Mississippi. She

Source: From *Coming of Age in Mississippi* by Anne Moody, copyright © 1968 by Anne Moody. Used by permission of Doubleday, a division of Random House, Inc.

was a good student and an excellent basketball player. Her athletic prowess got her a scholarship.

Her *Coming of Age in Mississippi* is one of the classic works produced about the movement. In this excerpt Moody recounts how, as a student at Tougaloo College, she first heard of SNCC's efforts during the summer of 1962 and decided to help. She was impetuous as well as idealistic, a combination that could lead to unanticipated danger. Her impromptu decision to integrate a bus station almost produced a riot.

During the summer a white student moved into the room across the hall from me. Her name was Joan Trumpauer, and she told me she worked for SNCC as a secretary. In a short time we got to know each other very well, and soon I was going into Jackson with Joan and hanging out at her office. SNCC was starting a voter registration drive in the Delta (Greenwood and Greenville) and was recruiting students at Tougaloo. When they asked me if I wanted to canvass every other weekend, I agreed to go.

The first time I went to the Delta, I was with three other girls. A local family put us up and we slept two to a room. The second time I was there I stayed at the Freedom House—a huge white frame house that SNCC was renting from a widow for sixty dollars a month. This time I was with Bettye Poole, who had been canvassing for SNCC for a couple of months, and Carolyn Quinn, a new recruit like me. We arrived at the Freedom House on a Friday night about twelve-thirty and found fifteen boys all sleeping in one large room on triple-decker beds. They were all sleeping in their clothes. Some of the boys got up and we played cards for a while. A couple of them were from McComb, Mississippi, which was only twenty miles from Centreville. We cracked jokes about how bad the whites were in Wilkinson County. Around 2 A.M. I started to get sleepy and asked where the girls were going to stay. I was told we were going to stay right in the same room with all those boys. I was some shocked. Now I understood why Bettye Poole was wearing jeans; just then she was climbing into one of the empty bunks and settling down for the night. Here I was with only a transparent nylon pajama set to sleep in. Carolyn Quinn wasn't prepared either. The two of us just sat up in chairs until some extra pairs of pants were found for us. The boys explained that they slept in their clothes because they had had bomb threats, and had to be ready to run anytime. They all slept here in this one big room because it was sheltered by another house.

The next morning I woke up to the sounds of someone banging on a skillet and hollering, "Come and get it! Come and get it!" When we walked in the kitchen, the boy who'd made the racket said, "All right, girls, take over. Us boys have been cooking all week." Most of the guys were angry because he had gotten them up in that manner, but they didn't make a big fuss over it. Carolyn and I started cooking. When we announced that the food was ready, the boys ran over each other to get to the kitchen. It seemed they thought the food would disappear. It did. Within five minutes, everything on the table was gone. The food ran out and three boys were left standing in line.

I really got to like all of the SNCC workers. I had never known people so willing and determined to help others. I thought Bob Moses, the director of SNCC in Mississippi, was Jesus Christ in the flesh. A lot of other people thought of him as J.C., too.

The SNCC workers who were employed full-time were paid only ten dollars a week. They could do more with that ten dollars than most people I knew could do with fifty. Sometimes when we were in the Delta, the boys would take us out. We did not finish with our work some Saturdays until ten or eleven, and all the Negro places had a twelve o'clock curfew. But we would have more fun in an hour than most people could have in twenty-four. We would often go to one place where the boys had made friends with the waitresses, and they would sneak us fifths of liquor. Those SNCC boys had friends everywhere, among the Negroes, that is. Most whites were just waiting for the chance to kill them all off.

I guess mostly the SNCC workers were just lucky. Most of them had missed a bullet by an inch or so on many occasions. Threats didn't stop them. They just kept going all the time. One Saturday we got to Greenville and discovered that the office had been bombed Friday night. The office was located up two flights of outside steps in a little broken-down building. It seemed as though a real hard wind would have blown it away. The bomb knocked the steps off, but that didn't stop the rally on Saturday night. Some of the boys made steps. When the new steps began to collapse, we ended up using a ladder. I remember when the rally ended, we found that the ladder was gone. For a few minutes we were real scared. We just knew some whites had moved it. We were all standing up there in the doorway wondering what to do. There was only one exit, and it was too high up to jump from. We figured we were going to be blown up. It seemed as though the whites had finally trapped us. The high school students were about to panic, when suddenly one of the SNCC boys came walking up with the ladder and yelled up to ask if the excitement was over. A lot of the other guys were mad enough to hit him. Those that did only tapped him lightly and smiled as they did it. "The nerve of those guys!" I thought.

Things didn't seem to be coming along too well in the Delta. On Saturdays we would spend all day canvassing and often at night we would have mass rallies. But these were usually poorly attended. Many Negroes were afraid to come. In the beginning some were even afraid to talk to us. Most of these old plantation Negroes had been brain-washed so by the whites, they really thought that only whites were supposed to vote. There were even a few who had never heard of voting. The only thing most of them knew was how to handle a hoe. For years they had demonstrated how well they could do that. Some of them had calluses on their hands so thick they would hide them if they noticed you looking at them.

On Sundays we usually went to Negro churches to speak. We were split into groups according to our religious affiliation. We were supposed to know how to reach those with the same faith as ourselves. In church we hoped to be able to reach many more Negroes. We knew that even those that slammed doors in our faces or said, "I don't want no part of voting" would be there. There would also be the schoolteachers and the middle-class professional Negroes who dared not participate. They knew that once they did, they would lose that $250 a month job. But the people started getting wise to us. Most of them stopped coming to church. They knew if they came, they would have to face us. Then the ministers started asking us not to come because we scared their congregations away. SNCC had to come up with a new strategy.

As the work continued that summer, people began to come around. I guess they saw that our intentions were good. But some began getting fired from their jobs, thrown off plantations and left homeless. They could often find somewhere else to stay, but food and clothing became a problem. SNCC started to send representatives to Northern college campuses. They went begging for food, clothing and money for the people in Mississippi, and the food, clothing and money started coming in. The Delta Negroes still didn't understand the voting, but they knew they had found friends, friends they could trust.

That summer I could feel myself beginning to change. For the first time I began to think something would be done about whites killing, beating, and misusing Negroes. I knew I was going to be a part of whatever happened.

A week before summer school ended, I was in town shopping with Rose, a girl from the dorm. We had planned to split cab fare back to campus, but discovered we did not have enough money. Cab fare out to Tougaloo was $2.50 and bus fare was thirty-five cents one way. We decided to take the Trailways back. When we got to the station. I suggested to Rose that we use the white side. "I'm game if you are," she said.

I walked in the white entrance. When I looked back, I saw that Rose had not followed. I decided I would not go back to see what had happened, because she would try and talk me out of it. As I was buying my ticket, she walked up behind me.

"Shit, Moody, I thought you were kidding," she said.

I didn't answer. I was noticing the reaction of the man behind the counter. He stood looking at me as if he were paralyzed.

"Make that two tickets, please," I said to him.

"Where is the other one to?" he said.

"Both to Tougaloo," I said.

As he was getting the tickets for us, another man had gotten on the phone. He kept looking at us as he was talking. I think he was reporting to the police what was taking place. The man that sold us the tickets acted as if that was the last thing in the world he wanted to do. He slapped the tickets down on the counter, and threw the change at me. The change fell off the counter and rolled over the floor. That bastard had the nerve to laugh as we picked it up. Rose and I sat opposite each other, so we could see what was happening throughout the terminal. The bus was to leave at three-thirty, and we had gotten there about two-forty-five. We had some time to wait. Rose had a watch, I asked her to keep a check on the time.

People came in and stared. Some even laughed. Nothing happened until a bunch of white soldiers sat with us and started talking. The conversation had gone on for some time when a Negro woman got off one of the incoming buses. She saw us sitting in there and walked right in. She had about six small children with her. The little Negro children started running around the station picking up things from the counter and asking if they could buy them. At that point the excitement started. A drunken white man walked into the station behind the Negro lady with all the children. He started cursing, calling us all kinds of niggers.

"Get them little dirty swines outta heah," he said, pulling one of the little boys to the door.

"Take your filthy hands off my child," the Negro woman said. "What's going on here anyway?"

"They got a place for you folks, now why don't you take them chilluns of yours and go on right over there?" the drunkard said, pointing to the Negro side of the bus station.

The lady looked at us. I guess she wanted us to say something: Rose and I just sat there. Finally she realized a sit-in or something was going on. She took her children and hurried out of the door. Instead of going to the Negro side, she went back on the bus. She looked as though she was really angry with us.

After that the drunkard started yelling at us. I didn't get too scared, but Rose was now shaking. She had begun to smoke cigarettes one after the other. She looked at her watch. "Moody, we have missed the bus," she said.

"What time is it?" I asked.

"It's almost four-thirty."

"They didn't even announce that the bus was loading," I said.

I walked over to the man at the ticket counter. "Has the bus come in that's going to Tougaloo?" I asked him.

"One just left," he said.

"You didn't announce that the bus was in."

"Are you telling me how to do my job?" he said. "I hear you niggers at Tougaloo think you run Mississippi."

"When is the next bus?" I asked.

"Five-thirty," he said, very indignant.

I went back and told Rose that the next bus left at five-thirty. She wanted to leave, but I insisted that we stay. Just as I was trying to explain to her why we should not leave, the white drunk walked up behind her. He had what appeared to be a wine bottle in his hand.

"Talk to me, Rose," I said.

"What's going on?" Rose said, almost shouting.

"Nothing. Stop acting so damn scared and start talking," I said.

The drunk walked up behind her and held the bottle up as though he was going to hit her on the head. All the time, I was looking him straight in the face as if to say, "Would you, would you really hit her?" Rose knew someone was behind her. She wouldn't have been able to talk or act normal if someone in the station threatened to shoot her if she didn't. The drunkard saw that I was pleading with him. He cursed me, throwing the bottle on the floor and breaking it. At this point, more people got all rallied up. They had now started shouting catcalls from every direction. Some bus drivers walked into the station. "What's wrong? What's going on heah?" one of them shouted. One took a chair and sat right in front of us. "Do you girls want to see a show?" he said. "Did you come here for a little entertainment?"

We didn't say anything.

"I guess you didn't. I'll put it on anyhow," he said. "Now here's how white folks entertain," putting his thumbs in his ears and wiggling his fingers, kicking his feet and making all kind of facial expressions. The rest of the whites in the bus station laughed and laughed at him. Some asked him to imitate a monkey, Martin Luther King, Medgar Evers. His performance went on for what seemed to be a good thirty minutes. When he finished, or rather got tired of, clowning, he said, "Now some of you other people give them what they really came for."

All this time the man was still on the phone talking to someone. We were sure he was talking to the police. Some of the other people that were sitting around in the bus station starting shouting remarks. I guess they were taking the advice of the bus driver. Again Rose looked at her watch to report that we had missed the second bus. It was almost a quarter to seven.

We didn't know what to do. The place was getting more tense by the minute. People had now begun to crowd around us.

"Let's go, Moody," Rose began to plead with me. "If you don't I'll leave you here," she said.

I knew she meant it, and I didn't want to be left alone. The crowd was going to get violent any minute now.

"O.K., Rose, let's go," I said. "Don't turn your back to anyone, though."

We got up and walked backward to the door. The crowd followed us just three or four feet away. Some were threatening to kick us out— or throw us all the way to Tougaloo, and a lot of other possible and impossible things.

Rose and I hit the swinging doors with our backs at the same time. The doors closed immediately behind us. We were now outside the station not knowing what to do or where to run. We were afraid to leave. We were at the back of the station and thought the mob would be waiting for us if we ran around in front and tried to leave. Any moment now, those that had followed us would be on us again. We were standing there just going to pieces.

"Get in this here car," a Negro voice said.

I glanced to one side and saw that Rose was getting into the back seat. At that moment the mob was coming toward me through the doors. I just started moving backward until I fell into the car. The driver sped away.

After we had gotten blocks away from the station, I was still looking out of the back window to see who would follow. No one had. For the first time I looked to see who was driving the car and asked the driver who he was. He said he was a minister, that he worked at the bus station part-time. He asked us not to ever try and sit-in again without first planning it with an organization.

"You girls just can't go around doing things on your own," he said. He drove us all the way to campus, then made us feel bad by telling us he probably would get fired. He said he was on a thirty-minute break. That's a Negro preacher for you.

Summer school ended the following week. I headed for New Orleans to get that good three weeks of work in before the fall term of my senior year began.

TESTIMONY OF MRS. DOROTHY MAE FOSTER

Even as SNCC and other civil rights organizations struggled to persuade Mississippi's black citizens to attempt to register, the Ku Klux Klan and other white supremacists sought to prevent them from doing so. The following testimony before the U.S. Commission on Civil Rights recounts an experience common to blacks brave enough to try to vote. The hearings took place more than a year after the events recounted here. The Commission was collecting evidence on the need for a federal voting rights act. The law passed. It was a direct outcome of the Freedom Summer.

MRS. FOSTER: My name is Dorothy Mae Foster. I live at Route 2, Box 166, Natchez, Miss., and I'm a housewife.

MR. TAYLOR: How many years of school did you complete, Mrs. Foster?

MRS. FOSTER: Ten.

MR. TAYLOR: How long have you lived in Jefferson County?

MRS. FOSTER: For 16 years.

MR. TAYLOR: Do you know of any Negroes who are registered to vote in Jefferson County?

MRS. FOSTER: Not that I know of.

MR. TAYLOR: Have you ever attempted to register to vote?

MRS. FOSTER: Yes, sir; I have.

MR. TAYLOR: When was that?

MRS. FOSTER: September 20, 1963.

MR. TAYLOR: When you went to try to register, did you go alone or did you go with someone?

MRS. FOSTER: No. My brother-in-law, his wife, my husband, and myself.

MR. TAYLOR: Now, did anything happen to you after you attempted to register?

MRS. FOSTER: Yes; a carload with four or five white men came to our house and asked the whereabouts of my husband. I told them I didn't know and they said they had a matter of important business to discuss with him, and I said, "Well, I don't know, where he is." They said, "Is he working?" I said, "Well, he has been." They said, "Is he off?" I said, "I don't know." They said, "Well, what time are you expecting him?" I said, "Well, I really don't know." So, some of the ones then in the car looked and saw a man coming and he said, "Here he ———" I said, "No, that's not my husband. That is someone hunting."

So, the ones, one of the two that was at the gate talking, he said, "She says that is not her husband, that is someone hunting." And, when the

Source: Testimony of Mrs. Dorothy Mae Foster, Jefferson County, Mississippi, before the United States Commission on Civil Rights, (hearings held in Jackson, Mississippi, February 16–20, 1965).

man got there and sit down, he said to the man, the other man, "Give her the information since she says she is his wife." So, the man passed me a card, a little white card and it read: "Ku Klux Klan," and it says, "There are thousand Klans watching you."

Mr. Taylor: Is that the card you have in front of you right now?

Mrs. Foster: Yes, it is.

Mr. Taylor: May I see that?

What happened then, Mrs. Foster?

Mrs. Foster: I said "Oh, Ku Klux Klan." He said, "Yes," He said, "You tell your husband—" I passed it to the man that was sitting on the porch. He said, "Don't be afraid." He said, "You tell your husband if he don't take his name off of that book, you would be afraid." So I said: "What book." He said: "Those names are signed in ink and they are there to stay." I said, "Are you coming back?" He said, "Yes." Then he said, "No, I won't, but someone will."

Mr. Taylor: I would like to have this card marked as an exhibit, Exhibit No. 8.

It reads: "Thousands of Klansmen Watching * * * waiting! Ku Klux Klan. Don't be misled. Let your conscience guide you." I would like to have it entered into the record.

Chairman Hannah: It is received into the record.

(Commission's Exhibit No. 8 was marked for identification and received in evidence.)

Mr. Taylor: How many white men were in this car?

Mrs. Foster: Four or five, it seemed like two gotten out.

Mr. Taylor: How soon was this after you had attempted to register?

Mrs. Foster: About 4 weeks.

Mr. Taylor: Did anything happen to your in-laws?

Mrs. Foster: Yes, they visited them the same way.

Mr. Taylor: Did you or any of your family pass the test?

Mrs. Foster: No.

Mr. Taylor: Have there been any other attempts by Negroes to register in Jefferson County since you attempted to register?

Mrs. Foster: Not that I know of.

Mr. Taylor: Mrs. Foster, have you talked to any of your neighbors about attempting to register?

Mrs. Foster: One or two.

Mr. Taylor: What do they say ?

Mrs. Foster: They don't give any answer. They just say they don't know.

Mr. Taylor: Do you think that people in your community know about this visit that you have told us about?

Mrs. Foster: I think some do.

Mr Taylor: Thank you.

2

Dry Run: The 1963 "Mock" Election

After more than two years of effort, the voting drive in Mississippi
had achieved little in the way of actual results. Six counties in the
state had no registered black voters. Six more had fewer than ten. In
other states, like Alabama, where Governor George Wallace led the
campaign against civil rights, almost 40% of eligible African Americans
had successfully registered. In Mississippi only 6% had. Worse, as the
experiences of Anne Moody and Dorothy Mae Foster and countless
others demonstrated, the levels of intimidation and violence were
actually rising. Occasionally a national newsmagazine or network
would report on white supremacists. Most of the time, the beatings
and threats were ignored.

SNCC and its associated organizations in COFO (the Council of
Federated Organizations) needed to do something dramatic. What
they hit upon was holding a mock election at the same time as
Mississippi's gubernatorial race. They nominated their own candidate,
Aaron Henry, president of the state NAACP (National Association for
the Advancement of Colored People). With Bob Moses as his campaign manager, Henry campaigned across the state. And Mississippi
whites and blacks both took his candidacy very seriously. In this mock
election were born the twin ideas that would shape the events of 1964.
One was the creation of the Freedom Democratic Party as a challenge
to the "regular" Democrats. The other was the use of out-of-state volunteers. During the 1963 race some seventy-five white students,
many from Yale, came to Mississippi to help organize the election. In
the summer of 1964 there would be hundreds of volunteers from
dozens of campuses.

"UNDERGROUND ELECTION"

Jeannine Herron

Jeannine Herron's story in the *Nation*, a liberal weekly, provided a useful summary of Aaron Henry's campaign and included several gripping illustrations of the harassment activists encountered as they tried to mobilize Mississippi's African Americans to participate in the "charade" election. She highlighted the role of the Yale volunteers but did not mention the name of Allard Lowenstein, the activist lawyer from New York, who recruited them and who first suggested the use of white volunteers to Bob Moses. Lowenstein would become one of the most important participants in the emerging New Left and in the opposition to the Vietnam War. Herron did mention the role of Norman Thomas. He was a longtime leader of the American Socialist Party and its perennial presidential candidate. When he wrote to President Kennedy that nothing in his experience prepared him for the virulent hatred he encountered in Mississippi, he was saying a great deal.

Jackson, Miss.

Bullets, beatings, arrests and fines drove the campaign of Aaron Henry, a Negro, for Governor "underground" as the 1963 gubernatorial campaign neared a climax in Mississippi. The outrageously "uppity" plan for a mock campaign of unregistered Negro voters to dramatize the flagrant totalitarianism of Southern politics was taken seriously by the white power structure. As a result of this, harassment and intimidation plagued Henry's campaign workers all over the state.

Despite the unexpected severity of these difficulties and a disappointing blackout by local news and national wire services, the Council of Federated Organizations (COFO) polled a highly significant 82,000 votes. COFO (consisting of NAACP, SCLC, CORE and SNCC), working on a state-wide project for the first time, managed to total the margin of difference between the Republican and Democratic votes in only three weeks of campaigning.

Two things undoubtedly worried Southern traditionalists. First, the integrated ticket—Dr. Aaron Henry, a Negro pharmacist, and Reverend Edwin King, white Tougaloo College chaplain—confounded their argument that Negroes, if allowed to vote, would "take over" the state.

Source: "Underground Election," by Jeannine Herron, from the December 7, 1963 issue of *The Nation*. Reprinted with permission.

Second, the platform of the Freedom Party raised issues at the heart of the depressing problems in Mississippi, a state that seems to rank fiftieth in almost every field. It is unprecedented to speak of justice, free elections, economics and education even in a game of "Let's Pretend We Have the Vote." In the official gubernatorial race, Rubel Phillips, the first Republican candidate since Reconstruction, repeated monotonously, "K.O. the Kennedys!" while Paul Johnson's Democratic pamphlet warned darkly, "DANGER, Two party system in Mississippi would END OUR WAY OF LIFE. Vote November 5 to stamp out Republicanism!"

But the final tally for Henry and King proved that Negroes are capable and willing to engage in the political affairs of their state, that they are vitally interested in a better society for *all* Mississippians and that they will have even greater resistance to overcome before the make-believe becomes real.

The unusual protest technique of a "mock ballot" was augmented and modified by the flexibility of such resourceful leaders as Robert Moses, campaign manager, in meeting unpredictable problems. In areas where threats had genuinely frightened local leaders and no churches or stores were available for polling places, he contrived "votemobiles," mobile ballot boxes carried in cars by campaign teams. Where even votemobiles were forced out and ballots confiscated, the campaign encouraged underground ballots, or mail-in votes. The committee made skillful use of an amazing contingent of more than seventy-five out-of-state students, mostly from Yale, who joined local workers to canvass and poll nearly every little town in the state.

The power of local authorities in exercising their whims was effective insofar as it kept the Negroes from realizing their goal of 200,000 votes. Nearly everyone actively working on the campaign was arrested, detained or fined. There were at least seventy arrests for everything from littering and vagrancy to sodomy. Bonds went as high as $1,000 for fictitious traffic violations. With only three or four lawyers daring to take civil-rights cases in all of Mississippi, several cases that should have been appealed were not contested. Had Negro citizens been free of fear, the vote most surely would have been doubled.

Among the particularly hazardous areas was Natchez. Bruce Payne, a Yale student, was pulled out of his votemobile and beaten by four white men in a gas station. They warned him to "stay out of Natchez." The next day Payne and George Greene, a SNCC worker, were forced off the road by the same men. Making a crucial decision, Greene reversed suddenly and got back onto the highway as three shots hit the car, one puncturing a tire. Speeding away on the slowly leaking tire, he somehow managed to lose his pursuers. The following day, in the same area, another votemobile was chased at speeds up to 115 mph.

In Picayune, three Hattiesburg Negroes and two white Yale students were detained by police for questioning. When they returned to their car, they found the gas tank full of water. The local garage could not repair the damage. A crowd of men and boys followed them while they hired a car and driver to take them out of town. Police and members of the crowd stopped the car north of Poplarville, and officials took the driver away in their car. In the confusion one boy was separated from the others and walked from 1 to 7 A.M. when he was picked up by a SNCC search car. The other four finally managed to flag down a Greyhound bus, which took them to New Orleans.

It took remarkable courage to enter a town like Belzoni where two Negroes have been shot in the last eight years for registering to vote. Willie James Shaw (they call him "preacher Shaw" at SNCC) was not going to be turned around. He sat on the hood of his votemobile and started singing freedom songs. The local Negroes stood in a silent, fearful group, not daring to vote in the presence of several police officers. Then Shaw got angry and began to preach.

"What's wrong with you? Negro, don't you know you got nothing left to lose? White man's got everything. Stand up and tell that white man you gonna be FREE!" The atmosphere of fear got thicker, but Willie preached on, seeming to have mesmerized himself, the crowd *and* the police. Then, miraculously, two women and a little girl joined Willie's singing. One by one they began to vote. Thirty-eight ballots were polled for Henry and King in Belzoni, but the police confiscated them as they took Willie off to jail for parking too close to a fire hydrant.

It may have all been make-believe, but both sides read it as a true story and as a portent of the future. Although the outcome of the Freedom Campaign had no effect on the actual gubernatorial race, the image of thousands of Negroes casting ballots for the first time for candidates they believed in could not be taken lightly by the white elite. With the issue of schools looming ahead next year they will let no challenge go by without battle. Their frantic efforts to submerge a mock campaign reveal their fear. They have left hasty, inadequate trenches behind them as they have backed away. . . .

Norman Thomas, who spoke for the Freedom Party in Greenwood and who narrowly escaped harassment himself, summed it up in a letter to President Kennedy: "We have in Mississippi a state obsessed with maintenance of segregation in support of white supremacy. It is a religion which, like communism to its believers, cleanses and sanctifies lies, perjury, perversion of law, perhaps even murder to maintain itself. This situation is America's business. I do not write as a sensationalist but as a veteran campaigner who has frequently covered the United States without finding a parallel or precedent for what I found in Mississippi."

"SOUTHERN DIARIES"

Ivanhoe Donaldson

Herron's article in the *Nation* afforded some sense of the risks SNCC and other workers ran in organizing the 1963 shadow election. Soon after her story appeared, *Freedomways*, a civil rights quarterly, published the following excerpts from Ivanhoe Donaldson's diary. He recounted, in horrifying detail, just how dangerous working in Mississippi was. Most frightening, perhaps, is Donaldson's stoical reflection on his experience: "There was simply nothing to do except chalk it up as something to be expected, especially when you're trying to bring the vote to the black man in Mississippi."

Jackson, Mississippi

The last two weeks of September and the month of October 1963 were spent organizing and campaigning for a mock election in which Negroes throughout the state of Mississippi were asked to participate. SNCC, in cooperation with other civil rights organizations, canvassed the entire state in an effort to bring the issue of the importance of political power to the Negro community. In many ways, both Negroes in various communities and SNCC field workers, were harassed and intimidated by the local police in an effort to discourage political activities of any kind. The following is an example of one of the methods that local police, under the direction of local political power structures, seek to make sure that workers are discouraged from taking part in political activity.

Charles Cobb and I arrived at the Jackson, Mississippi office (Henry-for-Governor Campaign Headquarters) at approximately 7 P.M. to talk with

Source: "Southern Diaries," by Ivanhoe Donaldson, from *Freedomways*, 1964.

Bob Moses (Mississippi SNCC leader) about the possibility of getting more manpower and a better means of transportation in and around the counties we were assigned to canvass. We had spent the entire day canvassing in Issaquena and Sharkey Counties. Moses decided that he would rent some cars to supplement the need to be more mobile in the counties. He asked us to wait around and go with him to the airport to pick up a couple of rented cars later that night. Around 11:15, Cobb, Jessie Harris, and I met with Moses in the office and left for the airport. We got into a 1963 Oldsmobile that Moses had rented earlier. We were to pick up two 1963 Ford Galaxies and leave the Oldsmobile for Moses. (He was taking a plane flight and would return in a few hours.)

We pulled into the parking space reserved for rented cars at the Jackson Municipal Airport. A green Valiant police car was parked with the motor running just a few cars away. As we got out of the car, a policeman came over and checked out the license on our car and told Bob Moses to "come here." The rest of us walked inside the terminal building where Moses joined us in a couple of minutes. Moses reported that the cop asked him if the Olds was rented. Bob then gave Jessie Harris one set of keys for the two rented cars (Fords) and myself the other set. Then he discovered that he only had papers for one Ford. Bob tried to call the office several times but the line either went dead or someone answered and said it was the wrong number. Finally we got a line through and someone from the office was to bring out the papers for the other Ford.

The policeman who had previously questioned Bob was now wandering around the terminal watching him board his plane. We returned downstairs to wait for the other papers. The policeman told us we would have to leave the airport or be arrested for *vagrancy*. Although we explained that we were waiting for someone, he threatened to arrest us again.

We all got into the white rented Ford for which I had papers and was driving. The policeman also got into his car and followed us out of the airport onto the highway. While we were on the highway the green Valiant police car passed us and two other police cars, both white, started following us. About a half mile from the Jackson City limits, one of the police cars flagged me off the road. One of the policemen got out of the car and told me to pull over to the gas station across the highway. All of us were ordered out of the car and searched. I gave the police my license.

There were four policemen. They told us to put our hands up. During this time, the policemen started a series of verbal harassments and intimidations. They threw in a couple of threatening gestures for good measure. Their language was abusive and vile:

. . . "Nigger, where you from . . . Boy! what's your name? . . . God-damned nigger twenty years old, ain't old enough, to register himself, come down here to get other niggers to register. . . . If you stay down here long enough, you gonna make a mistake. . . . Just like your mother paddled your behind, I'm going to have to paddle yours. . . . God-damned NAACP Communist trouble maker, ain't you, Boy? . . ."

After about twenty minutes of that and other forms of routine Mississippi cop interrogation, one of the policemen told me I was under arrest for having illegal plates on the car. I got into the back of one of the police cars while one of the policemen got in the front of the other car. The other three fellows were still standing in front of the gas station with their hands up. A policeman got into the front of the car in which I was sitting and turned around and looked at me as we were driving off. It seemed as though the harassment was to begin again.

". . . Nigger, what's your mamma's name?" I didn't answer. "Boy, if you feel so god damned [sic] sorry for these black son of a bitches, why don't you take them all up north with you? . . . Nigger, if I had your god damned ass over in Branden I'd kill you. Before you god damned black Communist sonofabitches started coming down here, everything was all right. Niggers down here don't need to vote—ain't supposed to vote."

All during this period of time I was just sitting, only answering questions which seemed half-way reasonable and that I felt were in his jurisdiction to ask. Finally, he told me that if the federal government ever sent troops down to Jackson, he would "kill every nigger he met. Boy, don't you know that whites are better than niggers?" I told him no. He unbuckled his holster, pulled out his gun and swung it at me. It caught me across the knuckles of my right hand.

"God damned black bastards think they're going to be taking over around here. Well, you and the other god damned Moses' niggers around here ain't gonna git nuthin' but a bullet in the haid!" With that, he swung his gun at me again and caught me on the other hand. "Black son of a bitch, I'm gonna kill you, nigger. God damn it, I'm gonna kill you!" He was almost hysterical as he lifted his gun and put it just inches from my face. He cocked the hammer and for a couple of seconds I felt it was just about all over. Just about the same time he was cocking the hammer, one of the other three policemen who were outside with the fellows, came in and told the other cop, "You just can't kill that nigger, heah."

They both just stared at me for what seemed like an eternity. I noticed that the other policemen were in the car and the fellows I was with had gotten back into the Ford. Finally, the cop who had arrested me threw my license in my face. "Don't let me catch your ass here in Rankin County agin, nigger, evah agin, or Ah'll kill you."

I got back into the driver's seat of my car and tried to calm my nerves which felt like they were about to explode. I explained to the fellows what happened. It was already after two o'clock. Moses had taken off at 12:32, so we had been out here on the highway for nearly two hours.

As I drove back to the office, I reflected over the incident just narrated. There was simply nothing to do except to chalk it up as something to be expected, especially when you're trying to bring the vote to the black man in Mississippi.

SPEECH AT STANFORD UNIVERSITY, PART TWO

Robert Moses

This speech was part of SNCC's recruitment efforts. As such it reflected the leadership style of Bob Moses. Moses candidly acknowledged that many of those active in SNCC in Mississippi did not want white volunteers coming into the state. He did *not* describe how he convinced them to go along, but he laid great emphasis upon the eagerness of Mississippi blacks in general to have the volunteers. One might speculate that he used that eagerness to persuade his coworkers. In any event, Moses made it clear that volunteers could expect a significant measure of suspicion, even hostility, from SNCC field-workers.

He also pointedly described the risks the volunteers would encounter from the white political structure in Mississippi. And he raised the question of his own responsibility should any volunteers be killed. It was not enough, in his mind, to blame Mississippi racists. They would be the killers, but he was the one who recruited the volunteers to run the risk. Nor was it enough that

Source: Speech at Stanford University, by Robert Moses, April 24, 1964.

he shared that risk fully. He, characteristically, referred to the work of Albert Camus, the French existentialist philosopher, whose *The Plague* helped him frame the question but did not provide a clear answer. He had to bear that responsibility. It did not stop him from doing what he thought right. But it was a "heavy" burden.

As this speech makes clear, Robert Moses and other SNCC workers had already formulated the challenge to the seating of the "regular" Mississippi delegation to the Democratic National Convention that August. Further, he and his coworkers already had come to view that challenge as a crucial test of the political system. Would the system bend? Could SNCC work for change within the system? Atlantic City would tell.

. . . By that time [1962] it was clear that the problems in Mississippi in terms of—were to be focused on political problems that what we had to do was somehow begin to tackle the political establishment in Mississippi—that the white citizens councils, the governor, the state legislature, the judiciary were all part of one monolithic system and that in order to find any kind of gaps in it we were gonna have to hit right at its heart. Well now, that phase in there was marked by several types of incidents and probably for us and for the workers, and still for the workers the acts of what we call symbolic terror figure most sharply in coloring all of the work because for us, Mississippi we believe deals in symbolic acts of terror, of killing.

It was, you roll off the names in 1956, it was a Mr. Lee in Belzoni who was shot and killed. The year after in that same city it was Gus Courts who was shot and ran out of the city. In 1960 it was a man on Brookhaven's Courthouse lawn who was shot and killed. In 1961 it was Herbert Lee in Amite County who was shot and killed. In 1963 it was Medger Evers in Jackson who was shot and killed. In 1964 it was Lewis Allen and three people in Wilkinson County and just recently another person in Wilkinson County all shot and killed. Always, the same type of people are found—they've been shot by white people. Only in Medger Evers' case was an indictment brought and an actual trial occurred. This kind of act of terror forces several very deep questions for the people who are working there because they have to in some sense or another come to grips with this. Workers who are working in Natchez, in Macomb, in Amite County who have to ride those roads by themselves who have already been shot at once, who may be every

The speech has been transcribed by Peter Bratt for the Voices of Freedom Web site at Stanford University. I have corrected several obvious errors in the transcription, for example, changing *streams* to *extremes* where it is clearly what Moses said.—ED.

time a headlight flashes up behind them, when they're riding at night, wondering if this is another time when somebody might take another shot at them, have to come to grips within themselves and turn to some kind of internal balance about that problem of violence.

All of that had to happen in that year between 1961–62 and on into 1963. But while that was happening what kept people going and what still keeps people going was that you were able to reach and make contact with the Negro farmers, with the people in the cities. You were able to actually grab a hold of them. There was some feeling that you had hit some rock bottom, that you had some base that you could work with and that you could build on and as long as you had that then maybe there was some hope for making some real changes someday.

Now, in 1963, after the summer and after the March on Washington, the Aaron Henry campaign issued in for us in Mississippi a new dimension. It wasn't a dimension devoid of problems. There were real, very tough problems with the sudden appearance of a number of students from Stanford and from Yale. But what they meant more than anything else was some type of involvement of the rest of the country on a different scale with a different kind of personal commitment and with a different possibility for organizing and working within the state. And it's the Summer Project which is the sequel to that and which is yet now being focused in a different way because if the Aaron Henry campaign had a bit about it, it was a big spontaneous thing and suddenly people rushed to join it. People were there for a week or two and then they vanished. The feelings of a lot of the kids who came down, perhaps, I'm not sure what their feelings were, because they were probably drawn up in a great big outburst of excitement on the campus and a very quick decision to move down and then down into something which maybe they really hadn't anticipated and couldn't have anticipated. This time what's at stake is something deeper. It's a question of whether in this country we can find people who are committed, who know, who care, who are willing to sacrifice, who are willing to say that they want to do their share, who are willing and able, perhaps, to look on this as somehow the country's business, not just as the Negroes' problems. Who are willing to look on this not as something maybe that just has to be done in Mississippi but something that will be carried back and will have to be done in places all across this country if we're really gonna get at the bottom of some of these problems. . . . The questions that we think face the country [are] questions that in one sense are much deeper than civil rights. They're questions which have repercussions in terms of whole international affairs and relations. They're questions that go to the very root of our society. What kind of a society will we be? What kind of a people will we be? It just happens that the civil rights question is at the spearhead of all of these. That all the questions about automation, all the questions about our schools, all the questions about our cities. What kind of cities will we have? All of these find their focus in the public eye in terms of some kind of civil rights demonstration or another; at a construction site, a school boycott, a rent strike, a stall-in. They're all gaining national focus and beginning to bring to the attention of the American people a wider cross section of problems. The problem is whether we will be able to really find solutions, whether we will be able if we find these solutions to take the steps that might be necessary in terms of the structure of our politics and economics to carry them through; whether if we're willing to take those steps; whether those steps can be carried through peacefully and with some kind of minimum amount of real frustration for millions of people. . . .

. . . In the Delta area of the Mississippi the people who work the plantations are facing the fact that every year there are 10% fewer jobs for them, that in probably five years, the automation of the plantations will be completed. The labor market on the plantation will be very well stabilized in at a very low point. And the people who come off those plantations will be unemployed and unemployable in our society. They will be permanently unemployed. Because, first they don't have the skills and there isn't anywhere in our whole country a system for teaching them say how to read and write because that was nobody's problem who had power, who had resources, who had money, who could tackle that problem. It's only since we've been down in Mississippi and since the civil rights movement has begun in the last few years that you've begun to get some concerted effort with very minimum resources. We got a grant, an anonymous grant mind you, of $80,000 to tackle the problem of literacy at the fundamental bedrock level and the person who gave it had to give it anonymously. Because the problem of literacy in the Delta and in Mississippi and the Deep South is a political problem. Because if you teach people how to read and write then they're gonna begin to want to govern themselves and they're gonna begin to want to govern themselves in an area where they formed the predominance of the population over more articulate, economically controlling white group. And that's a political problem in our country. The congressmen, the senators from those districts aren't interested in sponsoring literary problems. So there are no bills in Congress. We don't have a bill that has ever been introduced in Congress to deal with the problem of literacy for Negroes in the South. They're not interested. . . .

Now our feeling is that we have to be able to attack some of the specific structures which are visible, which we could see, which we may be able to move at. Certainly, the people who are in Congress from the South who don't belong there are such structures and part of that structure that need to be removed from office. And certainly, the whole country will be better off and better equipped to deal with these problems if they are. This does not beg the question of whether there will be Republican or Democrats or what will happen in terms of the political structure that will evolve; nobody knows. And the question should not be raised in terms of people who are afraid of what the political structure will be like if we get rid of those Dixiecrats. The problem is to get rid of them and begin to work on whatever evolves.

For our part this summer we're gonna go to the National Democratic Convention in Atlantic City and challenge the regular Mississippi delegation. We're gonna ask the National Democratic Party that they unseat that delegation; that they seat our people in its place and that they make a real structural change or the beginning of a structural change within their party. Our basis for doing that are three or four fold—we're carrying on within the state what we call a freedom registration. Some of the people who've come down this summer who are interested in politics will be working on that. We're setting up our own registrars in every one of the 82 counties, to have deputy registrars. We have our own forms. We're challenging the whole basis of the registration in Mississippi. We don't have any form or questions that will make people interpret some section of the Constitution. And we're making it simply as simple as we possibly can. We want to register upwards of 300,000 or 400,000 Negroes around the state of Mississippi. To dispel at least for once and for all the argument that the reason Negroes don't register is because they're apathetic. Because there are these 400,000 people to be registered. But for one thing people don't even know that they're there. And if they are and they do know they say well if so many people are not registering part of the reason and probably a large part of the reason must be their apathy.

With the freedom registration, we also have freedom candidates. We have three people who are running for Congress; one from the Second Congressional District, one from the Third and one from the Fifth, and then a person who's running against Senator Stennis. They have all filed, met all the qualifications and their names should appear on the Democratic primary on June 2nd. The idea is to begin to develop again within the people, the Negro people and some white people in the state, a different conception of their politics and to begin to see if we can't evolve a political organization within Mississippi. We also are gonna attend the precinct meetings that the regular Democratic delegates will be holding around the state. We figure that many of our people will be thrown out of these meetings because they're segregated. And we're gonna use this as part of the documentation as to why that delegation should not be seated. We also are gonna elect our own delegates, paralleling their procedures right from the start: precinct meetings, country conventions, district caucuses, a state convention, a total of 68 delegates representing 24 votes—2 whole votes and 22 half votes. We're gonna send them to Atlantic City. We're gonna ask that they be seated. We're gonna demand that they be seated. There most certainly will be demonstrations at Atlantic City. . . . I mean, we're trying to work as closely and as assiduously and as hard as we can within the political structures of this country—trying to see if they will bend, if they have any flexibility, if they give at some points, if they can really accommodate themselves to the demands of the people. The problem up to this point is that they haven't bent. They haven't given; they haven't been able to come up with real solutions. Everything has been patchwork and every time you put a patch on here, pressure mounts here, and something explodes. And you put a patch on it there and the pressure mounts here and something else explodes.

Now the questions that people keep asking are how long can this go on, how long are Negroes gonna maintain non-violence, how long are they gonna work in this fashion and the answer is I don't know. I really don't know. The problem now is that the call has really gone out to the rest of the country, not to Negroes now but the challenge now is to the rest of the country. In the same way, really, the challenge in the South is to the white people in the South. There's a sit-in at a lunch counter downtown. The question is how will the white people respond. See? What will they focus on? Will they focus on the fact that the Negroes shouldn't be down there and some of them are unruly and some of them approach violence and some of them do this and some of them do that or will they in turn focus on their just grievances and say o.k. this is what we've got to do. We've got to move over here and begin to accommodate them. That kind of call is going out across the country now.

And already the initial response is fearful because the initial response is not all in terms of re-examination of the country and its structures and how they can be changed and how they have to move and accommodate but rather focusing on the bad elements and using that as an excuse. . . . Theodore White wrote an article in *Life* magazine shortly after Kennedy was assassinated and he was describing the civil rights groups and picking out different facets of them and the one thing that he focused on was some of the civil rights groups, singling out SNCC in particular, who were gonna challenge the Democrats at their convention and we're gonna say to them if we can't sit at the table with you then we'll just chop off the legs and everybody sits on the floor. And he was saying that this is dangerous because he's essentially a man who looks for solutions, who tries to find ways out of impasses, who looks for the mean between each extreme.

But the problem is, what are the real solutions? And the danger is that the areas and the avenues that might be real solutions will simply be branded as acts of extremism. And exactly the same sense in which the first acts of a sit-in geared to a small Southern town were branded that way by southern politicians.

Well, I'd like to say just a little about the summer projects more concretely. And I'd like to do it in terms of some of the history as it evolved and some of the problems which happened in the state as the conception of the summer project came about. The staff in Mississippi were violently opposed to the Summer Project when it was first announced. They were opposed to an invasion of white people coming in to do good and to work for a summer and to essentially run projects without having any experience and basis for doing that. And we spent half of November and all of December and January and on into the very beginning of March in very heated, tough discussions about what the Summer Project could be, what it couldn't be, what kinds of hopes it held out for people in Mississippi and the country and what it didn't; essentially, what were its limits? What were the things that really might happen in terms of it that would be significant? And it was out of those discussions that we reached a very uneasy in many cases but at least tentative agreement among the majority of the staff to go ahead with concrete, specific programs and to try and channel people who are coming down into very specific jobs and tasks. An it was out of that agreement that the idea and the conception of the freedom schools and doing something to try and break psychological holds that Negroes have evolved and the concept of working in the community centers and the concept of working in the white communities, the concept of trying to provide some cultural dimension to the program and the concept of trying to buttress and further the legal work grew.

Now, on the other hand, the people in Mississippi did not have the reaction of the staff at all. The farmers and the people who lived and worked there welcomed the whole idea because they feel that any-body who comes down to help is good and that they need all the help that they can gain, since they're isolated, that they're alone, that they have no real tools, that they face an overwhelming enemy and any kind of help they can get is welcomed. So it was this more than anything else I think that swayed a lot of us because again, in the end, I think in many cases the instincts of the people and particularly some of the rural farmers' opinions about these things are truer, deeper, less clut-tered and less bothered by personal problems and things like that than the instincts, of say, the staff and the people who are working. So it was with this kind of background that we went into the project. And more and more as we've gotten into it we've come to the consideration that the people who've come down should be under some very well estab-lished controls—that they should have some idea of some very significant things they can do but very limited and perhaps significant because they are limited. And that some of the things that we would try to do would not be some of the things that we first envisioned doing. So, for instance, in the freedom schools we have one track which is basically just a set of questions which is devised to draw out of the Negro youngsters some ideas about themselves and the lives they lead. Questions which might ask them . . . Is their house painted? Does it have indoor toilets? Do they have pictures on their walls? How many kids live in a room? What are their schools like? Do they have libraries? What kind of teaching facilities do they have? Do they have laborato-ries? Questions which take them crosstown into white people's homes and try to get them maybe to imagine what the homes and schools over there are like. Questions which take them inside to their own minds, which try and get at attitudes that they have about themselves, that they have about white people. Questions which can be handled by people who have some sensitivity to other people, who have some con-cern about them, who are not so interested in projecting themselves but are able to try and reach out and really cross what is a really very wide gap between white people from the middle class backgrounds in the North and the Negro youngsters who've grown up in slums, rural or urban, in the South.

So that is one of the things we hoped to do. If we worked across the summer and if we touched in twenty freedom schools a thousand kids and began to draw some things like that out of them, then we felt that maybe we would have another layer, another stage, another base that we would have to operate from and on.

On the question of voting we decided that we would like to try and establish across the summer the right to picket at the courthouses in the downtown urban areas. We've had a picket line at Hattiesburg which started January 22nd when some fifty ministers from the National Council of Churches came in and joining a lot of our staff and young people and which went everyday from 9 till 5 and on Saturdays from 9 till 12 all through the month of March and on into the month of April. There were many significant things that came out of that picket line. For one thing, there was no violent white reaction, even though 50 miles away the Ku Klux Klan was burning crosses at 15 farmhouses and shooting 5 Negroes—in Hattiesburg no one was bothering the picket line. And even though the police the first day marched out in a platoon of 25 and stood up and down the streets and barricaded them, by the end of the week they were down to one or two policemen in shifts serving as observers. And the fact was the white people of Hattiesburg were not that upset about a picket line at their courthouse. Their attitudes about the rights of Negroes divulged did not reach that far. So that they were willing to form mobs in the street and conduct some kind of violence. So that the whole focus of the people who were really stopping voter registration could be narrow with something that many people thought already, but this corroborated it. I mean that the political establishment in Mississippi are the people who are really holding on and not letting Negroes vote—that if the white people were able or freer and were able to move and had more dimensions for themselves to move in, then it might be possible for Negroes to vote. We want to do this if we can in city after city around the state.

Now, we've already met obstacles to that. The state legislature about a week and a half ago passed a bill making it illegal to picket any public building. The governor signed it into law and the next day they arrested the whole picket line in Hattiesburg. And 44 people are now out on $1,000 property bonds each from Hattiesburg. But they are determined to start the picket line up again. And we're determined to gain that right this summer. Now in many cases, in many ways it's a very limited right but it's crucial in Mississippi because, if we gain the right to picket in integrated picket lines, then labor unions will gain the right to picket in integrated picket lines in Mississippi and will gain the right to picket and possibly the trade unions and the UAW and the Teamsters and the labor unions will move into Mississippi and begin to organize working people.

And if they move in, then they just might begin to move in behind them a whole host of other organizations in terms of beginning to meet and get to the working people in Mississippi. And that would be a bridgehead for the whole Deep South, if that were established.

If it's possible this summer to have interracial teams living and working in Mississippi and the Negro communities, it might change the whole conception around the country of how it might be possible to get at some of these problems in the Deep South. The federal government cannot have a real domestic peace corps. It's possible for our country to organize youth all over the country to give an elaborate training to spend millions and millions of dollars [in a] very worthwhile [cause] to train them and send them abroad to work in underdeveloped countries all across the world. It would be impossible for them to mount anywhere near that kind of program in this country. They could not send intregated teams into the South. The country wouldn't have it. They couldn't send integrated teams into the South. They couldn't guarantee their protection. They couldn't guarantee their protection! The federal government of this country can send people to Africa and get guarantees from the states that they go to [in] Africa they will have protection and that their lives will be safe. They couldn't get it from Alabama and they couldn't get it from Mississippi. They couldn't get it from Louisiana. They couldn't mount a domestic peace corps in this country. The country doesn't have available yet the tools to really get at this problem. It just doesn't have them. We don't even know how to put money intelligently into a state like Mississippi. The Ford Foundation, I bet, wouldn't know how to put ten million dollars into Mississippi without buttressing the system that already exists. I mean, how would they do it? How would you put money into the educational system of Mississippi without reinforcing what already exists there? We don't even have the beginnings of solutions. One thing that might happen out of this summer which could be very significant would be some idea of how people could go about beginning to make some break in the situation down there in the Deep South. . . .

The question comes up all the time about nonviolence and what it means. They're really deep moral problems which are connected already with the Summer Project. I realized one type of problem two and a half years ago when we first went down to Amite County. Because Herbert Lee who was killed that summer was killed just as surely because we went in there to organize as rain comes because of the clouds—if we hadn't gone in there he wouldn't have been killed. The action that was started in that county wouldn't have happened. So in some sense, if you're concerned about people and concerned about these kinds of questions, you have to dig into yourself to find out in what sense do you share responsibility, and what does it mean to be involved in that kind of action which might precipitate that kind of death. And I'm just posing that question now. I mean, Camus poses it on a historical scale in terms of whether people shall be victims or executioners; whether those people who are enslaved in order to get their freedom have to become executioners and participate in acts of terror and death and in what sense they do participate in it. And it takes place on maybe a very small scale down south in terms of that kind of activity which we carry on and perhaps one justification is that you are no less exposed than they are. So that at least you share that kind of exposure with them. But then, that's not equally so. The people who are currently working in Amite and Wilkerson and Pike Counties are more exposed than anybody. The people who've been working in Jackson organizing the office, which had to be done, are not as exposed as they are. And certainly the people who go down to Mississippi this summer—I mean that's the whole question of what will happen rests very heavy because nobody really knows what might happen and we're back in that same kind of dilemma which can be put maybe very nicely in terms of victims and executioners and philosophically, but when you come to deal with it personally it still rests very heavy.

© Stanford University 2001
August 8, 2001

3

Mississippi Summer

"A MISSISSIPPI JOURNAL"

Robert Penn Warren

Robert Penn Warren, author of *All the King's Men* and other well-received novels, was also a poet and essayist. As a young man he was one of the Southern Agarians, a group of intellectuals who collaborated upon a defense of white southern traditions in *I'll Take My Stand.* Warren became notably less conservative as he grew older and, perhaps, as he spent more time in the North. He also became an advocate of civil rights. This led to his *Who Speaks for the Negro*, a collection of interviews with black leaders interspersed with his own reflections. Warren's title reflects the growing differences between Dr. King and the Southern Christian Leadership Council and SNCC activists. To a considerable degree, these conflicts grew out of differing ideas about leadership. The SCLC was an organization built around the figure of Dr. King. SNCC, following the inspiration of Ella Baker, disliked top-down leadership. Instead it favored community organizing and consensus-based decisions. When Dr. King attempted to rein in SNCC initiatives, its members often rebelled. They sometimes scoffingly referred to him as "De Lawd." This split was symtomatic of other divisions within the civils rights movement. Some were over strategy, some over funding, and some over the viability of a multiracial movement.

Source: "A Mississippi Journal," in *Who Speaks for the Negro?*, by Robert Penn Warren, 1965. Reprinted by permission of the author. Copyright © 1965 by Robert Penn Warren, renewed 1993 by Eleanor Clark Warren. Reprinted by permission of William Morris Agency, Inc. on behalf of the author.

The interview with Robert Moses is particularly revealing. In it Moses, who rarely spoke about himself, discussed his upbringing and, especially, his very close relationship with his father. He also discussed the influence of Albert Camus, the French philosopher and novelist, upon his own thinking. In this context, he again candidly spoke of the tensions between white and black volunteers.

In his reflections on Camus' theories about "victims" and "executioners" and their relevance to the Mississippi Freedom Summer, Moses came as close as he ever did to formulating publicly his own understanding of the struggle and his own obligations as a leader. Given the very difficult decisions Moses made in organizing the Mississippi Summer, his thinking about the moral issues involved is especially important.

I have come to keep a nine A.M. appointment with Robert Moses. He is not here.

Moses comes, preoccupied, unsmiling behind his big glasses, blue denim trousers, white shirt, open collar, dark denim jacket; greets me, offers aimless abstract handshake.

Moses decides the office is too confused for an interview, and we go up the street to Number 1072, back into the now empty auditorium, where the meeting had been on Sunday. We set up the recorder on a small table in the rear.

WARREN: This is Robert Parris Moses.

MOSES: I am with the Student Nonviolent Coordinating Committee.

WARREN: In Jackson, Mississippi. Where were you born, Mr. Moses?

MOSES: In Harlem, raised in upper Harlem, went to school in Harlem until high school, and then I went to Stuyvesant High School, downtown. We took an exam, a city-wide exam to get in.

WARREN: What was the ratio of Negroes?

MOSES: Out of a graduating class of a few thousand, not more than a handful were Negroes.

WARREN: Did Negroes try for it?

MOSES: Over a city-wide basis my impression would be that there was usually no effort, really, in the Negro junior high schools to prepare people for the tests and encourage them to take it.

WARREN: Was there apathy among the students—the kids?

MOSES: They'd have the feeling it was something out of their range.

WARREN: I hear it said that part of the problem of voter registration is the fear of not passing.

MOSES: The fear of being embarrassed.

WARREN: Let's cut back to your career.

MOSES: I graduated from Stuyvesant in '52, then I went to Hamilton College. I graduated in '56, and went to graduate school, at Harvard, in philosophy, and stayed a year and a half. I picked up an M.A. at the end of my first year, then we had family trouble—my mother died the next year, my father was hospitalized, and I dropped out. Then I got a job teaching at Horace Mann—that was '58—and stayed there three years. Then came down here.

WARREN: Were you ambitious for an academic career when you went to Harvard?

MOSES: Well, I wanted to get the doctorate. I liked philosophy, I wanted to study. I wasn't sure I would teach—but there wasn't anything else at that time I wanted to do.

WARREN: How did you make the shift to active participation in the Movement?

MOSES: It was really a big break. I wasn't active at all until 1960, when the sit-ins broke out. It seemed to me something different, something new—and if—I had had a feeling for a long time—

WARREN: Before this you had a feeling?

MOSES: Yes. There was a continual build-up and frustration—back I guess as early as high school. And then in the teaching—confronting at every point the fact that as a Negro—I mean, first that you had to be treated as a Negro and you couldn't really be accepted as an individual yet—even at any level of the society you happened to penetrate.

WARREN: You wouldn't have felt it, you think, if you had taken your doctorate, then gone to a good college to teach?

MOSES: I don't know. But the fact was I gradually got the feeling that no matter what I did it would always be there, even though things were better and different than, say, my father's time.

WARREN: Had your father had ambitions like your own?

MOSES: Probably yes. But he was caught in the Depression, with two families to support. He had finished high school but he hadn't gone to college— there was no money—then he got a job in the armory and decided to keep that—I don't know, we had long talks about it, talks which I can now see were really about the question of opportunity, about whether he was satisfied or not—you know, his whole purpose in life. Anyway, he had decided to put his energies into his personal family. There were three of us and he wanted to see us all through school and college.

WARREN: It sounds as though you were very close to him.

MOSES: Yes.

WARREN: How do you respond to Dr. King's philosophy?

MOSES: We don't agree with it, in a sense. The majority of the students are not sympathetic to the idea that they have to love the white people that they are struggling against. But there are a few who have a very religious orientation. And there's a constant dialogue at meetings about nonviolence and the meaning of nonviolence.

WARREN: Nonviolence for Snick is tactical, is that it?

MOSES: For most of the members it is tactical, it's a question of being able to have a method of attack rather than to be always on the defensive.

WARREN: What about the effect King had at moments of crisis in Birmingham?

MOSES: There's no question that he had a great deal of influence with the masses. But I don't think it's in the direction of love. It's in a practical direction—that is, whatever you believe, you simply can't afford to have a general breakdown of law and order. And in the end everybody has to live together. Negroes understand this very well, but they put it in terms of "When they're all gone we'll still be here, and we have to live with the people here."

WARREN: "They all" being the workers who come in and then go away next week?

MOSES: Yes—but we try to send workers to communities where they can stay and live.

WARREN: The objection of the local Negro might have either of two meanings— a positive one, a vision of a society of men living together under law—and a negative one, a fear of reprisal after the outside workers have left.

MOSES: Exactly. They mean it largely in the negative sense. But in the end there can be an appeal they understand—that is, in the end the Negroes and the whites are going to have to share the land, and the less overlay of bitterness, the more possible to work out a reconciliation.

WARREN: Some Negroes say that such reconciliation may come more easily in the South, because of a common background and a shared history, than in the great anonymous Northern cities.

MOSES: Well—I really don't know. The country has such tremendous problems—I mean, every time you try and get a break-through in, say, the Negro problem, you run into a deeper, tremendous problem that the whole country has to face. Jobs, the question of education—these things are tied so deeply into problems that run deep into the major institutions of the country. And the whole question of automation, and armament. I get lost. I don't see ahead to what the shape of this country will look like in ten years. The fantastic changes—as deep, say, as the Industrial Revolution. . . .

WARREN: Have you suffered violence?

MOSES: Once I was attacked on the way to the courthouse—two Negro farmers and myself. Going to register, and walking down the main street three young fellows came up and began to pick an argument—they singled me out and began to beat on me. I had about eight stitches on the top of my head.*

WARREN: With their fists?

MOSES: Well, apparently—but it turned out after, he had a knife which was closed. We went to trial, and a couple of days later he was acquitted. We came back to town—this little town—Liberty—a town of maybe a thousand people. It has a long and vicious history. Just last week one of the farmers down there was killed and—

WARREN: He had consented to be a witness in a murder trial, hadn't he?

MOSES: Lewis told the truth to the FBI, but the local authorities, he had told them what they wanted to hear.

---

*The assailant was Billy Jack Caston, a cousin of the local sheriff and the son-in-law of a state representative, F. H. Hurst. Howard Zinn, *The New Abolitionists*.

WARREN: Then told the FBI the truth and was willing to testify if given protection?

MOSES: Yes, and we believe that the FBI leaked this to the local authorities, and the Sheriff, and the Deputy Sheriff came out, you know, and told them—Lewis—what they had learned.* And they had been picking on him ever since—that was in September '61. At one point a deputy sheriff broke his jaw—and then they killed him. With a shotgun.

WARREN: Have there been any arrests on that?

MOSES: I doubt that there will be.

WARREN: Do you believe that the leak was intentional?

MOSES: I believe that, and we said as much to the Justice Department.

WARREN: Back to you, have you had other attacks?

MOSES: Last year in Greenwood we were driving along.† Some white people had been circling the town—about three or four carloads. One followed us out of town—there were three of us in the car—and they opened up about seven miles out of town—just bullets rained all through the car—the driver had a bullet in his neck, and he was slumped over in my lap, and we went off the road. We had to grab the wheel and stop the car. He had a forty-five lodged about an inch from his spine. None of the rest of us were hit—just shattered with glass. This is all interesting because Beckwith—the fellow who was tried for killing Medgar—well, the people who shot us that the police arrested—there were some arrests on that—they answered to the same general description as Beckwith—middle-aged, middle-class people. They've never been brought to trial.

WARREN: The same type as Beckwith?

MOSES: I think there was a conspiracy up there—and we wrote letters and sent telegrams to the Civil Rights Commission asking for an investigation. Of course, they say there're no grounds justifying—no grounds.

WARREN: You are just married, aren't you?

MOSES: Yes.

WARREN: What view does your wife take of your hazardous occupation?

---

*The charge that in the South the FBI is packed with Southern-born agents and is racist is not uncommonly made by Negroes. It is alleged, for example, that Dr. King advised civil rights workers not to report to the FBI acts of violence in Albany, Georgia, because the agents were Southern. To this, Hoover replied that King is "the most notorious liar in the country," and asserted that four out of the five agents in Albany were Northern and "that seventy per cent of the agents in the South were born in the North." (*The New York Times*, November 19, 1964.)

Since that time Dr. King and Mr. Hoover have met for an "amicable discussion" of their differences. "I sincerely hope," King said, "we can forget the confusions of the past and get on with the job . . . of providing freedom and justice for all citizens of this nation." The issue, of course, is not really the percentage of Southern-born agents of the FBI working in the South. Negroes have not been alone in protesting against what the American Civil Liberties Union has called "the absence of a psychology of commitment [in the FBI] to enforcing laws which guarantee Negroes equal rights." The ACLU has suggested a separate unit in the FBI to investigate civil rights violations. (*The New York Times*, December 2, 1964.)

†The companions were Randolph Blackwell, of the Voters Education Project in Atlanta, and Jimmy Travis, twenty years old, ex-freedom rider, now member of the Snick staff. Travis was operated on and survived. The episode is one of a long series of acts of violence.

MOSES: Well—that's hard to say because she doesn't—I mean you don't really confront her. I mean, you just go on living.

WARREN: You take it day by day?

MOSES: Otherwise, there's no real way to confront that except to—within yourself, try to—you have to overcome the fear. And that took me quite a while, you know—quite a while.

WARREN: Can you put your philosophy to work on that?

MOSES: Not the Harvard seminar. It goes back when I was in college and I had a French professor who did a lot of work in twentieth century literature, and I read a lot of Camus. And I've picked it up again. When I was in jail this last time I read through *The Rebel* and *The Plague* again. The main essence of what he says is what I feel real close to—closest to.

WARREN: Will you state that?

MOSES: It's the importance to struggle, importance to recognize in the struggle certain humanitarian values, and to recognize that you have to struggle for people, in that sense, and at the same time, if it's possible, you try to eke out some corner of love or some glimpse of happiness within. And that's what I think more than anything else conquers the bitterness, let's say. But there's something else.

WARREN: What?

MOSES: Camus talks a lot about the Russian terrorists—around 1905. What he finds in them—is that they accepted that if they took a life they offered their own in exchange. He moves from there into the whole question of violence and nonviolence and comes out with something which I think is relevant in this struggle. It's not a question that you just subjugate yourself to the conditions that are and don't try to change them. The problem is to go on from there, into something which is active, and yet the dichotomy is whether you can cease to be a victim any more and also not be what he calls an executioner. The ideal lies between these two extremes—victim and executioner. For when people rise up and change their status, usually somewhere along the line they become executioners and they get involved in subjugating, you know, other people. Of course, this doesn't apply for us Negroes on any grand scale in the sense that we're going to have a political overthrow in which we are going to become political executioners.

WARREN: But it does apply in terms of inside attitudes?

MOSES: It applies very much, I think. We're going through a big thing right now even in terms of attitudes of the Negro staff towards the white staff, and it's very hard for some of the students who have been brought up in Mississippi and are the victims of this kind of race hatred not to begin to let all of that out on the white staff. And we just had a tirade—one staff person a few days ago just, you know, for about fifteen minutes, just getting—letting out what really was a whole series of really racial statements of hatred. And we sort of all just sat there. The white students were, in this case, now made the victims. You know it's a process mainly of cleansing, but the problem is whether you can move from one to the other—that is, whether you can move Negro people from the place where they are now the victims of this kind of hatred, to a place where they don't in turn perpetuate this hatred.

WARREN: What are the actual criticisms—I don't mean necessarily valid criticisms—of the white participants in this movement?

MOSES: Well, first, the white people come down and have better skills and have better training. The tendency always is for them to gravitate to command posts. But Negro students, you know, actually feel this is their own movement. This is the strongest feeling among the Negro students—that this is the one thing that belongs to them in the whole country; and I think this causes the emotional reaction toward the white people coming in and participating.

WARREN: What about the resentment against young white persons who come into such an environment as this, and then try to enter romantically into Negro taste in music, Negro taste in this, that and the other—who want to enter, to join, to become more Negro than Negroes.

MOSES: Well, it depends. The distinction that the students themselves use is where a person is white—that is, they make the distinction between white people who somehow carry their whiteness with them, and some white people who somehow don't.

WARREN: But this difference remains?

MOSES: Yes, well, the Negroes say that they're not really *white* white people. Some people transcend that distinction and move on a plane that people are human beings.

WARREN: I was referring to the sense of amusement, and perhaps even resentment, at the white man who tries to go Negro—

MOSES: The white person who carries his whiteness and who, in addition, may be trying to move into this area—that person becomes an object of amusement.

WARREN: Speaking of splits in identity, what of that split Du Bois speaks of—the tension between the impulse to Negro-ness, the *mystique noire*, and the impulse to be absorbed into the white West European-American culture—and perhaps blood stream?

MOSES: For myself I don't think the problem has been this kind of identity. It's not a problem of identifying with "Negro-ness." But neither do you want to integrate into the middle-class white culture, since that seems to be at this point in vital need of some kind of renewal. But in the struggle you find a broader identification, identification with individuals that are going through the same kind of struggle, so that the struggle doesn't remain just a question of racial struggle. Then you get a picture of yourself as a person, caught up historically in these circumstances, and that whole problem of identifying yourself in Negro culture—or of integrating into the white society—that disappears. . . .

WARREN: What relation, if any, do you see between your students and the Beats?

MOSES: One thing, the Beats were left without a people—without anybody they might identify with.

WARREN: Anti-social?

MOSES: Yes. Reacting against everything, they closed in on themselves—for their own values and things like that. What happens with students in our movement is that they are identifying with these people—people who come off the land—they're unsophisticated, and they simply voice, time and time again, the simple truths you can't ignore because they speak from their own lives. It's this the students are rooted in, and this is what keeps them from going off at some tangent. It's this that is put into opposition to what life is now. We had this meeting last Sunday—

WARREN: Yes, I was there.

MOSES: There are some in leadership who are against that kind of meeting.

WARREN: Why?

MOSES: They're for the kind of meeting where you get well-dressed, cleaned-up Negroes. They don't want the other people. They're embarrassed. Those people don't speak English well. They grope for words.

WARREN: "Red-ish" for "register."

MOSES: Right—they can't say that word. But it's that embarrassment the students are really battling against. For society needs to hear them, and as long as the students are tied in with these, their revolt is well-based. Not like the Beatnik revolt.

WARREN: Has there been a change in the climate of opinion—the white attitude toward the Negro, or toward the Negro problem?

MOSES: When I was at Hamilton the white attitude was: "Well, we have to do our part—the society has the overall problem, and our part as an educational institution is to try and open a door for two or three Negroes, and let's see what happens." The difference from the period before is simply that earlier they weren't interested in even opening a door. Well, while I was there I was glad to have the opportunity, but still I was deeply bitter about some of the realities of the campus and of the white attitude. You're getting another change now.

WARREN: Has the white man's picture of the Negro changed here?

MOSES: I'm sure it has. The Sheriff in Canton told some of our fellows, he told them, "Well, you all are fighting for what you believe is right, and we're fighting for what we believe is right." Now that seems to me to be a tremendous change.

WARREN: It surprises me, to tell the truth.

MOSES: That is the recognition of an equal status—that is, you're a person. Now these guys at Canton, they're not well-educated or anything like that. Just from the South—Negroes born right here—but here the Sheriff is saying to them, "You have something you believe in. So we both have sides—two sides of the same fence." That's a tremendous change.

WARREN: How do you give flesh in history to the concept "Freedom Now"?

MOSES: I don't know that that's a concept. It's an emotional expression, an attempt to communicate—we have a poster in our office and all it says is "Now!"

WARREN: I saw it.

MOSES: That's to say how we feel. This is the urgency.

WARREN: It's a poetic statement?

MOSES: Right.

I come out of Number 1072 Lynch Street and go toward town. I have an engagement for lunch, miles away at Tougaloo College. As I go down Lynch Street I am thinking of the conversation long ago between Robert Moses and his father.

And I am thinking of my own father. He was born in 1869, son of a Confederate veteran, and raised in the Reconstruction South. His mother died when he was quite young, and his father when he was in his teens, leaving several younger children, three of them by a second wife who was not much older than my father himself. He buckled down to run the family, postponing his own ambitions, studying at night, later taking courses at a little college at night—or rather, being tutored by an instructor at the college. I have his old Greek and German grammars, faded, yellow, falling apart. I have lost the old copy of Dante's *Inferno* with the illustrations by Doré, which had belonged, I think, to his father. I have the poems he wrote; I had an anthology in which one or two were printed, more than sixty-five years ago, but it is lost. He studied law by himself, the copies of Blackstone and Montesquieu were in the house for years. Meanwhile, he did his duty to the family left in his charge. He got married fairly late.

I am remembering what the father of Robert Moses said to him "about whether he was satisfied or not—you know, his whole purpose in life," and how "he had decided to put his energies into his personal family," and I hear in my head, clear as can be, my own father's voice—an old man's voice—saying to me that he had had to choose, had had to realize that certain things were not for him, but he was happy.

I think, then, that I understand something about Robert Moses.

THE MISSING MISSISSIPPI MODERATES: THE HEFFNERS OF MCCOMB

What made Mississippi the "most Southern place on earth"? Why was it "the heart of the iceberg" of white supremacy, as Bob Moses put it? Prize-winning novelist Walker Percy, member of a distinguished Mississippi family, wrote a thoughtful if sorrowful essay in the immediate aftermath of the "Freedom Summer."[1] His home state was now "mainly renowned for murder, church-burning, dynamiting, assassination, night-riding, not to mention lesser forms of terrorism." Why this was so derived from reasons "both obvious and obscure."

> What is obvious is that Mississippi is poor, largely rural, and has in proportion the largest Negro minority in the United States. But Georgia shares these traits. Nor is it enough to say that Mississippi is the state that refused to change. . . .

Mississippi had changed several times over its history, Percy pointed out. Why had its white citizens refused to change in the decade following the *Brown v. Board of Education* decision? One key to the answer, he thought, was "the total defeat of the old-style white moderate and the consequent collapse of the alliance between the 'good' white man and the Negro." Well-to-do whites had once sought to temper the more egregious expressions of white racism. They often failed, as the state's horrific record of lynchings demonstrates. But there had been a voice of moderation. By the mid-1950s that voice disappeared. The white moderates went into exile, as Percy did, or kept quiet—or, worse, joined the White Citizens' Council.

Why had this happened in Mississippi but not in Georgia or Alabama? They too had demogogic politicians who vowed to defend "segregation forever." Yet, by the end of 1964, about forty percent of Georgia blacks were registered to vote. In Mississippi the figure was six percent.

Percy pointed to the fact that Mississippi lacked a "big city which might have shared, for good and ill, in the currents of American urban life." Georgia had Atlanta. In Atlanta were large corporations with national, sometimes global, markets. Their executives dealt with New York bankers, London insurance carriers, and Washington bureaucrats. They knew that "segregation forever" was a lost cause and counseled obedience to federal court orders and racial accommodation. They did not silence the white supremacists, could not prevent violence and threats against civil rights activists, but

---

[1]Walker Percy, "Mississippi: The Fallen Paradise," *Harper's Magazine*, April 1965.

they did condemn those actions and call for peace. Over time their views prevailed. They had no counterparts in Mississippi.

One can see what happened to potential moderates in Mississippi in the saga of the Heffner family of McComb. "Red" Heffner was an insurance agent and local civil leader. He was also a lay reader in the Presbyterian Church. His wife was active in various women's organizations and charities. Their older daughter was Miss Mississippi in 1963, the same year Red won an award for most sales from his employer. The Heffners were an old Mississippi family and moderates on racial issues. When they heard that SNCC intended to launch a voter registration drive in McComb, they sought to broker an understanding among the city's business leadership, the white and black churches, SNCC workers, and the sheriff. The idea was to avoid the kinds of violence that had marked other SNCC campaigns. The following excerpts from local and regional newspapers show what happened instead.

Jackson, Miss. (AP)—The Albert Heffner family, parents of Miss Jan Nave, Miss Mississippi of 1963, left their ten-year home at McComb in South Mississippi because of what they called "unbelievable threats and intimidations." The mother of the past Miss Mississippi weaved a shocking tale Saturday explaining how her family was "run out" of their hometown because they associated with several civil rights workers.

Meridian Star, Sept. 6

Mrs. Albert Heffner told a news conference here the "series" of incidents began two months ago because she and her husband sought to "establish communications" between law officers in the southwest Mississippi town and civil rights workers involved in the Mississippi summer project.

Tupelo Journal, Sept. 7

Visibly choked with emotion she told of sleeping with guns beside the beds, of threats that their home would be bombed or burned, and of "at least 300 threatening or obscene phone calls."

"The fear was almost unbearable," she related. "One night when the highway patrol was watching the house we had to hide out at the Holiday Inn. The FBI told us not to leave the room for anything."

She said her daughter's three pets had been killed, and that when her daughter, Carla, 17, returned from a trip to New York she was repeatedly threatened and insulted.

"When I'd go downtown, people I had known all my life would treat me like I had leprosy. We just couldn't ask Carla to live in that atmosphere."

Meridian Star, Sept. 6

Albert W. (Red) Heffner Jr. of 202 Shannon Dr. issued a statement today in connection with reports that he had entertained two civil rights workers in his home Friday evening.

Heffner said, it is true that two white civil rights workers were in my home on this evening. But it was a conference and not a matter of entertainment. The purpose of the conference was to let the civil rights workers hear the Mississippi point of view.

"Nothing was done in my home or elsewhere which was not fully disclosed to law enforcement authorities at the time. I have worked closely with the authorities for the best interests of our town and state. I shall always work to this end for each and every member of my family is a native Mississippian, dedicated to the best interest of our people."

McComb Enterprise-Journal, July 22

Mrs. Hefner recalled with obvious terror the day she found out that her house was supposed to have been bombed the preceding night.

I learned about it while I was swimming at a motel pool. But I soon found out that I was about the only one in my neighborhood who didn't know about it," she said.

"A four-year-old child came up to me and asked, 'When is your house going to be bombed?'"

Delta Democrat-Times, Sept. 9

The city's mayor, Gordon Burt Jr., said the Heffner family never appealed to the city for assistance.

"It looks to me like Mrs. Heffner has made some observations and conclusions which she had not carefully considered before making them," Burt said when informed of her statements.

"I had no idea that anything like this was going on."

He added, "perhaps there are some differences in our basic attitudes with civil rights workers and they have never been welcome in McComb, but if the Heffners were threatened and intimidated, if they had spoken up, they might have been assisted."

Biloxi-Gulfport Herald, Sept. 7

He could not see it then, but Red Heffner took the first step on his road to ruin on July 7, five days after President Lyndon B. Johnson signed the Civil Rights Act.

In a move to establish communication between the races, he got in touch with two Negro business acquaintances and offered his services as a go-between to the white community in case of violence. He informed Police Chief George Guy of what he had done and promised to keep Guy posted.

. . . The Heffners are pure Mississippi. They look it, they sound it, they feel it.

Heffner, who is known as Red, was born 42 years ago in Greenwood, Miss., and was reared on a plantation. He traces his Mississippi ancestry back three generations. His great-grandfather was a Confederate army officer.

Heffner's wife, Malva, daughter of an attorney, also was reared on a plantation. Her family goes back even further into Mississippi history, having settled in the area before it became a state.

In 1957 Heffner received a community service award from the McComb Chamber of Commerce. He is a lay reader in the Protestant Episcopal Church. He is a past president of Mississippi Multiple Sclerosis Association and of the Pike County Little Theater Association. He was an organizer of the Pike County Association for Exceptional Children. His insurance firm gave him an award for an outstanding sales record in 1963.

Mrs. Heffner, 40, was president of the McComb Youth Center Association and was instrumental in raising $30,000 to build the city's first youth center. The project took six years. She also was vice president of the McComb Recreation Committee and was a member of the Junior Auxiliary for five years.

McComb Enterprise-Journal, Sept. 16

Source: From "Hounded from City Spreads," in *McComb Enterprise-Journal*, Sept. 16, 1964. Used by permission of the *McComb Enterprise-Journal* and the *St. Louis Post-Dispatch*.

"IT WILL BE A HOT SUMMER IN MISSISSIPPI"

Richard Woodley

With the moderates like the Heffners silenced, COFO and the forces of white supremacy prepared for battle. COFO's plans called for hundreds of volunteers, mostly white college students from affluent northern families, to fan out across the Delta. They would set up clinics, schools, day care facilities as well as launch voter registration campaigns. White Citizens' Councils, supplied

Source: "It Will Be a Hot Summer in Mississippi," by Richard Woodley, *Reporter*, May 21, 1964.

with intelligence reports by the State Sovereignty Commission, laid plans to drive the volunteers out. Members of the Councils, who tended to be merchants and other business leaders with a healthy representation of clergy and other professionals, would handle publicity, issue public statements calling upon volunteers to leave, and condemn their crusade as part of a Communist conspiracy to overthrow the American Way. They would also inform black clergy that cooperation with COFO might lead to violence which they would deplore but could not contain. They would explain to black school principals that their positions depended upon their discouraging their students from joining in COFO marches or other activities. The actual violence the Councils left to the Ku Klux Klan and local law enforcement officials.

The following account from the *Reporter* provides a vivid description of both COFO and white supremacist activists on the eve of the Freedom Summer, including COFO recruitment efforts and its plans for screening potential volunteers. Author Richard Woodley visited the Meridian COFO center and interviewed young New York volunteers Mike and Rita Schwerner. A month later the entire nation would hear of Mike (better known as Mickey) and Rita. He, another white northerner, Andrew Goodman, and a local black named James Chaney disappeared after an arrest in Philadelphia, Mississippi. COFO staff immediately presumed they were dead. The search for the bodies of Schwerner, Goodman, and Chaney dominated the headlines for weeks. As of May, however, Meridian impressed Woodley as being comparatively calm.

For some weeks, civil-rights forces and the state of Mississippi have been maneuvering in preparation for a summer confrontation. The civil-rights groups, united in Mississippi under the name of the Council of Federated Organizations (COFO), have announced plans to bring at least a thousand college students into the state from around the country. The state officials declare themselves firmly committed to maintain law and order on the one hand and to thwart COFO on the other.

Neither side is certain about the strategy of the other; neither seems entirely certain of its own. The COFO leaders talk of a peaceful program of political education for Negroes, while anticipating violence (and perhaps, in a way, desiring it, as a means of bringing in the Federal government). The state officials, with drastic new laws and police build-ups, hope by a show of force to keep up their harassment of civil-rights groups, keep down the violence, and keep out the Federal government.

College students are already being screened at the major recruiting centers at Yale, Harvard, the University of Illinois, Oberlin College, the University of Oregon, Stanford University, and the University of North Carolina. They are to staff the programs of what is blandly called the

Mississippi Summer Project. This will include possibly as many as fifteen Freedom Schools, concentrating on remedial and political-science classes for Negro high-school pupils and dropouts. Enrollees will be shown how to start school newspapers and organize student governments. There will be cultural programs in music and drama.

Community centers, with less formal programs for all ages, will be set up as long-term projects. They will provide job training and health education, and will serve as places where Negroes can gather for meetings or recreation. The programs started by the Freedom Schools will be continued after the summer, staffed by full-time COFO workers and volunteers from the Negro communities. The National Council of Churches, in co-operation with COFO, plans to establish a number of its own centers in the Delta area, at an estimated cost of $50,000. Two COFO centers are already in operation. In Meridian, Mike and Rita Schwerner, a young married couple from New York City, have transformed dingy second-floor doctors' offices into a pleasant five-room center with a 10,000-book library, a Ping-Pong table, a sewing machine, several typewriters, a phonograph, a movie projector, and drawing materials for children. The programs appear to be running smoothly. The Schwerners estimate that 150 people have used the center since it opened late last winter. They report no unusual harassment from city officials and are now busy setting up a system of block captains for canvassing Negro neighborhoods for voter registration.

In the tough Delta town of Greenwood, on the other hand, arrests for picketing to protest voter-registration abuses have kept the center's staff off balance, and the programs have been slower in developing. There is a large library, a nursery with three girls in charge, and off-and-on classes for voter registration and civic education. Downstairs in the two-story brick building, COFO maintains a distribution center for used clothing.

Among its special projects, COFO plans to employ summer workers to take polls of "attitudes" in white communities, toward both the racial problem and the COFO program itself. Leaders hope, of course, that the canvassers will also have some success in changing the attitudes of some of the white people. Several Harvard Law School students plan to join the summer project to prepare suits challenging discriminatory laws and to assist in the legal work resulting from the expected arrests. Ten Yale Medical School graduates will set up health clinics. In co-operation with Tougaloo College, a mainly Negro school near Jackson, COFO has already formed a repertory theatre with an integrated troupe that will travel throughout the state this summer to give performances in churches, community centers, and even in the cotton fields.

But COFO's chief purpose—and the one most controversial in Mississippi—is to work on voter registration. Negroes constitute forty-two percent of the state's population of two million, yet have only 25,000 registered voters. Despite sporadic efforts by the Justice Department and voter-registration work by the Student Nonviolent Coordinating Committee (SNCC), Mississippi has lagged far behind the rest of the South in the fight for the franchise. Two years ago, as a result of growing frustration among SNCC leaders, COFO was formed with SNCC and the other civil-rights organizations—the National Association for the Advancement of Colored People, the Congress of Racial Equality, the Southern Christian Leadership Conference—in order to co-ordinate the effort in Mississippi. Last August it ran a mock "Freedom Party" election in competition with the state's gubernatorial election. President Aaron Henry of COFO and the state NAACP, a forty-two-year-old Negro druggist, ran for governor, and a white chaplain from Tougaloo College, Edwin King, ran for lieutenant governor. They received 80,000 "votes," compared to the 125,000 won officially by Governor Paul B. Johnson, Jr.

Buoyed by this showing, COFO has entered three candidates for Congress in this year's Democratic primary. None are expected to win, but COFO intends to stage another mock election afterward and then contest the state's ballot in Congress on the ground that the state's voter registration was discriminatory.

To the state's officialdom, voter registration represents the most direct threat to the white power structure; to the Negro leaders, it is a prime source of frustration. Despite voting drives and work in preparing Negroes to pass the stiff registration tests, the registrars have been widely effective in blocking them.

"There is a kind of 'This is it' philosophy for Mississippi this summer," according to Peter Countryman, former president of the Northern Student Movement, which is helping recruit students for the summer project. "There is a feeling that they will do anything to get significant change now."

PLANS FOR A SUMMER

To direct the summer project, COFO has designated Robert Moses, a twenty-nine-year-old New York Negro with a master's degree in philosophy, who has been in charge of SNCC's operation in Mississippi since 1961. A soft-spoken former mathematics teacher, Moses has a reputation as one of the best civil-rights organizers and strategists in the country. His leadership is vital to the daily direction of COFO's state operation.

As the representative of all groups, COFO has overcome the competition that plagues civil-rights groups elsewhere, and finds it easier to attract the support of national agencies such as the National Council of Churches. Its leaders hope that the Federal government will it find easier to justify intervention with lawyers, money, and programs where COFO demonstrates the need. It is also expected that the broader-based effort will bring Federal marshals or troops more quickly should they be necessary.

In taking on the toughest of the segregationist states, where Emmet Till, Mack Parker, and Medgar Evers died, there is widespread repetition of the slogan "Crack Mississippi, and you can crack the South." It provides a rallying cry that expresses both the strategy of the project and its attractiveness to younger recruits in the civil-rights movement.

The full-time COFO workers, clad in dungarees and living on subsistence pay (food, lodging, and ten dollars a week), work long and frantic hours, stoically submitting to arrest and harassment and, occasionally, physical harm. One detects a tight knit group feeling of careless rapture among them, and an attitude of indifference to critics within and outside Mississippi.

The COFO headquarters in Jackson, a one-story white masonry building in the Negro section, with interior walls of plasterboard covered with posters, maps, newspaper clippings, and progress reports from all over the state. On one wall under the red-crayon title "The opposition," there is an array of newspaper clippings with background information on state and local government officials. Leaning against a wall in another room is a tall green blackboard that carries chalk reports on police action in various towns ("Hattiesburg—Pete Stoner in Jail"). Key staff people moved in and out on their way to or from other towns where mass meetings were to be held and plans discussed. The four office telephones were kept busy, but always with the possibility that the lines were tapped. There is also suspicion that much of the mail is opened. Hence, very little of importance is discussed outside the closed executive-committee meetings.

The branch offices have even more the atmosphere of unarmed outposts in hostile territory. Only in Meridian, where an unofficial biracial committee has kept down the tension, was the community center comparatively relaxed. In Greenwood, harassment has created an atmosphere of suspicion. After several arrests recently during voter-registration demonstrations, the office became a confused center of activity as workers tried to find out who was in jail and on what charges. Affidavits were taken from Negroes who had been at the scene.

At times like this, there is no certainty that help will be sent. Jackson headquarters will be notified, and there will be attempts to get lawyers (there are reportedly just four lawyers—all Negroes—in Mississippi who will take civil-rights cases). In case of mass arrests or arrests of key leaders this summer, COFO plans to call in other leaders immediately from outside the state.

"If real money comes through," said Moses, "it'll be one kind of program. If it doesn't, it'll be another." Along with an estimated $50,000 the National Council of Churches will put into the Delta, COFO is trying to raise an additional $100,000. SNCC is conducting fund-raising drives at a number of colleges (Yale is trying to raise $15,000), and appeals are being made to the New World, Taconic, and Field Foundations, which have donated in the past. The college students coming to Mississippi are expected to pay their own fare and expenses (about $20 a week), though there may be scholarship grants for needy Negro students from the South.

COFO leaders are less worried about attracting a sizable number of volunteers this summer than about sreening them. With the strong emotions involved on both sides, there will be danger, Moses said, in accepting anyone who greatly misunderstands himself, the movement, or Mississippi. At the orientation session in Berea, Kentucky, the latter half of June, there will be concentration on, as Moses put it, "recognizing our own attitudes and the attitudes of the people here." Economic and educational differences between Mississippi and the areas from which the students come will be studied and Mississippi's laws analyzed. Nonviolence will be an important subject for training. "In Mississippi," said a free-lance photographer who has been observing the Mississippi scene, "you don't even go limp when they arrest you. You co-operate, brother."

The screening process will serve to eliminate types of people who could hurt the program. Professor John Maguire of Wesleyan University in Connecticut, who is recruiting students for the summer project, has explained: "We are largely worried about two types: those who are looking for a new kind of 'kick,' sexual or otherwise; and those evangelical souls who will arrive in Mississippi with no more understanding of the situation than to turn their eyes skyward and say, 'Lord, here I am.'"

Moses candidly admitted that much depends on what the Federal government does. Critics suggest that this means the students will be used primarily as bait for intervention by Washington. On the COFO application forms, students are advised to have access to money for bail, and are asked to list names of persons to be contacted should they be arrested.

In the COFO strategy, even staff people are occasionally used as pawns. Recently one COFO worker, an M.I.T. graduate known not to drink, was arrested on a charge of drunkenness. The fine was only $40, but the worker remained in jail for a week while COFO pleaded vainly for Justice Department intervention, "We'll wait until Saturday," said field worker Jesse Morris, "and if nothing happens by then, we'll pay his fine." Morris explained that the summer workers will be expected to let COFO make such decisions if they are arrested.

THE COUNTERPLANS

The strategy on the state's side appears to be equally hardheaded. The prospect of COFO's student invasion has provoked extensive political and police preparations. Governor Johnson has been working to unite racists and moderates behind him. In his inaugural address in January, Johnson called for an end to hate and violence and an increase in understanding, reminding Mississippians that they are a part of the Union. In March, he asked the legislature for an increase of from 275 to 375 in the number of state highway patrolmen, and additional powers to employ them in maintaining order. The governor told the legislators: "If we allow these invaders to succeed in their dastardly scheme; that is, if we allow them to commit violence or to provoke our own citizens to violence, we will be guilty of a very costly error." There was plenty of room at the state penitentiary, he declared, for "overflow prisoners."

Besides increasing the patrol, the legislature passed several measures aimed at restricting COFO's operations this summer: a bill to permit municipalities to "lend" fire equipment and personnel to each other to quell civil disturbances; a "quarantine" bill that permits municipalities to restrict movements of citizens "when there is imminent danger to the public safety"; a bill making it a felony to circulate material that encourages boycotts; and a bill to prohibit picketing or demonstrations when they "interfere" with entrance ways to public buildings or with the "free use of public streets or sidewalks."

This last law, already used to arrest nearly fifty pickets in Hattiesburg, is being challenged in Federal court. But the constitutionality of these laws has caused little concern at the state capitol.

The Jackson police force is being expanded, but Assistant Chief M.B. Pierce insisted that the complement of men is simply being brought up to "regular size." He says the force has 390 men, and

Jackson newspapers have reported a dozen being added. Mayor Allen Thompson reportedly bought two hundred shotguns last year and has ordered fifty more. Shotgun mounts have been installed in squad cars and on motorcycles. Three flat-bed trailer trucks have been converted into paddy wagons and two city trucks into troop carriers. The crowning piece of weaponry is an armored car called "Thompson's Tank." It has twelve-gauge steel walls and bulletproof windows behind which are seats for ten men with shotguns, tear-gas grenades, and a machine gun.

Deputy Chief J.L. Ray said that all this is just good business for a city the size of Jackson, and that none of it is aimed at civil-rights activities this summer. "If a man goes berserk and barricades himself in a building," said Ray, "this car [the tank] will be the safest way for the police to do their job and get him out." Ray believes that this will be quietest summer in three if COFO workers stick to their program of schools and community centers. "Spread them across the state," he said, with a wave of his hand, "and a thousand ain't so many." Ray said that "harassment" is a word being grossly overused by civil-rights workers in Mississippi. "Every time one of them gets arrested for anything," he argued, "they call it harassment."

The most ominous question for Mississippi this summer is, "Who will be protected, how well, and by whom?" There is no clear Federal policy on intervention in civil-rights matters, and it is not known how far COFO will push to force it or what Mississippi will do to prevent it. Though both Henry and Moses said that no demonstrations are planned, it is apparent that picketing will play a role in voter registration. "We are definitely not interested in filling up the jails this summer," Henry said. "But who can say there won't be some marching around the courthouse?"

Some state officials argue that the extensive preparations and armaments could just as well be viewed as a means for protecting COFO as persecuting it. It is known that the Ku Klux Klan is reorganizing in southwestern Mississippi, a troubling fact both to the police and to COFO.

Will the summer project succeed? It is certain that the invasion of students will leave an indelible mark on the state, either as the start of a massive and continuing Negro political-education program or as in eruption of violence. A great many arrests could cripple the program, according to Moses, but he maintains that anyone who thinks it will be stopped underestimates the spirit and commitment of the movement.

"'TIRED OF BEING SICK AND TIRED' . . ."

Jerry DeMuth

More than anyone else, Fannie Lou Hamer came to symbolize the determination of Mississippi blacks to overthrow the state's system of racial segregation. She became active in the voter registration campaign in 1962 when she first attempted to register. Faced with Mississippi's requirement that she correctly interpret a section of the state constitution, her application was rejected. Just the attempt, however, cost her and her husband their jobs. She went back, took the test again, and then again until she finally was able to register in January 1963. By then she was working full time for the movement. Bob Moses had insisted from the beginning that it would be Mississippi blacks who would ultimately free themselves. He had in mind people like Hamer.

Hamer was one of the key figures in the creation of the Freedom Democratic Party that challenged the all-white "regular" party. Her testimony before the Credentials Committee at the Democratic National Convention in August 1964 made her a national figure. The following interview dates back to the late spring of 1964 when she was challenging long-time Mississippi Congressman Jamie Whitten for the party's nomination for the House of Representatives. Her account of her life and her decision to fight Jim Crow to the death, if necessary, provides a case study in courage.

About 20 feet back from a narrow dirt road just off the state highway that cuts through Ruleville, Miss., is a small, three-room, white frame house with a screened porch. A large pecan tree grows in the front yard and two smaller ones grow out back. Butter bean and okra plants are filling out in the gardens on the lots on either side of the house. Lafayette Street is as quiet as the rest of Ruleville, a town of less than 2,000 located in Sunflower County, 30 miles from the Mississippi River. Sunflower County, home of Senator Eastland and 68 percent Negro, is one of twenty-four counties in the northwestern quarter of the state—the Delta—that make up the Second Congressional District. Since 1941, this district has been represented in Congress by Jamie Whitten, chairman of the House Appropriations Subcommittee on Agriculture, who is now seeking his thirteenth term.

Source: "Tired of Being Sick and Tired . . .", by Jerry DeMuth, *Nation*, June 1, 1964. Reprinted by permission of the author.

From the house on the dirt road there now comes a person to challenge Jamie Whitten: Mrs. Fannie Lou Hamer. Mrs. Hamer is a Negro and only 6,616 Negroes (or 4.14 percent of voting-age Negroes) were registered to vote in the Second Congressional District in 1960. But in 1962, when Whitten was elected for the twelfth time, only 31,345 persons cast votes, although in 1960 there were more than 300,000 persons of voting age in the district, 59 per cent of them Negro. Mrs. Hamer's bid is sponsored by the Council of Federated Organizations, Mississippi coalition of local and national civil rights organizations.

Until Mississippi stops its discriminatory voting practice, Mrs. Hamer's chance of election is slight, but she is waking up the citizens of her district. "I'm showing people that a Negro can run for office," she explains. Her deep, powerful voice shakes the air as she sits on the porch or inside, talking to friends, relatives and neighbors who drop by on the one day each week when she is not out campaigning. Whatever she is talking about soon becomes an impassioned plea for a change in the system that exploits the Delta Negroes. "All my life I've been sick and tired," she shakes her head. "Now I'm sick and tired of being sick and tired."

Mrs. Hamer was born October 6, 1917, in Montgomery County, the twentieth child in a family of six girls and fourteen boys. When she was 2 her family moved to Sunflower County, 60 miles to the west.

> The family would pick fifty-sixty bales of a cotton a year, so my father decided to rent some land. He bought some mules and a cultivator. We were doin' pretty well. He even started to fix up the house real nice and had bought a car. Then our stock got poisoned. We knowed this white man had done it. He stirred up a gallon of Paris green with the feed. When we got out there, one mule was already dead. T'other two mules and the cow had their stomachs all swelled up. It was too late to save 'em. That poisonin' knocked us right back down flat. We never did get back up again. That white man did it just because we were gettin' somewhere. White people never like to see Negroes get a little success. All of this stuff is no secret in the state of Mississippi.

Mrs. Hamer pulled her feet under the worn, straight-backed chair she was sitting in. The linoleum under her feet was worn through to another layer of linoleum. Floor boards showed in spots. She folded her large hands on her lap and shifted her weight in the chair. She's a large and heavy woman, but large and heavy with a power to back up her determination.

> We went back to sharecroppin', halvin', it's called. You split the cotton half and half with the plantation owner. But the seed, fertilizer, cost of hired hands, everything is paid out of the cropper's half.

Later, I dropped out of school. I cut corn stalks to help the family. My parents were gettin' up in age—they weren't young when I was born, I was the twentieth child—and my mother had a bad eye. She was cleanin' up the owner's yard for a quarter when somethin' flew up and hit her in the eye.

So many times for dinner we would have greens with no seasonin' . . . and flour gravy. My mother would mix flour with a little grease and try to make gravy out of it. Sometimes she'd cook a little meal and we'd have bread.

No one can honestly say Negroes are satisfied. We've only been patient, but how much more patience can we have?

Fannie Lou and Perry Hamer have two daughters, 10 and 19, both of whom they adopted. The Hamers adopted the older girl when she was born to give her a home, her mother being unmarried. "I've always been concerned with any human being," Mrs. Hamer explains. The younger girl was given to her at the age of 5 months. She had been burned badly when a tub of boiling water spilled, and her large, impoverished family was not able to care for her. "We had a little money so we took care of her and raised her. She was sickly too when I got her, suffered from malnutrition. Then she got run over by a car and her leg was broken. So she's only in fourth grade now."

The older girl left school after the tenth grade to begin working.

Several months ago when she tried to get a job, the employer commented, "You certainly talk like Fannie Lou." When the girl replied, "She raised me," she was denied the job. She has a job now, but Mrs. Hamer explains, "They don't know she's my child."

The intimidation that Mrs. Hamer's older girl faces is what Mrs. Hamer has faced since August 31, 1962. On that day she and seventeen others went down to the county courthouse in Indianola to try to register to vote. From the moment they arrived, police wandered around their bus, keeping an eye on the eighteen. "I wonder what they'll do," the bus driver said to Mrs. Hamer. Halfway back to Ruleville, the police stopped the bus and ordered it back to Indianola. There they were all arrested. The bus was painted the wrong color, the police told them.

After being bonded out, Mrs. Hamer returned to the plantation where the Hamers had lived for eighteen years.

My oldest girl met me and told me that Mr. Marlowe, the plantation owner, was mad and raisin' Cain. He had heard that I had tried to register. That night he called on us and said, "We're not ready for that in Mississippi now. If you don't withdraw, I'll let you go." I left that night but "Pap"—that's what I call my husband—had to stay on till work on the plantation was through.

In the spring of last year, Mr. Hamer got a job at a Ruleville cotton gin. But this year, though others are working there already, they haven't taken him back.

According to Mississippi law the names of all persons who take the registration test must be in the local paper for two weeks. This subjects Negroes, especially Delta Negroes, to all sorts of retaliatory actions. "Most Negroes in the Delta are sharecroppers. It's not like in the hills where Negroes own land. But everything happened before my name had been in the paper," Mrs. Hamer adds.

She didn't pass the test the first time, so she returned on December 4, and took it again. "You'll see me every 30 days till I pass," she told the registrar. On January 10, she returned and found out that she had passed. "But I still wasn't allowed to vote last fall because I didn't have two poll-tax receipts. We still have to pay poll tax for state elections. I have two receipts now."

After being forced to leave the plantation, Mrs. Hamer stayed with various friends and relatives. On September 10, night riders fired sixteen times into the home of one of these persons, Mrs. Turner. Mrs. Hamer was away at the time. In December, 1962, the Hamers moved into their present home which they rent from a Negro woman.

Mrs. Hamer had by then begun active work in the civil rights movement. She gathered names for a petition to obtain federal commodities for needy Negro families and attended various Southern Christian Leadership Conference (SCLC) and Student Nonviolent Coordinating Committee (SNCC) workshops throughout the South. Since then she has been active as a SNCC field secretary in voter registration and welfare programs and has taught classes for SCLC. At present, most of her time is spent campaigning.

In June of last year, Mrs. Hamer was returning from a workshop in Charleston, S.C. She was arrested in Winona, in Montgomery County, 60 miles east of Indianola, the county in which she was born. Along with others, she was taken from the bus to the jail.

> They carried me into a room and there was two Negro boys in this room. The state highway patrolman gave them a long, wide blackjack and he told one of the boys, "Take this," and the Negro, he said, "This what you want me to use?" The state patrolman said, "That's right and if you don't use it on her you know what I'll use on you."
>
> I had to get over on a bed flat on my stomach and that man beat me . . . that man beat me till he give out. And by me screamin', it made a plain-clothes man—he didn't have on nothin' like a uniform—he got so hot and worked up he just run there and started hittin' me on the back of my head. And I was tryin' to guard some of the licks

with my hands and they just beat my hands till they turned blue. This Negro just beat me till I know he was give out. Then this state patrolman told the other Negro to take me so he take over from there and he just keep beatin' me.

The police carried Mrs. Hamer to her cell when they were through beating her. They also beat Annelle Ponder, a SCLC worker returning on the bus with her, and Lawrence Guyot, a SNCC field secretary who had traveled from the Greenwood SNCC office to investigate the arrests.

They whipped Annelle Ponder and I heard her screamin'. After a while she passed by where I was in the cell and her mouth was bleedin' and her hair was standin' up on her head and you know it was horrifyin'.

Over in the night I even heard screamin'. I said, "Oh, Lord, somebody else gettin' it, too." It was later that we heard that Lawrence Guyot was there. I got to see him. I could walk as far as the cell door and I asked them to please leave that door open so I could get a breath of fresh air every once in a while. That's how I got to see Guyot. He looked as if he was in pretty bad shape. And it was on my nerves, too, because that was the first time I had seen him and not smilin'.

After I got out of jail, half dead, I found out that Medgar Evers had been shot down in his own yard.

Mrs. Hamer paused for a moment, saddened by the recollection. I glanced around the dim room. Faded wallpaper covered the walls and a vase, some framed photos, and a large doll were placed neatly on a chest and on a small table. Three stuffed clowns and a small doll lay on the worn spread on the double bed in the corner. Both the small doll and the larger one had white complexions, a reminder of the world outside.

We're tired of all this beatin', we're tired of takin' this. It's been a hundred years and we're still being beaten and shot at, crosses are still being burned, because we want to vote. But I'm goin' to stay in Mississippi and if they shoot me down, I'll be buried here.

But I don't want equal rights with the white man; if I did, I'd be a thief and a murderer. But the white man is the scardest person on earth. Out in the daylight he don't do nothin'. But at night he'll toss a bomb or pay someone to kill. The white man's afraid he'll be treated like he's been treatin' Negroes, but I couldn't carry that much hate. It wouldn't solve any problem for me to hate whites just because they hate me. Oh, there's so much hate. Only God has kept the Negro sane.

As part of her voter-registration work, Mrs. Hamer has been teaching citizenship classes, working to overcome the bad schooling Delta

Negroes have received, when they receive any at all. "We just have nine school buildings," she says. In Sunflower County there are three buildings for 11,000 Negroes of high school age, six buildings for 4,000 white high school students. In 1960–61, the county spent $150 per white pupil, $60 per Negro pupil. When applying to register, persons as part of the test must interpret the state constitution but, Mrs. Hamer says, "Mississippi don't teach it in school."

The Negro schools close in May, so that the children can help with the planting and chopping; they open again in July and August, only to close in September and October so that the children can pick cotton. Some stay out of school completely to work in the fields. Mississippi has no compulsory school-attendance law; it was abolished after the 1954 Supreme Court school-desegregation decision. Many Negro children do not attend school simply because they have no clothes to wear.

Mrs. Hamer has helped distribute clothing sent down from the North. 'We owe a lot to people in the North," she admits. "A lot of people are wearing nice clothes for the first time. A lot of kids couldn't go to school otherwise."

One time when a shipment arrived for distribution, the Ruleville mayor took it upon himself to announce that a lot of clothes were being given out. More than 400 Negroes showed up and stood in line to receive clothes. Mrs. Hamer, combining human compassion and politicking, told them that the mayor had had nothing to do with the clothing distribution and that if they went and registered they wouldn't have to stand in line as they were doing. Many went down and took the registration test.

"A couple weeks ago when more clothes arrived," she relates, "the mayor said that people could go and get clothing, and that if they didn't get any they should just go and take them. I went and talked to the mayor. I told him not to boss us around. 'We don't try to boss you around,' I told him."

Obviously, Fannie Lou Hamer will not be easily stopped. "We mean to use every means to try and win. If I lose we have this freedom registration and freedom vote to see how many would have voted if there wasn't all this red tape and discrimination." If Mrs. Hamer is defeated by Jamie Whitten in the primary, she will also file as an independent in the general election. . . .

In addition to Mrs. Hamer, three other Mississippi Negroes are running for national office in the 1964 elections. James Monroe will challenge Robert Bell Williams in the Third Congressional District, the Rev. John E. Cameron faces William Meyers Colmer in the Fifth, and Mrs. Victoria Jackson Gray is campaigning for the Senate seat now held by John Stennis.

This extensive program provides a basis for Negroes organizing throughout the state, and gives a strong democratic base for the Freedom Democratic Party. The wide range of Negro participation will show that the problem in Mississippi is not Negro apathy, but discrimination and fear of physical and economic reprisals for attempting to register.

The Freedom Democratic candidates will also give Mississippians, white as well as Negro, a chance to vote for candidates who do not stand for political, social and economic exploitation and discrimination, and a chance to vote for the National Democratic ticket rather than the Mississippi slate of unpledged electors.

"We been waitin' all our lives," Mrs. Hamer exclaims, "and still gettin' killed, still gettin' hung, still gettin' beat to death. Now we're tired waitin'!"

"FIELD REPORT—TELLING IT LIKE IT WAS"

John Due

John Due, a Florida attorney, worked on the Voting Education Project, a privately funded campaign to help register voters in the Deep South. In April of 1964 he and Emma Bell, a field-worker for COFO in Jackson, Mississippi, gathered evidence for a hearing before a subcommittee of the U.S. Commission on Civil Rights to be held in Natchez, Mississippi. What Due and Bell wanted were first-hand accounts of violence against African Americans who tried to register. This quickly brought Due and Bell to the attention of the Ku Klux Klan and other white supremacist organizations and individuals, including local sheriffs.

This portion of Due's report begins after he had been arrested for refusing to stop at a road block. Civil rights workers always feared stopping for the police who routinely used alleged traffic violations to harass and sometimes harm them. Due had decided not to stop. But he did, once Mississippi state troopers ordered him to do so.

They let Emma sit in the car. When we entered the lighted room, only Sheriff Daniel Jones was there. I wondered to myself where the other two men were who had been with the sheriff down the highway when he had first searched the car. Jones was looking through my legal pads, one for Pike County, the other for Amite County. Also in his possession were statements and affidavits, and also the COFO materials concerning intimidation and brutality in Southwest Mississippi. He also asked for whom I worked, and I repeated the same story but being a little more explicit that I had been researching the "economic conditions" in Amite County, knowing where my notes were going to lead him. By that time, Butler had demanded my billfold and spent much time going through my cards. He found my membership card to the Florida Bar, my NAACP membership card, and my CORE membership card and threw them to the sheriff, saying, "that communist organization."

The sheriff took my Florida Bar card and asked me if I was an attorney. I said yes. He then said, "Well, attorney, what good is being a lawyer doing you now?" I admitted that it was not doing me much good. Sheriff Jones went briefly through my report on Amite County and said, "Well, we don't want Bobby Kennedy down here, so I will give these papers all back to you nice and pretty." I don't think he noticed where he had been involved in [two of the affidavits].

The state trooper then motioned the sheriff into another room and discussed something about which I could not hear. The sheriff then came out, took my papers and placed them in his safe. The trooper then left. After I had been charged with reckless driving and failure to stop for an emergency vehicle, the sheriff then said that my cash bond was $100, and asked whether I wanted the trial in the morning or in the afternoon on Wednesday. I chose the afternoon. He then said for me to be there at 3 P.M., warning me that he wanted me to be there.

I was free. I got in the car, and Emma drove off. She drove past the place where Lewis Allen was shot, which I really didn't care to see at that time; and she searched for the road that would lead out of Liberty other than the highway toward McComb. It had been two years since she had been in the area, and she couldn't find it. We drove back into the main part of Liberty and went past the courthouse into the highway toward McComb. It was now after 1 A.M., and it seemed that no one was stirring. Emma drove slowly, both of us keeping close eyes to the side of the road. About 15 miles away from Liberty, we drove past a building behind which a state trooper was parked. About six or seven miles away from McComb, lights of a car approached us from behind. We were traveling only about 40 mph. The car passed us, and with our bright lights shining into it, we could see six tall men sitting ramrod-straight—who seemed to be farmer types—all of them wearing wide-brim hats. Emma in about a mile turned off from the highway onto a county road which leads to Magnolia, Mississippi. From Magnolia, we entered McComb from the side. Emma said that if we had gone farther on the highway, they probably would have met us at an underpass where the highway divided with no place to turn around.

As we drove into McComb, we passed a . . . gasoline station, at which Mr. C.C. Bryant had said earlier that he does not like to do business because he believed that the owner was a member of the Klan. There were several cars of people gathered at the station, but we did not tarry there in order to determine whether Mr. Bryant's belief was true or not.

Emma then dropped me off by the Negro hotel. I told her to return at 6 A.M. I wanted to be out of Amite County before the sheriff would get to his office. Also, we had to get all the information as soon as we could out of Wilkinson County and get to Natchez, Mississippi, so that I could report . . . about the sheriff stealing my papers.

I had a very restless night; however, I was dressed and ready to go when Emma came by. I decided not to take the most direct route to Centreville and Woodville, Wilkinson County, which was by Liberty, Amite County; but rather, we drove south out of the way and then took the county road to Centreville. One pick-up truck followed our car for about five miles, but it went on to Liberty when we turned off into a very rugged county road that finally led into Centreville.

We soon reached the home of Mother O'Quinn, 94 years old, but seemed to be in her 70's. When we introduced ourselves, she invited us in her half-lighted living room. We explained to her why we were there. She understood and was eager to cooperate. The daughter-in-law . . . who we were looking for was in Florida; so we decided to take her statement.

Her own son was shot-gunned one dark night as he was coming into his driveway, over five years ago. [His son], Clarence O'Quinn, who had made his home in Florida and was teaching, came to Centreville to live and comfort his grandmother. Around the first of April of this year, he came home and told her that [a] chief of police had beaten him. She asked what happened. Clarence said that he was only going in the post office and was on the steps when the chief approached him without any explanation or cause and said, "You damn uppity nigger, you think you own the town," and began to beat O'Quinn. Clarence asked his grandmother what he should do. She said, "You have a life worth living; you should not throw it away. You have no rights and privileges here." She told him to get all his things and leave Centreville that day. Clarence did leave Centreville that day to save his life and is presently living in Florida.

In this work, I had been objective, not emotionally involved with the particular person, but tears came to my eyes as Emma and I turned to leave. I had almost become used to stories of beatings and "mysterious shotgunnings." I had not become used to a grandmother telling her grandson to leave her—in order to live—because he had no rights and privileges. I suddenly remembered the hot argument I had with a high school chum back in 1951. He had volunteered for the Air Force rather than waiting to be drafted in the infantry. He argued that he did not want to die in Korea fighting people of his color, when here in the United States he was not even treated as a human being. I do not remember the counter arguments I used, but whatever they were, they are implicit in the activity of Emma and I trying to get statements before the Mississippi Advisory Committee to the United States Civil Rights Commission; but moist eyes belied the same old frustrations felt by my old high school chum.

It was a relief to arrive in Natchez. Emma didn't understand my feelings because the very reason the hearing was being held in Natchez is that most of the known cases of brutalities and beatings have occurred in Natchez. After a while, we finally arrived at the funeral home of Mr. Archie Curtis, the place where I was to meet Siceloff. Curtis is a Negro who seemed to be in his 50's. He has an Adenauer-type face resulting from having recently suffered from a stroke. It had not incapacitated him except to require him to speak slowly and to write slowly. He welcomed us into his private study. Although it was already planned that he appear before the Advisory Committee, he told us what had happened to him. One night in March of this year, he received a telephone call for him to pick up a body. He and his assistant, Willie Jackson, took the hearse wagon and drove in the direction of the given address. He said to Jackson, "We must have the wrong address" because they were in a deserted area when a car drove up behind them and they were ordered to stop. Curtis told me that six armed men in hoods got out of their car, and one of them demanded from him his NAACP membership card. Curtis told them that he had no NAACP card (it so happened that his new one had not yet arrived). They proceeded to beat him and his assistant. He begged them to stop beating him, telling them that he had had a stroke, but they continued until they were tired of it and then left him and his assistant in the street. This same "trick" happened to another Negro funeral director, George West. Mr. Curtis is actually not active in any NAACP but has been active with Natchez Negro Business League which has been urging Negroes to register. Their success which would arouse the KKK to be excited is that only about 200 Negroes are registered.

Mr. Siceloff arrived, and while eating a lunch brought by Emma, I told him what happened. He expressed a great concern about my papers because now in jeopardy were all the people I talked with, being that they were in the possession of the sheriff, Daniel Jones . . . Rather than forfeiting or even getting consent that I could forfeit the bond, I decided to return to Liberty and appear for the trial and stand mute; but at the same time, I believed that I should present a written demand for my papers.

Upon the advice of Mr. Wiley Branton, I asked Mr. Siceloff to be a witness or ascertain whether a member of the FBI would be present. Siceloff was willing but said that he had to call Washington to make sure that they were on notice. As it was after 2:00 and the trial was at 3:00, Emma and I left Natchez.

When we arrived in Liberty, I already felt like a martyr. I had solemnly prepared written motions, such as, appearance to stand mute, demand for papers, and request for an attorney and a jury trial. I gave copies to Emma, putting them in an envelope which she hid. I anticipated that they would deny that I ever presented the motions.

When I arrived in the office of Sheriff Jones, a quite sullen deputy sheriff was waiting for me. Soon, I heard the voice of Mr. Siceloff, and I felt as if the U.S. Marines had arrived. Mr. Siceloff identified himself and expressed an interest in the papers which Sheriff Jones had. The sheriff, in a surprised voice, said, well, he was going to give the papers back anyway. I had information which was useful for his investigation, he said. We all then went up to the Justice of Peace's office.

The Justice of Peace was an elderly man who seemed almost gentle. After reading the accusation, he asked me for my plea and I told him that I stood mute and explained what that meant. Sheriff Jones interfered, saying that in Mississippi, there is no such plea, that *nolo contendere* took the place of "standing mute." I admitted that I was not all that familiar with Mississippi law except that it was a common-law state, and "standing mute" is part of the common law. I then presented the written motions and the demand for my papers. I may have made a mistake, but I proceeded to explain my action on account of the fact that the sheriff had taken my papers without my consent. Sheriff Jones exclaimed that he was going to return my papers regardless of whether I plead guilty or not guilty; so he hurriedly went downstairs and restored to me my papers.

I then pleaded "guilty" after a long pause of thinking. It seemed unreasonable to fight both the traffic case and the sheriff's action.

I decided to fight Mississippi's methods of dealing with traffic violations another day. The Justice of Peace then gave a statement about the seriousness of what I had done and that the maximum sentence included 30 days; but because I was so "reasonable and fair," so said the Justice of Peace, I was fined $50 for both charges and $19 for the cost of court. After paying the fine, we all left. Soon Emma and I were leaving Liberty.

Around 6:30 Wednesday morning, Emma and I left McComb going to Liberty to pick up Evelina Tobias. We again wanted to be out of Liberty before too many people stirred around. We then remembered that we had procured no real information about the Lewis Allen killing of February of this year. During the excitement evolving around my situation, we had relied upon the Jackson COFO office to follow through in reaching Mrs. Allen in Louisiana. Emma called her and told her as I had promised, that we would pay for her expenses if she would come to Natchez, but Mrs. Allen told her that she didn't want to have anything to do with Mississippi. However, we still had hopes that she might come.

After we picked up Evelina Tobias, she told us about how the Sunday before, a high school boy by the name of John Harris was beaten by the Klan. Evelina knew where the family lives, so we went there to talk to them. They lived in the town of Gloster, 12 miles west of Liberty on a small farm. In reaching their home, we had to pass the homes of Sheriff Jones and the deceased Lewis Allen. Both of them had been neighbors. We turned into the driveway of the Harris' home, and Evelina went to the door and brought to the car Mrs. Lillie M. Harris, the mother of John Harris. I told her what we were doing and asked her what happened to her son. She said that on Sunday, April 19, her son, the members of the family, and members of the choir were coming home from church when hoodlum whites, without their hoods, drove up in their car and stopped, ordered John Harris to come to them and proceeded to assault him with the blunt end of their pistols. He screamed for his mother and then begged for them to kill him. Without hearing more, I asked her whether she and her son would go with me to the hearing in Natchez. She said yes, and in a short while we had picked up her son, who wore a cap to cover the stitches on his head wounds. We then picked up Mr. Franklin Robinson at Mr. Westly's farm, and finally reached Natchez about 11 A.M.

When we arrived at the place of the hearing at the Natchez Post Office, Mr. Siceloff asked us to return later because members of the Mississippi Advisory Committee were having a preliminary discussion. We went to a Negro restaurant, and while there I met Mr. Archie

Curtis, who notarized my affidavit that I witnessed personally the signatures on the signed statements I had in my possession. He also brought with him a man . . . [who] had somebody for me to see. I told Emma to take everybody on down to the U.S. Post Office, and that I would be there later.

Even Mr. Curtis could not come because it was a secret hiding place, and with him already having been beaten, he could be beaten again in order to tell the Klan where the place was. [The man] brought me to the place, and as I entered a bedroom, there was lying on the bed a young Negro of about 25 years of age. (Whereas only *this* person is in *immediate* danger as distinguished from the other persons who gave me their statements, and who are in probable danger only, I shall not expose this person's name.)

He had worked as a general handyman for a white farmer. On April 13 of this year, on a Sunday night, he was in the barn. He was trying the ignition because the truck had not been starting. He just happened to turn around and stared in the barrel of a shotgun. A man in a black hood holding the gun said, "Get out, boy." The Negro pushed the gun out of the window and quickly rolled the window up. He turned around to roll the window up on the other side of the truck and looked into the barrel of a rifle. This man also in a black hood told him, "You better do as he says." Each of them got to the side of him and began marching him to the back of the barn. As soon as he came to the edge where he could see the back of the barn, he said about six more men in hoods were all armed with guns. One man said, "We have been waiting for this a long time." He immediately pushed the two by his side together and turned, sprinting toward the house. He was able to get one side of the barn between him and them for awhile, but he had at least 50 yards to reach the porch of the house. He ran screaming for Mrs. X (the owner of the farm), and had attained about 20 yards when he received shot in his shoulder and back. The force of the bullets spun him slightly around when he was dropped by a shot in his leg.

Mrs. X ran out screaming, "What is the matter, what is the matter?" She saw that he was covered with blood. She told him to "play" like he was dead, and she ran and got a raincoat to cover him up with. With both of them straining together, they were able to get him on the floor of a car and she drove him to the hospital.

Why did this happen? He is the only Negro in Kingston who has been registered and he has been voting since 1960. Whites have made pointed remarks about this, his voting being a common known fact. Because of this, he has acquired a personal debt of more than $435 medical expenses incidental to four bullet wounds.

I then returned to the hearing of the Advisory Committee. While the hearing was in session, I saw now that there remained only one more hurdle—to get my witnesses back safely in Liberty and McComb, and then get back to Jackson. Courtney Siceloff was worried about this. So was William Taylor, the General Counsel to the U.S. Civil Rights Commission, who was there with the Advisory Committee. We also were worried about retaliation by the Klan against these people.

When we first had arrived in Natchez and when my party first got out of the car, I noticed how we attracted the attention of curious people, such as the white attendant, who in the service station next to the bus station "studied" us and then made a phone call and talked to someone while still "studying" us.

On my return to the post office and when I went back to the car to get the cross out [a charred Ku Klux Klan cross picked up as evidence], and as I carried the cross down the block across the street, going to the hearing room, I deliberately avoided looking into the face of the same attendant or other white persons standing about. I left the cross outside the door of the hearing room, not wanting to take it in. I felt that it might just interrupt the proceedings.

Pretty soon two carloads of men drove up to the post office, disembarking their passengers. Although there were a few thin high school youths and a thin man about 40 in a business suit, the most of them were husky white men in their 20's and 30's wearing tight levis and khakis, western hats, string ties, and sunglasses. One wore sun-mirrored glasses which he wore throughout the hearing, and sat in the front row easily frightening the members of the Committee. However, most of them were in good spirits, even joked about the cross standing in the doorway. When they first came to the door, they hesitated when they were confronted by the scene of an integrated panel presided over by the Negro, [Dr. A.B.] Britton. Not wishing them to be standing by the door because of my example, I pointed to vacant seats. They nonchalantly took their seats, even next to Negroes— some preferring to cluster together and some preferring to sit in the front row, as did the one with mirrored sunglasses.

They remained quiet, but they were still an ominous group by their mere presence. One of them got a pad out and as each witness would identify himself, the "cowboy" would busily write down the person's name, address, etc. I received a hidden joy to see the members of the committee become a little unnerved. I was glad the Klan was there because that was exactly what we wanted to show the committee, and eventually the American people, fear and intimidation produced by the Klan. Only Dr. Britton, although wet with beads of perspiration on his forehead—which I cannot blame only because of all the stuffiness of the hearing room—seemed brave when he dryly stopped the proceedings. He indicated that the committee noticed the presence of new people who had just arrived. He explained the purpose of the committee and indicated that if any of them had any information to present, such as being injured by violations of their civil rights, etc., the committee would hear them.

In a few minutes, I saw Attorney William Taylor abruptly leave and then return. Dr. Britton then called a short recess and asked everyone to leave. I then saw the local police come into the room. At first I thought he was after my charred cross, but I learned later that Taylor had received a bomb warning.

After my people from Pike and Amite Counties testified, I presented my statements and explained to them why some of them were not notarized. I also produced the charred cross, since some of the members of the committee had never seen one.

For the closed session, Dr. Britton asked everyone except the witnesses and their families to leave. After a short recess, the closed session was called and more testimonies were taken.

By this time, Robert Moses and his wife had made their appearance. Dr. Britton acknowledged their presence and asked Bob whether he had anything to say. Bob then gave a run-down of all the cases and killings and brutalities which had been reported to COFO and demonstrated the need for federal protection in the area. Dr. Britton then asked Bob a leading question about the kind of people doing violence: Bob told the Committee that these people believe that the U.S. Government is an illegal government and that their actions are a response to their beliefs.

It was now after 4 P.M., and by an unspoken unanimous agreement, it was decided that we terminate the hearing so that everyone would be able to get home before dark. Because my people had to go to Liberty, Amite County, and McComb, Pike County, I was able to persuade Dr. Britton, with his carload of committee members, and Courtney Siceloff, both of whom were going to Jackson, to go out of the way and go as far as Bude, Franklin County, following us. This would leave only about 30 miles for us to go, but this 30 miles was all in Amite County. Robert Moses and his wife were also in a car. It was clear that a caravan of five cars was attracting attention; but at a very slow pace, we finally reached Bude and waved goodbye to Dr. Britton and Siceloff, who continued on their way to Jackson. Mr. Robinson, who was in my car, offered that I should go only as far as Mr. Westly's farm and that he would take Miss Tobias and the Harrises home. I appreciated that, realizing that my black car was well known in Liberty, and it would be safer if they were in Mr. Robinson's car. We reached Mr. Westly's home and I said goodbye to these good people of Amite and Wilkinson Counties. I was glad that I had given to Mr. Taylor of the USCRC the names and addresses of persons I brought to the hearing.

Our caravan of three cars went by an out-of-the-way country road until we were about six miles from McComb, and then we said good-bye to Mr. Thompson and Mr. C.C. Bryant who drove their car on to McComb. . . .

TESTIMONY OF WILEY A. BRANTON

Wiley A. Branton, director of the Voter Education Project (VEP) of the Southern Regional Council, provided a useful summary of the sorts of dangers, and the endless frustrations, faced by those seeking to register black voters in Mississippi. The Southern Regional Council was a project of white liberals who sought to bring the eleven states of the Confederacy into compliance with federal law by encouraging black voting. The council represented a minority view among southern whites, but a very important one. It reflected the views of those who believed that the South could no longer maintain segregation. More importantly, its members believed that the South should voluntarily abandon Jim Crow and work to create a genuinely multiracial society.

As Branton's testimony makes clear, the VEP was an important source of funding for voter registration projects. In general, these projects proved quite successful. The exception was Mississippi. According to VEP figures, 6.7 percent of Mississippi's eligible black voters had registered. The next lowest percentage was in Alabama (23 percent). In many southern states, the proportion of African American voters had doubled. In Mississippi the proportion had barely changed, despite long and heroic efforts.

Discouraged, the council largely abandoned its efforts in Mississippi. This helps explain COFO's decision to move away from traditional registration efforts and embark upon the Freedom Summer.

Source: Testimony of Wiley A. Branton, Director, Voter Education Project, Southern Regional Council, hearings before the United States Commission on Civil Rights, Volume I: Voting (hearings held in Jackson, Mississippi, February 16–20, 1965).

TESTIMONY OF WILEY A. BRANTON, DIRECTOR, VOTER EDUCATION PROJECT, SOUTHERN REGIONAL COUNCIL

MR. TAYLOR.   Mr. Branton, will you state your full name and address for the record?

MR. BRANTON.   My name is Wiley A. Branton. I presently reside in Atlanta, Ga. My voting residence is in Pine Bluff, Ark.

I am a lawyer and at the moment director of the Voter Education Project of the Southern Regional Council.

MR. TAYLOR.   Would you describe what the Voter Education Project is?

MR. BRANTON.   The Voter Education Project is a special project which was organized about January of 1962 to make a study, over a period of approximately 2½ years, of the causes for low voter registration and participation in 11 Southern States. We were given a rather substantial grant by three foundations, and we started into the business of voter registration and education about April 1 of 1962. We terminated the active registration programs in the 11 States where we were working in October of 1964 and made a study of election returns following the November 1964 election.

Since that time we have been in sort of a phasing-out proposition, studying and analyzing the data which we have secured during the past 3 years.

MR. TAYLOR.   Thank you.

If I might, I would like to direct your attention to that chart for a moment and ask Mr. Humpstone if he would explain what the figures are?

MR. HUMPSTONE.   The chart shows estimated Negro voter registration in 11 Southern States as it was in 1956 and as it is in 1964.

In Alabama, the 1956 figure is 11 percent registered. The 1964 figure is 23 percent registered.

In Arkansas, the 1956 figure is 36 percent registered. In 1964, 49.3 percent registered.

In Florida, the 1956 figure is 32 percent. The 1964 figure is 63.7 percent.

In Georgia, the 1956 figure was 27 percent. The 1964 figure is 44 percent.

In Louisiana, the 1956 figure was 31 percent. The 1964 figure, 32 percent.

In Mississippi, the 1956 figure was 5 percent. The 1964 figure is 6.7 percent.

In North Carolina the earlier figure is 24 percent. The more recent, 46.8 percent.

In South Carolina the earlier figure is 27 percent; the 1964 figure, 38.8 percent.

In Tennessee, in 1956, 29 percent of the voting age Negroes were registered. In 1964, 69.4 percent.

In Texas, in 1956, 37 percent. In 1964, 57.7 percent.

In Virginia, in 1956, 19 percent of the voting age Negroes were registered. In 1964, 45.7 percent were registered.

MR. TAYLOR.   Thank you.

Mr. Branton, both these 1956 and 1964 figures, I believe, are estimates which your Voter Education Project has made.

MR. TAYLOR.   Mr. Branton, these figures and what you have said about them would indicate that there has been a good deal of progress in voter registration in a number of places.

They would also indicate that there has not been very great progress in this State. I wonder if you could tell us about the activities of the VEP in Mississippi—I understand the project was ultimately withdrawn— what the reasons were for the withdrawal, and why the progress elsewhere, but not here.

MR. BRANTON.   When we started into the registration business—principally we have operated by making grants to other organizations to finance their nonpartisan registration activities.

In the case of some organizations because of the fact they were engaged in activities other than voter registration we had a rather clear understanding that any funds which we provided were to go solely for voter registration and education, and we sort of rode herd on the grant to make sure that the terms of the grant were not violated. We tried to be as equitable as possible, in the beginning, by making grants under a complicated formula, which we adopted, which would make money available in each of the 11 Southern States, with some relationship to the total number of unregistered Negroes of voting age in those States, and Mississippi is a place where we had a rather early start. One of the reasons for it was that I happened to have already known a great deal about Mississippi. I lived most of my life in Arkansas and I have relatives in Mississippi and visited here very often and knew a good many of the people in the organizations here.

I was personally acquainted with the indigenous leadership and so, even before the projects were started, I came in to Jackson for a regional meeting of NAACP which was held, I believe, in February of 1962. So that by the time we were able to really start business on April 1, 1962, we made funds available on a 90-day crash-program basis to several different organizations—NAACP, Southern Christian Leadership Conference, CORE, and SNCC—for work in Mississippi, most of it in Mississippi and in the delta region, and up in Marshall County. And following that 90-day period we sort of took a look-see at that project, which we had sponsored at the time, and with other projects which we had sponsored at the same time across the South. And we even—after the first 3 or 4 months, we saw these startling differences where we were getting measurable results in other places but not in Mississippi.

We then started coming into Mississippi. I made several trips in. We sent our field staff in to find out the reasons why, and at this time we were approached by local Negro leaders in Mississippi, who felt that the problems in Mississippi were so complex that perhaps it would be better if everything was coordinated, rather than having each organization go its separate way.

I talked with the late Medgar Evers and he and some of his coworkers had drawn up, on paper, a program which bore the name Mississippi Council of Federated Organizations. They said to us that the only way that they could really expect to see a breakthrough in the problems of Mississippi, and those problems at that time were identified primarily as fear, fear of economic intimidation, fear of physical violence and harassment, etcetera, would be for everybody to work under some umbrella organization and they asked us if we would make our grants through COFO. Well, we went along with separate organizations for awhile and then in fall of 1962, at my suggestion, a meeting was called in Clarksdale to discuss with all of the Mississippi leaders the possibility of really making COFO a working organization.

Now, one thing that I would like to set the record straight on, if I might: Many people have talked about COFO being an outside organization, but I don't know whether it is outside now or not, but certainly in the beginning, and for as long as we were involved in it, COFO was made up of the Mississippi Negro leadership of organizations which had been in existence, here in Mississippi, for long periods of time and the people who came from the outside were primarily field workers and canvassers and door knockers who came in at the request of the local Negro Mississippi leadership.

Well, we sponsored this meeting in Clarksdale, and had representatives there, and decided then to channel any grants which we might spend in Mississippi through that organization. It was at that time that Mississippi COFO really came into being. But, even on the very night that we organized, the harassment intensified. This meeting, because of the fact that everybody wanted to get back to their respective area, didn't break up until almost 12 o'clock at night and as we left the meeting at 12 o'clock at night in Clarksdale a number of people were going to their respective towns. I think the occupants of some three or four different automobiles were arrested as they left there and many of them were locked up in jail. I happened to spend the night on that occasion in Clarksdale with Aaron Henry and we received a call, oh, at 2 or 3 o'clock in the morning that several of our workers were in jail. I went down personally at 2 or 3 o'clock in the morning to try to see about obtaining their release. I couldn't get anywhere.

The next morning I went down, some were in city jail and some in county jail, and I obtained the release of several of them. There were six occupants in one car. This car was going to another city. This car had been stopped about three blocks from where we were meeting. All occupants were held in jail all night and when I got them out the next morning and asked the nature of the charges, I was told they were all charged with loitering. Well, I had practiced law for about 11 years before I went to this project and I must admit I have never heard of a charge of loitering in a moving automobile.

The occupants of a car were put into police cars and taken to jail.

Now, there was no mechanical defect, no mechanical defect of the vehicle they were riding. Nevertheless, the local police had a wrecker and sent to have the car picked up to tow it about six blocks to a garage in Clarksdale and the next day after obtaining the release of the charges of the occupants all charged with loitering, we came over to pick up the car and I believe the bill came to about $40 for towage and special handling. Nothing wrong with the car but the only way we could get the car was either pay the money or file some replevin action which probably would have been much more time consuming. The trial was set for, I believe, the following afternoon at 4 or 5 o'clock in the afternoon and I took off then to investigate some matters down around Greenville. Some of the workers who had been released went to Indianola, Miss., to hand out leaflets of a voter registration mass meeting that very night and they were arrested and locked up in jail for distributing handbills without a permit.

Now, these were the people who were due in court 5 o'clock in the afternoon in Clarksdale. Because I am a lawyer and because I went around first and tried to obtain some local lawyer to represent them—I could not find any lawyers who would accept employment and because I am a lawyer and had practiced in a number of Mississippi courts, always, of course, with permission of the judge, when I explained that I was from out of the State—I was permitted to represent the defendants and to our great surprise the city moved to dismiss the charges against the people who had been loitering but charged the driver with driving in a hazardous manner.

Well, we explained that we couldn't get the people out of jail down at Indianola and, of course, they accepted this and dropped the charges as to them also. I don't know the reason for withdrawing the charge. It was rather ridiculous, and the trial for the other men who were still in jail in Indianola was set for 7 o'clock the next morning. They keep ungodly hours at most of these courts in Mississippi. And, I drove to Indianola the next morning where these people were charged with distributing handbills without a permit. There was what I would really describe as a mob in the courthouse at the time. The defendants were brought in one at a time. They were all Negro, and I asked for additional time in which to employ local counsel to represent them and this request was granted. But then in the full presence of the chief of police and the judge, somebody came in with one of these aerosol insect bombs, walked over to where I was sitting and the defendants and started spraying this thing in our faces with the loud statement, "I have got to de-niggarize this," and, of course, this brought a lot of laughs from the court, but the judge did nothing about stopping this.

A day or two later when we arranged for local counsel, a Negro lawyer from Jackson, to represent them, the word had gone out that these people were coming there for a trial and the fear for the personal safety of this lawyer and of his clients was so strong at that time that the lawyer and his clients were afraid to even walk in the court room. They drove on to another town and phoned back and arranged for a plea of guilty on the telephone with the right of appeal which Mississippi procedure provides for where you have a trial de novo.

Now, I have gone at great length to describe these incidents because from there on out it appeared that we were subjected to this kind of harassment and intimidation every single week. Because of the fact that so many people in Mississippi knew me personally, whenever they would get in jail, even though this was not a part of our responsibility, they would phone us first, all hours of the night, asking for help.

These problems were not confined to Clarksdale and Indianola. They happened at one time all up and down the delta. Almost nobody could get out in an automobile and drive anywhere without fear of being arrested for some trumped-up traffic violation and in practically every instance the simple thing to do was to go ahead and pay the fine.

The problem of bail for getting people out of jail was a tremendous problem because in Mississippi as a general rule you can't post a cash bond. It requires a property bond, though in some instances, the Attorney General had agreed to the posting of cash bail, and I had the problem, for example, in Greenwood going around door to door of property owners in Greenwood trying to convince 20 or more Negro property owners that they should sign the bond for some of their local residents who were being held in jail on very frivolous charges.

I might add, in most respects, these people were quite willing to put up their property and their own income as bail for those people, but the problems really became acute and we were not getting anybody registered.

In Greenwood, for example, we sent down several hundred people to the registrar's office and then when we would check back with them to find out whether or not they had been notified if they passed or not, they don't know. They would go down to the courthouse and they couldn't find out, and the number of Negroes who had gone on down to the courthouse in Greenwood during the past $2^{1}/_{2}$ years probably exceeds 1,500, but very few of them have ever been notified as to whether or not they had passed the test. The harassment by county and city officials in Leflore County is a typical example of where they have some kind of auxiliary police force that is tied in with civil defense. And you have private citizens who work at other jobs, but they are furnished some kind of helmet, little white helmet, and they can wear billy clubs and they get in their private automobiles. And at one time it was rather common sight to see carloads of local white private citizens wearing these helmets driving through Negro sections with their windows rolled down and making very nasty remarks to Negroes on the street. You perhaps know as much as I do of the use of police dogs in Greenwood.

Numbers of people were arrested there. And when the people started going down in rather large numbers they were arrested for parading. And then, as a source of information perhaps to use in court, to show that there was no discrimination, and to manufacture evidence to show that these so-called marches interfered with the orderly process of traffic, I have personally witnessed firetrucks in Greenwood, Miss., screaming down streets where Negroes were walking to the courthouse and I have followed these firetrucks and they went nowhere but around the corner and stopped and all the firemen would get off and laugh. But, while the firetruck was going by screaming, with Negroes going to the courthouse, local police would be there with photographers to take pictures, supposedly to take pictures, to show to the courthouse that there was a fire and the parading of Negroes interfered with local emergencies. This happened many times.

Finally, we found we were spending money in Mississippi far out of proportion to what we were spending in the other States and despite the fact we were following the same methods and techniques and even trying to find a novel approach to the problem in Mississippi, it became apparent to us that conditions in Mississippi were such that you were not going to get any meaningful registration no matter how much money this project spent. And it appeared to me it was a waste of money to further spend VEP funds in that State, with one possible exception, and I don't think that you can underestimate the value of it: We think that the money spent in Mississippi by our project, though it did not result in substantial increases in registration, did a great deal to help the people of Mississippi overcome the climate of fear, particularly in Leflore County and some of the other counties. And we think that just doing this was money well spent because we think that at least in Leflore County, not to mention some others, a great deal of the fear has now been eliminated and if you can just get the meaningful court decrees which are vitally necessary, that you have a vast reservoir of people who are ready to move in and ask for the right to register.

I don't think you are going to get any meaningful registration in Mississippi until there is a strong definitive court decree enjoining the use of the literacy test and enjoining the use of this new law which was passed, I believe about 1962, which requires the publication of each name and address of each voter applicant to be run in the local paper once a week for 2 weeks before he can even complete the application form.

This is designed purely for harassment and intimidation and until that's knocked out, you are not going to get any meaningful registration in this State. It was for this reason that in November of 1963 we decided to withdraw all financial support of projects in Mississippi with the exception of a continuing program here in the city of Jackson which was under the auspices of NAACP. And later in the spring of 1964, following the issuance of a Federal court decree in Panola County, we made a grant to SNCC so that they might go into Batesville in Panola County. And we think it was largely due to funds from the Voter Registration Project following the decree in that county which enabled an increase in the registration up there.

But, other than that, we withdrew earlier in Mississippi than any other State in the South which we have worked.

Chairman HANNAH. Thank you.

Map of Mississippi Project.

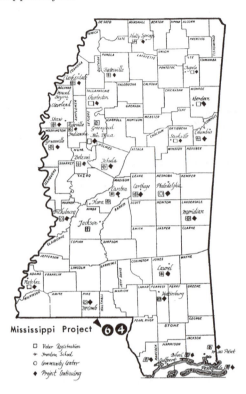

Source: Map of Mississippi Project, from *Freedomways* V, Spring 1965, 217.

THE RIVER OF NO RETURN: THE AUTOBIOGRAPHY OF A BLACK MILITANT AND THE LIFE AND DEATH OF SNCC

Cleveland Sellers (with Robert Terrell)

COFO set up its training program for volunteers for the Freedom Summer project at Western College for Women in Oxford, Ohio. Cleveland Sellers was a SNCC field worker who went to Oxford to help in the training. He and

Source: From *River of No Return* by Cleveland Sellers and Robert L. Terrell, pp. 94–107. Copyright © 1973 by Cleveland Sellers and Robert Terrell. Reprinted by permission of HarperCollins Publishers, Inc.

others had to get the thousand or so volunteers ready to cope with all they would encounter in Mississippi, and they had to accomplish this within one week. Sellers was not sanguine about their success. "When we tried to explain the rural South to them, they would nod as if they understood, but their eyes remained blank, uncomprehending."

This first excerpt from his autobiography is noteworthy for his portrayal of Bob Moses and for his description of the impact on everyone at Oxford of the news of the disappearance of James Chaney, Michael Schwerner, and Andrew Goodman. Schwerner and wife Rita, as noted above, directed CORE'S efforts in Meridian. Chaney was a local black who volunteered to work with them. All three had attended the first week's training where they met Andrew Goodman, a volunteer from New York City. As the first week ended, the Schwerners and Chaney received word that a church in which they had held meetings had burned. Mickey Schwerner, James Chaney, and Andrew Goodman decided to leave immediately for Meridian to find out what had happened and to try to rally the local community. Rita Schwerner agreed to stay to help out in the training of the second week's batch of volunteers. Two days after their departure, word reached Oxford that the three were missing.

The "Stokely" Sellers referred to was Stokely Carmichael, another SNCC field-worker and director of one of five regional centers in Mississippi, who would play a leading role in moving the organization to adopt a "Black Power" program in 1965.

There were a lot of problems in Oxford, most of them stemming from the innocence of the white volunteers. When we tried to explain the rural South to them, they would nod as if they understood, but their eyes remained blank, uncomprehending. Many of them talked about Mississippi as if it were somehow the same as the romanticized scenes they had read about in *Gone with the Wind*.

Communication was further complicated by the fact that only about 135 of the 900 student volunteers were black. Feeling outnumbered and misunderstood, most of the black students withdrew. Bob Moses communicated best with the white students. Most of them had heard about the work he had been doing in Mississippi long before they got to Oxford. He was a *culture hero* to them and they talked about him all the time. By the time they had been in Oxford a couple of days, many of the white students had begun to emulate Bob's slow, thoughtful manner of speaking. Others rushed downtown and purchased bib overalls like his.

In all fairness, I must admit that Bob had almost the same effect on blacks. There was something about him, the manner in which he carried himself, that seemed to draw all of us to him. He had been where we were going. And more important, he had emerged as the kind of person we wanted to be. He was speaking to us that night when the news arrived.

"Our goals are limited. If we can go and come back alive, that is something. If you can go into Negro homes and just sit and talk, that will be a huge job. We're not thinking of integrating the lunch counters. The Negroes in Mississippi haven't the money to eat in those places anyway. They still don't dare go into the white half of the integrated bus terminals—they just weigh that against having their houses bombed or losing their jobs."

He was patiently explaining the scope of the Summer Project and the nature of the problems we would encounter. He knew Mississippi backward and forward. He picked his words carefully. During those moments when he stood before us deep in thought, we waited quietly.

"You may find some difficult limiting situations. If you were in a house which was under attack, and the owner was shot, and there were kids there, and you could take his gun to protect them—should you? I can't answer that. I don't think that anyone can answer that."

He paused again. Shifting slowly on the balls of his feet, he looked up and began to speak again.

"We've had discussions all winter about race hatred." The auditorium was completely quiet. We knew that he was about to get to the heart of a problem that could divide and destroy us during the dangerous months ahead.

"There is an analogy to *The Plague,* by Camus. The country isn't willing yet to admit it has the plague, but it pervades the whole society. We must discuss it openly and honestly, even with the danger that we get too analytical and tangled up. If we ignore it, it's going to blow up in our faces."

He had paused to gather his thoughts when one of SNCC's staff members sprang to the stage and whispered in his ear. A look of extreme concern spread slowly across his normally impassive face. I sensed that something terrible had happened. After a long moment, Bob told us what it was.

"Yesterday morning, three of our people left Meridian, Mississippi, to investigate a church-burning in Neshoba County. They haven't come back, and we haven't had any word from them. We spoke to John Doar in the Justice Department. He promised to order the FBI to act, but the local FBI still says that they have been given no authority."

An anguished murmur passed through the auditorium. Bob left the stage immediately and a slight woman whose face was furrowed with deep worry lines took his place. She told us the names of the three missing workers: James Chaney, Andrew Goodman and Michael Schwerner. Her name was Rita Schwerner. Michael was her husband.

Some wanted to believe that the three men were only missing. I had no such illusions. I was one of those who volunteered to search for their bodies.

Our search party was divided into four teams. Each team was given money for food and gas and a map with three alternate routes marked off. We knew that Mississippi's highway patrolmen were trying to keep civil rights workers out of the state, so we used different entry routes: they couldn't patrol all the roads.

We left Oxford at about three in the afternoon and arrived at the Mississippi border early the next morning. There was a big green sign on the side of the road adorned with cotton plants: "Welcome to the Magnolia State."

"The point of no return," I murmured to my team.

Each team had been instructed to phone the SNCC office in Meridian as soon as it entered the state. We had been instructed to call from SNCC's office in Holly Springs. There was a skeleton crew of three at the office when we arrived. They were expecting us.

"No word yet," they replied to our anxious eyes.

Three of the four teams arrived in Meridian before our one o'clock check-in time. Stokely and Charlie Cobb were late. We knew that they were in the state because they had called early in the morning from the SNCC office in Greenwood. Although some us wanted to go out and look for them, we weren't allowed to.

We spent the afternoon being briefed on the three missing men.

Mickey Schwerner, who had arrived in Mississippi with his wife Rita on January 17, 1964, was the key figure. He was twenty-five years old and had done some work at Columbia University's School of Social Work. He was also deeply committed to the movement.

Mickey and Rita were members of CORE. Soon after they arrived in Mississippi they went to Meridian, where they set up a community center. The center became very popular with Meridian's young blacks, who loved to go there to read, relax and discuss politics.

Although Mickey and Rita had problems identical to those of every other civil rights worker attempting to crack a new town, they refused to be intimidated. They shrugged off the harassment of local police and tried to reason with those whites who criticized them.

In the spring of 1964, James Chaney, a twenty-one-year-old black high school dropout, joined the staff at the community center. He was from the Meridian area and wanted to do what he could to improve conditions for local blacks.

Mickey and James made a good team. Mickey had a good understanding of formal politics and shared his knowledge with James. Although he didn't know a great deal about formal politics, James understood the art of survival in Mississippi. He shared this knowledge with Mickey.

Mickey, Rita and James went to Oxford, Ohio, in mid-June to help run orientation sessions for the Summer Project. While there, they met Andrew Goodman. Like Mickey and Rita, Andrew was from New York. He was also a student at Queens College, Rita's alma mater. Although he was only twenty-one years old, he was mature and appeared to be a bit more confident than most of the student volunteers. Noticing these qualities, Rita, Mickey and James asked him to come to Meridian and work with them. Honored by their request, he accepted.

On Wednesday, June 17, Mickey got word that one of the churches he and James had been working in had been firebombed. Because they were concerned about the bombing's effect on the local people, Mickey and James decided to leave Oxford early and return to Meridian. Although Rita wanted to join them, they persuaded her to remain in Oxford for another week, training the volunteers.

On Saturday, June 20, Mickey, James and Andrew packed their car and headed south. It was three in the morning when they left. There was no way for Rita to know when she said good-bye that they would be dead in a few hours.

The three tired men arrived in Meridian at about 5 A.M. Sunday morning. After getting a couple of hours' sleep, they made plans to drive to Neshoba County and inspect the ruins of the church. Just before leaving, they instructed Louise Hermey, one of the girls working in the office, to call COFO headquarters in Jackson, the local police and the FBI if they were not back by 4 P.M.

That was the last time she saw them alive.

Louise, an attractive black girl, was one of the people in the Meridian office who briefed us. She was terribly upset and had a difficult time talking. She nearly burst into tears on several occasions. Although she still hoped that the missing men would be found alive, she *knew* what the rest of us knew: they were already dead.

"BASIC TRAINING"

Sally Belfrage

One of the earliest, and one of the best, accounts of the training white and black volunteers received before going to Mississippi is that of Sally Belfrage. She arrived in Oxford, Ohio, just as the news broke of the disappearance of James Chaney, Michael Schwerner, and Andrew Goodman. Belfrage's memoir, like Sellers', focused upon the impact of the disappearance, and likely murder, upon her fellow volunteers and upon those training them. She captured much of their confusion, anger, fear, and determination. Her account is one of the fullest available in detailing much of the specific sorts of training volunteers received. She also testified to the influence Bob Moses exerted over all.

1. BASIC TRAINING

All one Sunday in June they arrived at the college in Ohio. Their cars pulled in past the sign crayoned ORIENTATION, down the grassy drive to a cluster of dormitories and administration buildings. The atmosphere of campus, brick and ivy, matched them nearly perfectly: their ages fit, their haircuts, dress, and choice of words, and their baggage, books, guitars. It might have been the start of summer school.

They left the stuff in the cars or in heaps on the lawn and went inside to register. Their names were taken; meal tickets, mimeographed literature, name badges, and room assignments distributed; powers of attorney signed; and then they were sent singly down the hall to have their pictures taken—two poses each, holding numbers under their chins. Out on the lawn again afterwards, they formed in haphazard circles around the guitars, looking at each other self-consciously as they sang the words they scarcely knew.

Then there was a change: a woman whose badge read "Mrs. Fannie Lou Hamer" was suddenly leading them, molding their noise into music.

> If you miss me from the back of the bus,
> You can't find me nowhere,
> Come on up to the front of the bus,
> I'll be ridin' up there. . . .

Source: Sally Belfrage, "Basic Training" from *Freedom Summer.* (first published in 1965 by The Viking Press, Inc. for University Press of Virginia printing 1990). Copyright © 1965 by Sally Belfrage. Reprinted by permission of the Irene Skolnick Literary Agency.

Her voice gave everything she had, and her circle soon incorporated the others, expanding first in size and in volume and then something else—it gained passion. Few of them knew who she was, and in her plump, perspiring face many could probably see something of the woman who cleaned their mothers' floors at home. But here was clearly someone with force enough for all of them, who knew the meaning of "Oh Freedom" and "We Shall Not Be Moved" in her flesh and spirit as they never would. They lost their shyness and began to sing the choruses with abandon, though their voices all together dimmed beside hers.

> Paul and Silas, bound in jail,
> Had no money for to go their bail,
> Keep your eyes on the prize,
> Hold on, hold on.

"Hold on," they bellowed back, "Hold o-o-on. Keep your eyes on the prize, hold on."

The music had begun—the music that would have to take the place for them, all summer, of swimming, solitude, sex, movies, walking, drinking, driving, or any of the releases they had ever grown to need; and would somehow have to come to mean enough to drive off fear.

It was the second of two training periods for six hundred student volunteers en route to Mississippi, at the Western College for Women in Oxford, southwest Ohio. The teachers—SNCC field secretaries, guest speakers, some native Mississippi movement workers, and "resource people"—had a week in which to give the volunteers, eighty-five per cent white, one hundred per cent middle-class, some introduction to the foreign land which they were going to try to change.

On the paths to the dining room, the volunteers greeted each other and smiled as though they had met and were already friends. They had come from all ends of the country, having developed in as many vacuums; and were astonished to discover one another. There was the predictable vague division between the radically inclined, sandaled sophisticates from New York and California, and what one of them called "the girls from Wichita who have very straight teeth and say 'nifty,' 'grisly,' and 'neat.' "But they had more in common than not—on one level, three hundred indestructible innocents, apostles of Dr. Pangloss, ludicrous in their unfashionable idealism; on another, complicated heroes who could acknowledge the world's evil in themselves, confront it, and speak the words that everyone else was gagging on: "I am responsible." Few could explain what it was, in the middle of their generation's apathy, that had made them care, but the fact that they did seemed a phenomenon of as much hope for America as the Negro revolution they were coming to join.

They left possessions carelessly around, concerned with something else besides the theft of their cameras, and joined the cafeteria line. Conversation began without introductions—about what the work would be, where the places were, how the system worked.

"I wanted to do voter registration, but my parents said they wouldn't let me go and I'm not twenty-one yet."

"They're not taking any more girls for voter registration anyway. I wanted that too."

"What are you going to do?"

"Teach. I taught in Harlem last year and I guess I was pretty good at it, so I'll have to do it again."

"What's the matter with that?"

"I hate teaching."

"But it's important"

"I know. But what we really have to do is get people registered."

"It isn't going to be that easy to get people registered. Have you seen the test? It depends completely on some registrars' interpretation— you couldn't pass it with a Ph.D. if the guy says no. And then the people who try lose their jobs and get shot at—"

"Are you scared?"

"Sure I'm scared. You'd have to be out of your mind not to be scared."

Then a new voice, a Negro in CORE T-shirt: "You talk about fear—it's like the heat down there, it's continually oppressive. You think they're rational. But, you know, you suddenly realize they want to *kill* you."

Giggles (nervous).

"And the thing is, it's not funny. That's why I'm laughing."

The college was built for the academic year and was not equipped for heat waves. Volunteers who came to the "optional" meeting— every one of the three hundred—sat in packed liquid rows in paralyzing heat. They were welcomed by Bruce Hanson on behalf of the National Council of Churches—sponsor of the orientation—with the words: "Any of you who don't want to go to Mississippi can leave."

"Is this meeting about why *aren't* we going?" said someone behind me.

Vincent Harding, a compact, squarely built Negro Mennonite, who was to lead the discussion, rearranged the question: the "Why?" that would keep being asked throughout the week. No one was being seduced into Mississippi; the slimmest private doubts were encouraged, and Bruce Hanson's welcome began each day like the pledge of allegiance.

"Are you going," Vincent Harding started, "as 'In' members of the society to pull the 'Outs' in with you? Or are we all 'Outs'? Are you going to bring the Negroes of Mississippi into the doubtful pleasures of middle-class existence, or to seek to build a new kind of existence in which words like 'middle-class' may no longer be relevant? Are we trying to make liberal readjustments or basic change?" The floor took over.

White boy: "For me there is only one race, the human race. It's one nation. Mississippi is our back yard as much as Harlem. I've had it good for a long time. But I've seen too many people hungry for too long."

Negro boy: "We have to try to change the South so that the people of the North will want to do better. The South is a battlefield: the North is in a stalemate. For us, it's all intolerable. But we have to work where the situation is flexible enough for change. Open hate is preferable to hypocrisy—it can be moved."

White girl: "There's not enough justice and not enough liberty. There's not enough truth and there's not enough beauty. Who will work to make these things? It's everyone's job."

Southern white boy: "I'm involved in this for my own freedom. We have to build a new South, a South ruled by law, democracy, and humanity. I couldn't not have come."

White boy: "I'm going because the worst thing after burning churches and murdering children is keeping silent."

Mrs. Hamer stood, reducing the audience to intense silence. "We need you," she said. "Help us communicate with white people. Regardless of what they act like, there's some good there. How can we say we love God, and hate our brothers and sisters? We got to reach them; if only the people comin' down can help us reach them."

A Negro girl with a Northern accent spoke then from another source. "It's been part of our education to distrust white people," she began quietly, "and no matter how hard we try, we can't get rid of the remnants of suspicion." Then, fiercely: *"You're going to have to make your position very clear if you're going to cross the line."*

Vincent Harding tried to draw these poles together. "There is an ambiguous feeling. . . . The Negroes would like you to know what it's like to be a Negro. They want it to be well with you; but at the same time they want something to happen to you." He didn't mean white deaths and mutilations, he meant white comprehension. A feeling had persisted in the group that had preceded us in Ohio, and had left the day before for Mississippi, that they were being sent as sacrificial victims. Although they recognized that publicity and federal involvement could be achieved only if the victims were white—in a state where the beating and murder of Negroes was endemic and a matter of no national interest—there was resentment. "We think all these problems must be aired now, before they explode on us in Mississippi." That was part of what the week was for.

All were left with more questions than had ever occurred to them before. But there were still songs. Mrs. Hamer led the first chorus:

> Go tell it on the mountain,
> Over the hills and everywhere,
> Go tell it on the mountain
> To let my people go.

When the verses came, they clapped.

> Who's that yonder dressed in black?
> Let my people go.
> Must be the hypocrites turnin' back.
> Let my people go.

Then:

> Who's that yonder dressed in red?
> Let my people go.
> Look like the children Bob Moses led. . . .

They didn't know about Bob Moses yet.

A general meeting the next morning established the routine for the week. Volunteers had continued to arrive through the night; now the full complement was assembled in the auditorium, expectant and prompt, clipboards in their laps and pencils sharpened. Their listening, questioning, and note-taking habits were those of college students, and helped one forget that the lessons were not altogether removed from experience. "I." appeared on the top of innumerable sheets of paper; "(a), (b), (c)." The first a, b, and c were for the areas of work, outlined by the staff members in charge:

Community centers: ten or fifteen were planned, with facilities for arts and crafts, recreation, libraries, literacy classes for adults, health, and day care.

Freedom Schools: to supplement and complement the regular schools, there would be a general academic curriculum with remedial work, but also emphasis on Negro history and current events.

The political program: a major voter registration drive in all the projects, with a parallel organization of the Mississippi Freedom

Democratic Party, working toward a challenge to the seating of the regular Mississippi Democrats at the national party convention in Atlantic City in late August.

Then Bob Moses, the Director of the Summer Project, came to the front of the floor. He didn't introduce himself, but somehow one knew who he was. Everyone had heard a little—that he was twenty-nine, began in Harlem, had a Master's degree in philosophy from Harvard, and that he had given up teaching in New York to go South after the first sit-ins. He had been in Mississippi for three years, and he wore its uniform: a T-shirt and denim overalls, in the bib of which he propped his hands. He began as though in the middle of a thought. "When Mrs. Hamer sang, 'If you miss me from the freedom fight, you can't find me nowhere; Come on over to the graveyard, I'll be buried over there . . .' That's true."

Moving up to the stage, he drew a map of Mississippi on a blackboard and patiently, from the beginning, outlined the state's areas and attitudes. The top left segment became the Delta: industry was cotton; power in the Citizens' Councils; and opposition to the movement systematic and calculated, aimed at the leadership (including Moses himself—in 1963, the SNCC worker beside him, Jimmy Travis, was shot in the neck and the shoulder as they rode together in a car outside Greenwood), and at decreasing the Negro population by the expedient of automating the cotton fields, thereby "getting it down to a livable ratio." The segment beneath the Delta was the hill country, mostly poor white farmers who had been organizing since the March on Washington, Amite County, McComb: Klan territory, where violence was indiscriminately aimed at "keeping the nigger in his place" and no one was safe. Five Negroes had been murdered there since December. No indictments.

Mississippi gained texture and dimension on the blackboard. Moses put down the chalk, paused, then looked out at us, his eyes reflective behind horn-rims. When he began again he seemed to be addressing each one separately, though talking to no one at all, just thinking aloud. "When you come South, you bring with you the concern of the country—because the people of the country don't identify with Negroes. The guerrilla war in Mississippi is not much different from that in Vietnam. But when we tried to see President Johnson, his secretary said that Vietnam was popping up all over his calendar and he hadn't time to talk to us." Now, he said, because of the Summer Project, because whites were involved, a crack team of FBI men was going down to Mississippi to investigate. "We have been asking for them for three years. Now the federal government is concerned;

there will be more protection for us, and hopefully for the Negroes who live there."

He stood looking at his feet. "Our goals are limited. If we can go and come back alive, then that is something. If you can go into Negro homes and just sit and talk, that will be a huge job. We're not thinking of integrating the lunch counters. The Negroes in Mississippi haven't the money to eat in those places anyway. They still don't dare go into the white half of the integrated bus terminals—they must weigh that against having their houses bombed or losing their jobs."

He stopped again, and everyone waited without a sound. "Mississippi has been called "The Closed Society." It is closed, locked. We think the key is in the vote. Any change, any possibility for dissidence and opposition, depends first on a political breakthrough."

He frowned, then said a few words on the subject of nonviolence. No COFO workers, staff or volunteers, would be permitted to carry guns. The police could murder the armed and then claim self-defense. "We don't preach that others carry guns or refrain from carrying them. You may find some difficult, limiting situations. If you were in a house which was under attack, and the owner was shot, and there were kids there, and you could take his gun to protect them—should you? I can't answer that. I don't think anyone can answer that. . . .

The question of arrest. In Mississippi a charge is not necessary. It can be made up later. There will be many arrests; but I think it should be avoided. The work you are going for can't be done in jail. We have a staff of volunteer lawyers who are coming during the summer. Now, among these lawyers there are some who people say are politically less desirable than others. This kind of thing bogs us down. I don't want to get caught up in a discussion of communism in the movement. It's divisive, and it's not a negotiable issue with us.

"Money. We don't have any. But where you have people and programs and the minimum materials, a lot can be done."

He stood pondering something, quite still. The next words came, almost disembodied from him. "We've had discussions all winter about race hatred." The audience had become absorbed in him, an extension of his soft voice; he no longer had color—but the words gave our flesh a tint again and opposed it to his. "There is an analogy to *The Plague*, by Camus. The country isn't willing yet to admit it has the plague, but it pervades the whole society. Everyone must come to grips with this, because it affects us all. We must discuss it openly and honestly, even with the danger that we get too analytic and tangled up. If we ignore it, it's going to blow up in our faces."

There was an interruption then at a side entrance: three or four staff members had come in and were whispering agitatedly. One of them walked over to the stage and sprang up to whisper to Moses, who bent on his knees to hear. In a moment he was alone again. Still crouched, he gazed at the floor at his feet, unconscious of us. Time passed. When he stood and spoke, he was somewhere else; it was simply that he was obliged to say something, but his voice was automatic. "Yesterday morning, three of our people left Meridian, Mississippi, to investigate a church-burning in Neshoba County. They haven't come back, and we haven't had any word from them. We spoke to John Doar in the Justice Department. He promised to order the FBI to act, but the local FBI still says they have been given no authority."

He stood, while activity burst out around him. In the audience, people asked each other who the three were; volunteers who had been at the first week of orientation remembered them. Then a thin girl in shorts was talking to us from the stage: Rita Schwerner, the wife of one of the three.

She paced as she spoke, her eyes distraught and her face quite white, but in a voice that was even and disciplined. It was suddenly clear that she, Moses, and others on the staff had been up all the night before. The three men had been arrested for speeding. Deputy Sheriff Price of Neshoba claimed to have released them at 10 P.M. the same day. All the jails in the area had been checked, with no results. The Jackson FBI office kept saying they were not sure a federal statute had been violated.

Rita asked us to form in groups by home areas and wire our congressmen, that the federal government, though begged to investigate, had refused to act, and that if the government did not act, none of us was safe. Someone in the audience asked her to spell the names. She erased most of Moses' map of Mississippi from the blackboard and, in large, square capitals, printed:

JAMES CHANEY—CORE STAFF
MICHAEL SCHWERNER—CORE STAFF
ANDREW GOODMAN—SUMMER PROJECT VOLUNTEER

Underneath, she printed: NESHOBA COUNTY—DISAPPEARED.

California and New York split out the left and right doors; others formed by states inside. We composed telegrams, collected money and sent them, and tried to rub out the reality of the situation with action. No one was willing to believe that the event involved more than a disappearance. It was hard to believe even that. Somehow it seemed only a climactic object lesson, part of the morning's lecture, an anecdote to give life to the words of Bob Moses. To think of it in other terms was to be forced to identify with the three, to be prepared, irrevocably, to give one's life.

The volunteers broke up into their specialized units—Freedom School, community center, voter registration—in the afternoons, and met again in the auditorium for general lectures in the mornings. Each day began with an announcement like Vincent Harding's on Tuesday: "There has been no word of the three people in Neshoba. The staff met all night. When we sing 'We are not afraid,' we mean we are afraid. We sing 'Ain't gonna let my fear turn me round,' because many of you might want to turn around now." For three days no one cleaned the blackboard on the stage; the names were still there, over the partially erased map of Mississippi.

Tuesday was about Southerners, black and white. Harding talked of the three centuries of slavery and segregation in America— "the great melting pot where color evidently didn't melt"—and the symptoms produced in the victims. "Some have a broken spirit— 'I been down so long that down don't bother me.'" Afraid of whites, they seek at any cost to stay on good terms with them, "always agreeing, never honest, therefore never human with you—and underneath it there is a deep distrust and hatred of you because they have to behave this way."

Others become black supremacists. Harding's advice to his largely white audience was to tackle them with: "'Yeah, baby, I know you think black is great. Well, I think white is great,' You got a dialogue going there," he said, "and that's a beginning."

Still others react with sexual aggressiveness. "Some Negroes think the only way that whites can prove they're really in the movement is by going to bed with a Negro." Harding thought this might be a particular problem for the white girls who were "going for 'my summer Negro.' The summer Negro is no different from the token Negro in the school. We're going to Mississippi because men have been using other men. Using people sexually is no different from using them politically or economically."

And finally, among the Negroes we were to meet would be the freed: "some in their old age, some freed even from the need to hate, to deceive. When you find them, hold them tightly."

From the other side came Charles Morgan, the white Birmingham lawyer forced to leave his home because of his public stand on the 1963 church-bombing in which four children were killed. "In white Mississippi," he said, "you have a little house on a little green plot in a little town. For them, the worst thing in the world is controversy—because, you see, they're just like the family you left behind next door. But in the South, controversy means only one thing: being on the wrong side of the race question. When faced with it, nice people commit crimes in the name of a great cause. They have their own rationality. What they're concerned with is Main Street: 'Let's keep it just as it is.' What you're talking about is power, and they got it. And they have a bunch of people who are going to convince you that you are wrong—one way or another."

He dug into the volunteers, attacking the martyr instinct and any remnants of fearlessness among them, and somehow reconstructed the Southern white as a human being, an image long gone in most of his audience. Once liberated from bigotry, they were unable to mind their own business, and ultimately, like Morgan, had had to leave their friends, their towns, their states. But how were Morgans made? What was the process, and how could it be encouraged?

There was no time to pursue it. A gaunt, fierce-eyed young man raised his hand and was recognized. When he began to speak it was in waves approaching hysteria. "It's hell in Mississippi!" he said, his voice breaking. "And you've got to realize that nobody *cares. We* care. We've got to change the *system*. It's hard. It's just like one person beating his head against this building to tear it down. It's impossible, but we have got to *do* it. They say that democracy exists in America. But it's an idea. It doesn't function. You have got to make it function in Mississippi, so that it can function in the rest of the country, and in the world."

There was a silence resembling fear in the room. "Who is it?" someone craned around and asked my row. "Jimmy Travis," another whispered. "The one who was shot. Didn't you see the scar on his neck?"

"The three people," Travis said. I think he was crying. "I don't know. I hurt. These people are lost. I don't know where they are. What can we do? The *system!* The system is the reason these people are missing. It's easier to know that someone is in jail, even that some-one is dead, than to wait and wonder what happened."

He pointed to Chuck Morgan. "This cat is from Birmingham, Alabama. This cat knows what's going on. I'm black. You're white. If you're going down there, you're going to be treated worse than black. Because you are supposed to be free. But I say that no one is free until everyone is. And until we can show the people of Mississippi that we are willing to make the extreme sacrifice, we can't change the world.

"It's hard. So hard. But all we have is each other. When something happens to you, we care. We really *care.*"

He slumped against the door behind him, then disappeared through it. There was a second's silence, then a splattering of applause which grew, wavered, died out. A girl stood in the uncomfortable quiet that followed, Morgan still at the podium, no one looking at anyone else. "You've got to understand Jimmy," she said. She was a Mississippi Negro. "He was nearly killed. It was something he had to say. You shouldn't applaud."

The lectures and classes continued, and there was no news from Neshoba. The tension clouded us in until it was all there was to breathe. In free time we composed letters and telegrams to anyone conceivably influential enough to get the government to act: to send federal marshals and outside FBI agents to Mississippi. Moses explained, "The inside agents, Mississippians, are psychologically incapable of carrying on the necessary investigations. We need the FBI before the fact. We have them now after the fact." It wasn't a question of military occupation, as Southerners were claiming: "We're not looking for generalized chaos in which troops can come and take over. We're looking for a framework in which people can do their work—for the summer, and then afterwards, a means of extending it to the Negroes of the state."

There was one television set on the campus, and the floor around it was jammed for news broadcasts. But when the next news arrived, it was during dinner on Tuesday night. Bob Moses came in quietly, turned on the microphone and said, "The car has been found outside Philadelphia. It's badly burned. There is no news of the three boys."

Bayard Rustin, the next morning's speaker, had the crowd's respect before he began—not only for his organization of the March on Washington, but for his principled nonviolence based on a pacifism tested in many jails. "All mankind is my community," he said, and: "When I say I love Eastland, it sounds preposterous—a man who brutalizes people. But *you* love him or you wouldn't be here. You're going to Mississippi to create social change—and you love Eastland in your desire to create conditions which will redeem his children. Loving your enemy is manifest in putting your arms not around the man but around the social situation, to take power from those who misuse it—at which point they can become human too."

He suggested that our difficulties in connecting with white Mississippi might not be insurmountable. "One can evaluate others in the light of one's own experience, see them in one's self, understand how one can become that bestial." He smiled and bummed a cigarette off a volunteer in the first row. "Last week I was smoking and wondering why a white Southerner can't act on what he believes. Then I took another puff. I *know* cigarettes will give me lung cancer. Well, I can understand him. In this we are one. We are both intensely stupid."

The President sent two hundred sailors to search for the missing boys. Rita Schwerner and all the staff members who could be spared were in Meridian and Philadelphia. Nothing visible was being done by the authorities to prevent the same thing from happening to anyone else. We clung to the television set.

On Thursday there was a TV special: "The Search in Mississippi." Classes were scheduled for the same time, but everyone, thinking himself alone, was in the lounge—a couple of hundred in a space meant for a third that many, crammed in the room and out through the hall. On the screen appeared the faces of the enemy, the friend, the one who sat beside us now, the one who had gone ahead reporting how it was. The program contained interviews filmed the day before in the room where we sat.

The voice was SNCC Executive-Secretary James Forman's, and he was speaking in the auditorium where we had spent half the week. The camera played around the audience, at the volunteers like us, some of them the same—staff and holdovers—and finally came to rest on a very young, dark, thin but tender face. Only when it was gone was it identified as Andrew Goodman's.

But then the face was Senator Eastland's—whose children we would redeem? "Around where I live it's seventy-five percent colored," he was saying. "Many's the time I've slept at home with the doors unlocked. We don't have any racial fiction, uh, friction."

Aaron Henry, head of the Mississippi NAACP, and also of COFO: "Fifty-one percent of the people in the Delta earn less than a thousand dollars a year. This is the fiftieth state economically. The reason we're fiftieth is because that's how many states there are. We used to be forty-eighth."

Senator Eastland: "There is no attempt to prevent Nigras registering. You go by what some agitator claims. They're perfectly free to go to the clerk's office to register to vote."

Mrs. Hamer: "I tried to register in 1962. I was fired the same day, after working on the plantation for eighteen years. My husband worked there thirty years. When my employer found out I'd been down to the courthouse, she said I'd have to withdraw or be fired. 'We are not ready for this in Mississippi,' she said. 'Well, I wasn't registering for you,' I told her. 'I was trying to register for myself.' "

Governor Johnson: "The hard core of this [COFO] group is your beatnik-type people. Nonconformists, hair down to their shoulder blades, some that you'd call weirdos. . . . (They don't realize that they're following a group of professional agitators, many of them with criminal records, people who've been in trouble all their lives—you can see it in their face. We're not going to tolerate any group from the outside of Mississippi or from the inside of Mississippi to take the law in their own hands. We're going to see that the law is maintained, and maintained Mississippi style."

The audience in the lounge joined in the show, expressing some unequivocal opinions of the speakers. At the end, under the titles, we ourselves appeared, standing, singing "We Shall Overcome." We stood and joined our own voices:

> Black and white together now—
> Oh deep in my heart, I do believe,
> We shall overcome someday.

For a long time after the program had finished we remained there, while Mrs. Hamer led more stanzas, more songs.

There was one side still to be heard. John Doar of the Justice Department's Civil Rights Division came from Washington to speak, as he had the week before. I got to the auditorium early, after an 8 A.M. class, and found a seat near the front while volunteers drifted in. Near me a group began to sing in slow rhythm. "We need justice, Lord, come by here. Oh, Lord, come by here." An old Negro woman was weeping into her handkerchief. Behind her a white girl with high cheekbones and dark hair pulled severely back sang gravely while tears fell down her cheeks, oblivious of a movie camera on the stage poised on her face, just as it had been on Andrew Goodman's the week before.

Moses urged us to be polite to Doar, an effort at which the previous group had apparently failed. "A year ago this week Medgar Evers was buried. It was a near riot situation, and Doar was sent in to prevent worse. He has helped us." The camera buzzed behind his words. Doar arrived.

"This is a serious operation that you are involved in," he said straight off. "I wish the world were different; I don't like it any better than you do." He was tall, blue-eyed, narrow-shouldered, and his face wore a steady, concerned frown. He outlined the reasons why "there is no possible way that anyone can be completely protected from violence." Suggesting that there were many native white realists in the state, he asked us to "help them correct a problem that they must realize they want to get behind." On his own forces: "If we don't make good sound judgments and imaginative investigations, we should be criticized."

Perhaps some felt that this man and his government represented them, but in the past week many who had started out as ordinary college students with respect for all the ordinary institutions had learned about cynicism. Because of Moses' admonition, however, most of the muttering remained only that, and when Doar asked for questions just two hands were raised.

"How is it that the government can protect the Vietnamese from the Viet Cong and the same government will not accept the moral responsibility of protecting the people in Mississippi?"

"Maintaining law and order is a state responsibility," Doar said.

"But how is it"—the questioner persisted—"that the government can accept this responsibility in Vietnam?"

"I would rather confine myself to Mississippi."

Next was Staughton Lynd, a professor of history at Yale, who would run the statewide Freedom School program. "In 1890," he began, in his dry, quiet voice, "during the railroad strike, the government went into Illinois. Its right to do so was upheld by the Supreme Court. In a crisis, the President does have the established power to send a police force into a state, whether the state wants it or not. The question is, is the situation in Mississippi a crisis? What we are trying to communicate is that it *is*. . . . It's a moral question. If you have this power to act, and if you have the moral responsibility yet choose not to act, how in the world do all of you live with this responsibility?"

"I believe we are a government of law," Doar said. "I have taken a vow to uphold the law. I just try to do the best I can under law. I have no trouble living with myself. The people I know in the federal government and administration are fine people, and they have no trouble living with themselves either."

On this, the meeting adjourned. "What a lot of junk," a girl said on the walk to lunch. A few days before she had told me that her plans to join the Peace Corps had been interrupted because of the urgency of Mississippi. "I don't know who I'm fighting any more. To think that I nearly *worked* for those people. There are a lot of great words, but where is their conscience? They just want to keep the Southern vote for the Democrats. They're not going to do a damn thing they don't have to." She kicked at the ground.

We had been given our choice of job and area. I was to be a librarian in Greenwood. The library coordinator, who had a degree but no experience, said, "Some of you are going to be worrying about being black or white; I'm just worried about being green." The Freedom School teachers had received thick folders of lesson material and had discussed their approach; the voter registration workers had learned techniques of canvassing and means of gathering evidence for federal lawsuits. COFO lawyers had let us all in on some of the law's mysteries, the charges Mississippi was able to bring, how to insure one's right to appeal, when to stand mute or plead *nolo contendere*. In general sessions we had been prepared for everything, usually the worst.

On the last day, the Oxford barbershop had lines three deep for every chair, and the beards and "hair down to the shoulder blades" vanished. The students gleamed as though they had been polished. They were packed, scared, cheerful, and ready. A few had gone home. Two psychiatrists among the "resource people" had mixed with us all week and scrutinized every volunteer. Parents had been phoning hysterically; the bulletin board outside the dining room was buried in messages which had gone unanswered. At least one mother came to collect her daughter. An Oklahoma boy was forced to drop out after receiving a letter from his father saying, "If you think you're going to liberate Mississippi, I'm getting a posse and coming to liberate *you.*" In the end, only ten went home. The rest gathered in the evening for a last general meeting.

Jim Forman had just arrived back from Mississippi. A large, rumpled, dark-brown man who needed a haircut, he had the good speaker's urgency, power over a mood. His volatility was the other side of Moses' pensive strength, but both earned an audience's total attention, total sympathy. He wanted to give us a little history and background. "I know, Moses spoke on Monday, but he is a very shy person." Moses, crouched against the stage with his head down, smiled. It was the first time I had ever seen him smile.

Forman asked us to rise and to sing "Well Never Turn Back," with our arms around each other, and then he repeated some of the lines very carefully:

> We have hung our head and cried
> For those like Lee who died,
> Died for you and died for me,
> Died for the cause of equality,
> But we'll never turn back—

The song was written by a young SNCC worker in memory of Herbert Lee, shot to death in Amite County, Mississippi, by a member of the Mississippi State Legislature who was never indicted. Forman went over the details of the case, how the only witness to the crime, Louis Allen, was shotgunned dead in January 1964, on the night before he was to leave the state. He named these deaths as punctuations in the life of the Mississippi movement, as was Medgar Evers', and the five newest murders in as many months. Despite these events, he said, SNCC had developed from the first sit-ins to "Moses and His Boys, the Nonviolent Guerrillas," the Delta voter registration program, and, after the Civil Rights Bill, the Summer Project.

There was danger, and work to do. "You've got to get down to the nitty gritty. You've got to be willing to sweep the floors," He smiled and his voice took on a sarcastic tone. "Of course you're *teachers*, so you're more so*phis*ticated than the voter registration workers. In fact, some of you probably signed up because you think it's safer work. But you can't start shouting, 'Hey, I'm a Freedom School teacher, I'm all right.' Because in Mississippi nobody has any rights.

"All of you should have nervousitis. If you have doubts, we'll admire you for dropping out. But I think the best thing to say is, you know, we'll be there with you, and . . . we'll never turn back."

It was Moses' turn. As he stood, he swayed slightly, then held the microphone. His head dropped, and the voice was so soft it seemed to stroke us. He wondered if any of us had read Tolkien's *The Fellowship of the Ring*. "There is a weariness . . . from constant attention to the things you are doing, the struggle of good against evil." I thought of what one of the volunteers had said that day of Moses: "He's like someone you only read about in novels. He has great currents of moral perplexity running through him."

Then Moses said, "The kids are dead."

He paused—quite without regard for dramatic effect. But long enough for it to hit us: this was the first time it had been spoken: they are dead. Up to now they had simply "disappeared." There had been no reason for us to believe anything else.

"When we heard the news at the beginning I knew they were dead. When we heard they had been arrested I knew there had been a frame-up. We didn't say this earlier because of Rita, because she was really holding out for every hope." Rita had gone to Meridian now.

"There may be more deaths." He waited, seeking the words he needed. "I justify myself because I'm taking risks myself, and I'm not asking people to do things I'm not willing to do. And the other thing is, people were being killed already, the Negroes of Mississippi, and I feel, anyway, responsible for their deaths. Herbert Lee killed, Louis Allen killed, five others killed this year. In some way you have to come to grips with that, know what it means. If you are going to do anything about it, other people are going to be killed. No privileged group in history has ever given up anything without some kind of blood sacrifice, something."

He sank into his tiredness again and the volunteers just watched him. He wasn't looking at us, but at a space between him and the floor.

"There are people who left today, went home. I was worried yesterday because no one had left and that was bad, it was unreal.

"The way some people characterize this project is that it is an attempt to get some people killed so the federal government will move into Mississippi. And the way some of us feel about it is that in our country we have some real evil, and the attempt to do something about it involves enormous effort . . . and therefore tremendous risks. If for any reason you're hesitant about what you're getting into, it's better for you to leave. Because what has got to be done has to be done in a certain way, or otherwise it won't get done.

"You have to break off a little chunk of a problem and work on it, and try to see where it leads, and concentrate on it."

His voice had faded almost to a whisper, and it was as if he were speaking out of his sleep, out of his unconscious directly into ours.

"All I can say really is . . . be patient with the kids, and with Mississippi. Because there is a distinction between being slow and being stupid. And the kids in Mississippi are very, very . . . very slow."

He finished, stood there, then walked out the door. The silence which followed him was absolute. It lasted a minute, two; no one moved. They knew, now, what could not be applauded. Suddenly, a beautiful voice from the back of the room pierced the quiet.

> They say that freedom is a constant struggle.
> They say that freedom is a constant struggle.
> They say that freedom is a constant struggle.
> Oh, Lord, we've struggled so long,
> We must be free, we must be free.

It was a new song to me and to the others. But I knew it, and all the voices in the room joined in as though the song came from the deepest part of themselves, and they had always known it.

CHAPTER 3

"THE UNTOLD STORY OF THE MISSISSIPPI MURDERS"

William Bradford Huie

As Sellers' and Belfrage's memoirs make plain, the disappearance of Schwerner, Chaney, and Goodwin haunted everyone connected with the Summer Project. It also dominated news coverage, a fact that intensified pressure upon the local FBI to solve the crime, or, at least, locate the bodies.

Forty-four days elapsed after Michael (Mickey) Schwerner, Andrew Goodman, and James Chaney disappeared. Then an informant told FBI agents exactly where to dig in a new earthen dam. Forensic evidence indicated that Schwerner and Goodman had each been shot once, execution style. There were no bruises on their bodies or other evidence of struggle. James Chaney was shot three times and his shoulder fractured; his body had significant bruising. This gave rise to speculation that Chaney had been severely beaten before being killed. An alternative explanation, favored by William Bradford Huie, a journalist who wrote extensively on the murder of Emmet Till, was that Chaney had tried to escape—hence the three shots rather than one—and that the broken shoulder and bruising arose from his body being run over by a tractor in the process of burying it.

The comparative absence of blood at the dam indicated that the murders occurred somewhere else. The difficulty of reaching the dam—there was no road—suggested that the three were buried some ten or twelve hours or more after their deaths. Huie's detailed account tells what was known about the murders at the end of August.

At dusk two cars met on a narrow, lonely red-clay road. They stopped side by side. One driver passed a shoe box to the other. Then they sped away. In that box was $25,000 in $20 bills, belonging to the people of the United States. It was paid for three bodies which had been hidden 44 days in an earthen dam.

Who were these two anxious men who met at dusk?

There is little curiosity as to the identity of the payer. He acted for the United States Government. In seeking the bodies of murder victims, he employed avarice, and avarice can overpower hate and fear. He

Source: "The Untold Story of the Mississippi Murders," by William Bradford Huie, *Saturday Evening Post*, September 5, 1964.

played one emotion against others and found the bodies in the only way they could have been found.

But everyone, who has followed this story, or is part of it, is curious about the payee. He may never be identified. He may live in legend. He is one of perhaps a dozen citizens of East Central Mississippi who knew where the bodies were; and he has bet his life that the other 11 will never believe that he is the one who informed.

Consider the risks he took. His deal with the Federal Bureau of Investigation was C.O.D. So he had to map the location of the bodies for them, then wait for his money until they found and identified the bodies. How could he be sure they'd pay him, once they had the bodies? He had to risk their recording his conversations with them. He had to risk their photographing his receiving the payoff.

How does he know his money isn't marked, perhaps with chemicals which will cause it to turn red next month? How can he ever sleep soundly again, when one piece of tape or film slipped into the right hands could cause him to be riddled with buckshot in his own bed?

In Philadelphia, Miss., a week before the bodies were found, one of its citizens said to me, "I don't believe a million dollars could buy those bodies."

"I think they can be bought for twenty-five thousand or less," I said. "Just go down the list of suspected lynchers. Some of the scum of this county. They'd sell their mothers or children."

"But this is different," he insisted.

"This is a hate lynching. To these lynchers their victims were an agitating nigger and two Jew-atheist-Communist-beatnik-nigger-lovers. Hell, these killers think they are patriots. They think they killed to protect the Mississippi way of life. This lynching is the only act in their crummy lives which they think becomes them. This is their finest hour. I can't believe that a million dollars would cause one of them to squeal to the bureau or to any other representative of Lyndon Johnson or Bobby Kennedy or Martin Luther King."

"Maybe the informer will be a man who wasn't party to the lynching," I suggested. "One way or another he might learn where the bodies are. Assuming the bureau never identifies him, he could inform with little risk."

Neshoba County is 25 miles square. It is hill country, mostly piney woods and pastures. At its center is its county seat, Philadelphia, and half of the county's 20,000 population lives in or near Philadelphia, which is industrializing, growing and prospering.

The countryside looks vacant: There has been an exodus. "Cotton," as the saying goes, "has moved to town." Since 1945 rural Neshoba

County has lost 10,000 residents. The sharecroppers have gone with the row crops. There are only 5,000 nonwhites left in the county, half of whom are Choctaw Indians living on a reservation. Of the 2,500 remaining Negroes, about 1,500 live around Philadelphia in "nigger towns." They work in the three lumber mills. The other 1,000 Negroes live in several rural pockets. They own small patches of land. They cluster about their tiny Baptist and Methodist churches and graveyards. They "scratch out a little cotton." The young ones are in a hurry to get old enough to go to Chicago: the old ones wait to die, to be buried next to Mamma and Papa and Grandpa and Grandma in those old graveyards.

These few remaining Negroes are no real threat to any white man. They are only a psychological threat. If they all voted, they couldn't elect a candidate: Their bloc support would only assure his defeat. But, as one man put it, "If niggers aren't gonna be kept in their place in Mississippi, then what's a pore white man gonna feel he's superior to?"

During May and early June, Michael Schwerner, 24, white, of New York, and James Chaney, 21, Negro, of Meridian, made several trips to Longdale, an all-Negro farm community eight miles east of Philadelphia. They asked the Negro farmers to let them speak at the Methodist church, and in their speeches they urged the Negroes to allow "freedom meetings" to be held in the church, meetings in which Negroes would be instructed in how to register to vote.

On a Tuesday evening in June, as 30 Negroes were leaving the church, a dozen white men struck back. They beat four of the Negroes, including one woman. They shouted, "Keep that Red Jew nigger-lover out of here, or you'll all wind up in the river." They drove the Negroes off and burned down their church.

Schwerner and Chaney were in Oxford, Ohio, when the church burned, training recruits with money furnished by the National Council of Churches. But the church burners had descriptions of them. They had photographed the youths' blue Ford station wagon. They broadcast its license number and description. They let it be known that "We're laying for that bearded Red Jew agitator. We'll get him the next time he comes in here."

On one point the Negroes who were beaten and threatened at the church are unanimous: One of the white men wore a uniform.

Two men in Neshoba County wear sheriffs' uniforms. Lawrence A. Rainey, the sheriff, is a formidable figure; At 41, he is six-foot-two, 240 pounds, meaty, barrel-chested, and keeps a fist-sized chaw of Red Man tobacco in his jaw. He wears a khaki uniform with calf-length boots and a cattleman's hat turned up on the sides; his belt line bulges with polished leather, burnished brass-and-lead ammunition and a heavy, holstered gun. He drives a new, tan Oldsmobile, which has a powerful red light on top and is filled with guns, nightsticks and extra cartons of Red Man.

The sheriff was born on a farm in adjoining Kemper County. By profession he is an automobile mechanic: He learned it and worked at it in Canton, Miss. A kidney ailment is said to have kept him out of military service. In 1957 he became a Canton city policeman, and in 1959 he killed his first Negro. "A Chicago nigger," Rainey explained to me. "He had me down choking me." He then moved to Philadelphia where, in 1961, he became a sheriff's deputy. He killed a second Negro. "A crazy nigger. We were taking him to the state hospital. He grabbed a gun out of a glove compartment, and I killed him in an exchange of gunfire." In 1963 he was elected sheriff, and in January, 1964, he assumed office.

The only deputy, Cecil Price, is a younger and slightly less formidable copy of the sheriff. Only 27, he came from Madison County (Canton) to Philadelphia eight years ago as a salesman of dairy supplies. He has traveled every back road and pig trail in the county and knows it like the back of his hand. As fire chief of Philadelphia for two years, he served as a weekend policeman, handling ball games and dances. When Rainey became sheriff, Price was his first choice for deputy. Like Rainey, Price and his wife are southern Methodist; they are expecting their first child in October.

A sheriff and his deputy are particularly close in Mississippi, because neither is salaried. The sheriff works on a fee system, and he himself hires, fires and pays his deputy.

A third, but not uniformed, law-enforcement figure in Neshoba County is a justice of the peace, Leonard Warren. His office is in the courthouse, and most miscreants are first brought before him. He is the physical opposite of Rainey and Price: skinny, no more than 140 pounds, chicken-necked with a prominent Adam's apple. But he, too, likes to don the cattle-man's hat, the gun and the nightstick and work as a part-time cop.

Of these three it was Sheriff's Deputy Price who, on Sunday afternoon, June 21, apprehended the civil-rights workers on the eastern outskirts of Philadelphia.

Everyone familiar with the story knows how Schwerner, Chaney and others, in the blue Ford station wagon, arrived back in Meridian from Ohio on Saturday, June 20. Around noon on Sunday Schwerner, who headed the Meridian office, decided to drive the 32 miles into Longdale to try to persuade the Negro farmers to continue holding "freedom meetings" in the open air at the site of the burned church.

He took with him Chaney, and also Andrew Goodman, 20, white, of New York, who had ridden from Ohio with him and had been in Mississippi less than a day.

The three reached Longdale safely, talked with Negroes at the church site, and left sometime after three P.M. Obviously they decided to return to Meridian by way of Philadelphia, so from Longdale they drove eight miles due west and reached the city limits of Philadelphia.

From this point on it must be understood—indeed it is conceded in Mississippi—that all information comes from persons who hated these three young men. The police do not claim objectivity; they believe that they were dealing with "invaders who had no right to be here."

Price says he stopped the station wagon for driving 65 miles an hour through a 30-mile zone.

Maybe he did, but the three were unlikely speeders. They had a policy of never stopping the car in Neshoba County other than in all-Negro areas. They always left Meridian with a full tank of gas, so they wouldn't have to stop at an "unfriendly" filling station.

They stopped on the eastern edge of Philadelphia because they had car trouble. They stopped on a main highway at about 3:30 P.M. in Sunday-afternoon traffic. They were conspicuous for two reasons: They were young white men traveling with a young Negro, and both Michael Schwerner and Andrew Goodman wore the beatnik sneakers and blue jeans, and Schwerner wore the beatnik beard. So they were publicly noticed and recognized as "the enemy."

Sheriff Rainey told me that the station wagon was moving and speeding when Deputy Price saw it, that Price flagged it down in front of the First Methodist Church, and that "they all noticed the tire going down while Price was standing there talking to them."

Price's car stood parked behind the station wagon while the three changed the tire. Price had radioed the Mississippi State Highway Patrol for "help in making the arrest." So two patrolmen who live in Philadelphia, Earl R. Poe and Harry J. Wiggs, arrived, and the state car also parked, making three *very conspicuous* parked cars.

When the tire had been changed, one of the patrolman drove the station wagon the six densely populated blocks to the county jail, with the county car and the state car following, making a conspicuous three-car caravan.

So there is no doubt that Schwerner, Goodman and Chaney *reached* the jail safely. The jail is one block from the courthouse, half a block from the city hall and police station, and half a block from the Benwalt Hotel where the Rotary Club meets. And any witness to the procession of automobiles would have conluded that Mississippi lawmen had captured John Dillinger, Pretty Boy Floyd and Jesse James.

The hours from 4:30 P.M. to 10:30 P.M. or later, on Sunday, June 21, 1964, are shameful hours for Neshoba County, for Mississippi and for the United States. These are hours of hypocrisy, injustice and tragedy . . . hours in which a ghastly lynching could have been prevented.

What makes this lynching a high crime against humanity is the role of the police. The three young men were not criminals. They were unarmed. They were well-intentioned. They were peaceful and peace-loving. Mississippi requires no visa for an American citizen to visit it. So they were in Mississippi by legal right, and they had violated no law.

This is conceded by the state's highest law-enforcement agency. So why were the young men jailed, and why did their co-workers not hear from them?

Chaney, driver of the station wagon, was said to have been speeding. Unless a driver is drunk, he is not ordinarily jailed for speeding anywhere in the United States, until he has had a chance to make bond. Speeding is a misdemeanor, not a felony. When a speeder is arrested in Mississippi, he is carried before a justice of the peace. If he needs it, he is allowed to telephone for counsel or money. He pays his fine or makes bond and is freed.

I asked Rainey why Price didn't carry Chaney before Justice of the Peace Leonard Warren.

"It was Sunday afternoon," Rainey said. "I was in Meridian at the hospital with my wife. So Price just telephoned Warren."

"What did the justice say?"

"He finally told Price to let him go for twenty dollars."

"It took the justice six hours to reach that decision?"

"Well, it was Sunday afternoon and night. I wasn't here. Price was holding the fort alone. Things just don't move very fast on Sunday."

The passengers in a speeding car are not guilty of speeding; only the driver is guilty. So Schwerner and Goodman were jailed on "suspicion." Suspicion of what?

Officials of the Mississippi State Highway Patrol knew that the three were in the Neshoba County Jail after dark, and therefore knew that they were in grave danger. Officers Wiggs and Poe are in radio communication with the patrol substation at Meridian, which, in turn, is in communication with the headquarters at Jackson.

One telephone call by a patrol official to Philadelphia might have prevented the lynching. Since Officers Poe and Wiggs had been party to the arrest, why weren't they ordered to prevent a lynching by safeguarding the prisoners when and if they were released?

In Meridian young associates of the three began telephoning the FBI and Justice Department lawyers at nine P.M. The federal officials were anxious to demonstrate that the FBI is not a federal police force but only a criminal investigative agency. They insist that "law enforcement within her boundaries is Mississippi's responsibility." So they told the callers that they could do nothing yet; that the three had not been missing long enough to be officially missing; and that there was no reasonable evidence that any "civil rights had been abridged."

Since so many persons in Philadelphia knew that the three hated "agitators" were in the jail, the six or more hours provided ample time for *the few men capable of killing* to communicate, to assemble from far away as 50 or more miles, and to plot seizure, murder and body disposal. . . .

And the three prisoners during these critical hours? There is no reasonable doubt that they shuddered at the approach of darkness.

Price, the arresting deputy, says, "I took twenty dollars from the nigger and turned them loose at 10:30 P.M. They got in their car. I followed them a piece. The last I saw of them was their taillight disappearing down Highway 19 toward Meridian."

Sheriff Rainey told me that a city policeman, Richard Willis, was in the car with Price and also witnessed the disappearing taillight of the station wagon.

It is 35 miles from Philadelphia to Meridian. Highway 19 is a broad and heavily traveled road. Along it there are many homes, an Indian Agency headquarters and school and several tiny communities, none large enough to have a traffic light.

Were the three stopped by roadblock? No one believes this. Not on such a highway. The three would have crashed the station wagon, run, fought: They would not have submitted meekly to clandestine terrorists. Were they stopped by gunfire? No. The burned station wagon bore no evidence of gunfire, and the recovered bodies of Michael Schwerner and Andrew Goodman were incredibly free of any evidence of struggle: just one pistol bullet through their hearts, fired from directly in front of them.

Then how were they seized?

In the Mississippi Highway Patrol are some able investigators. In this case, from the beginning, they have considered three possibilities:

1. That the young men were seized at the jail entrance.

2. That they were allowed to reach the station wagon, which was parked on a hill just below the city police station, and then surrounded.

3. That they were allowed to proceed down Highway 19 for several miles, then flagged down by a police car and delivered to the murderers.

This third theory has been abandoned because of the unlikelihood that the three, once they were in the station wagon, would have stopped for anything short of gunfire or being pushed off the road. The second theory came into question when the bodies of Schwerner and Goodman showed no signs of struggle. Even if they had been looking into gun barrels, it seems unlikely that they would have surrendered to a mob without some effort to break and run.

Two key questions about the murders are when and where. Were they shot Sunday night or after daylight on Monday? And were they shot at the site where they were buried or elsewhere?

There are reasons to believe that they were shot within half an hour after they were released and seized—which may not have been at 10:30 P.M. The murderers apparently had nothing else in mind except to kill them; and a mob bent on murder doesn't waste time.

WAS CHANEY BEATEN?

I don't agree that Chaney was beaten and the other two forced to watch. This belies character. Had the killers paused to beat anybody, they would have beaten Schwerner or Goodman. A "nigger" in Mississippi would never be beaten in preference to a "nigger-lover." Because he found Chaney's shoulder and arm crushed, a New York pathologist concluded that Chaney had been beaten with a chain or blunt instrument.

Here, I think, is a more likely explanation: The three bodies were buried with a bulldozer. When the bulldozer began work, the bodies may have been covered with several inches of dirt or with no dirt at all. The bulldozer track could have passed over one of the bodies, or a portion of it, and missed the other two.

It's true that Chaney was shot three times while the others were shot once—with remarkable accuracy. An explanation is that Schwerner and Goodman were standing before a flashlight, in handcuffs and leg-irons. Struggle was useless, so they stood unflinching as . . . Chaney watched his companions die, struggled and tried to dodge, and was shot three times with much less accuracy.

My own feeling is that the three were murdered in darkness, perhaps near the Bogue Chitto swamp where the burned station wagon was found, and that the burial was by daylight.

The 250-acre farm owned by Olen Burrage, is six miles southwest of Philadelphia and a mile off the paved road leading to Sebastopol. It is known as the John Townsend place, and it isn't really a "farm" anymore. Like most such farms, it now grows pine trees and cattle, with some corn to feed the cattle.

Mr. Burrage, a big, jovial man, lives in Philadelphia, where he operates freight trucks. The only house on the farm—300 yards from the burial spot—is occupied by Lamar Smith, with his wife and seven children. Mr. Smith, a wrinkled, red-faced man in his 40's, is a caretaker, and he has five lean and barking dogs.

Late in May Mr. Burrage contracted with Herman Tucker to build a cattle pond on his place. There are scores of such ponds in Neshoba County. To build a pond you generally dig a ditch may be 30 feet wide and five feet deep. Into this ditch you pack red clay, and it hardens. Then you scoop up, push up and pile up an earthen dam, sloping the sides, to whatever height is needed.

Mr. Tucker talks reluctantly. He said most of the work on the dam was done by two of his employees using a bulldozer and an endloader. The dam, begun in late May, was completed "sometime along in July."

The bodies were found on August 4, in the center of the dam, 14 feet and 10 inches below the crest. They were lying face down, side by side. Goodman and Schwerner were head to head and feet to feet; and Chaney, on the outside, was in the opposite position; his feet were at Schwerner's head. The two white men's arms were above their heads, indicating that they were dropped or laid into the dirt by one man holding wrists and another holding ankles. Chaney's arms were at his sides, probably because a bullet had broken his right wrist and forearm: It would have been bloody and slick, so he would have been handled by the shoulders or by hands in his armpits.

All of this means that one of the lynchers—or *an adviser to the lynchers*—knew that this out-of-the-way dam was being built. He knew that it was half built on June 21–22, and he knew exactly where to put the bodies. When the FBI got its tip from the informer, it used a dragline and cut into the dam with remarkable precision.

Three factors indicate to me that the burial may not have been in darkness:

1. Lamar Smith's five dogs. They were accustomed to activity at the damsite during daylight. But nocturnal activity would have set them to the sort of barking which isn't easily silenced.

2. Access to the damsite from the nearest road was barely cleared. The pathway was adequate for tracked vehicles but difficult for wheeled vehicles. Before they moved the huge dragline and a pickup truck along the path. FBI agents used a bulldozer for further

clearing. So it seems questionable that the killers would have driven in there at night in a passenger car, or a station wagon or even a pickup.

True, the three victims could have been walked to the site and shot there. If so, the FBI will know it from the amount of blood beneath the bodies. The agents collected a ton or more of dirt, in garbage cans, and flew it to the Washington laboratory.

3. The precision of the informer indicates daylight burial to me. If the burial was at night, and the dam builders never discovered it, how could the informer be so precise? He might have been reasonably accurate, but how could he have been so *precisely* accurate?

This possible delay in burial, along with the method and the place, convinces me that at least one and perhaps as many as four men, who were not members of the mob, could have learned the location of the bodies.

"AN ADDRESS BY MRS. FANNIE LEE CHANEY OF MERIDIAN, MISSISSIPPI"

Intimidation had always worked. Violence had always worked. Killing Schwerner, Goodman, and Chaney did not work. COFO did not back off. The volunteers continued to pour into the state. And Mississippi blacks began to believe that this time things would be different, that this time they could effect real change. Chaney's mother and his younger brother embodied this new determination and hope. About a year after her son's murder, Mrs. Chaney talked about the struggle in Mississippi and particularly in Meridian.

I am here tell you about Meridian, Mississippi. That's my home. I have been there all of my days. I know the white man; I know the black man. The white man is not for the black man—we are just there. Everything to be done, to be said, the white man is going to do it; *he* is going to say it, right or wrong. We hadn't, from the time that I know of, been able to vote or register in Meridian. Now, since the civil rights workers have been down in Mississippi working, they have allowed a lot of them to go to register. A lot of our people are scared, afraid. They are still backward. "I can't do that; I never have," they claimed. "I have

Source: "An Address by Mrs. Fannie Lee Chaney of Meridian, Mississippi," from *Freedomways*, Second Quarter, 1965.

been here too long. I will lose my job; I won't have any job." So, that is just the way it is. My son, James, when he went out with the civil rights workers around the first of '64 felt it was something he wanted to do, and he enjoyed working in the civil rights Movement. He stayed in Canton, Mississippi, working on voter registration from February through March. When he came home he told me how he worked and lived those few weeks he was there; he said, "Mother, one half of the time, I was out behind houses or churches, waiting to get the opportunity to talk to people about what they needed and what they ought to do." He said, "Sometime they shunned me off and some would say, 'I want you all to stay away from here and leave me alone.'" But he would pick his chance and go back again. That is what I say about Mississippi right now. There is one more test I want to do there. I am working with the civil rights Movement, my whole family is, and my son, Ben, here, he is going to take his big brother's place.

He has been working for civil rights. Everything he can do, he does it. For his activities, he had been jailed twice before he was 12 years old. He told me when he was in jail he wasn't excited. He is not afraid; he would go to jail again! I am too, because we need and we've got to go to jail and we've got to get where the white man is. The white man has got Mississippi and we are just there working for the white man. He is the one getting rich. And when he gets rich, we can be outdoors or in old houses and he is going to knock on the door and get his rent money.

This is not something that has just now started, it has been going on before my time and I imagine before my parents' time. It is not just *now* the white man is doing this; it was borne from generation to generation. So, as I say, Ben is going to take his big brother's place, and I am with him and the rest of the family also. You all read about Mississippi—all parts of Mississippi, but I just wish it was so you could just come down there and be able to see; just try to live there just for one day, and you will know just how it is there.

THE RIVER OF NO RETURN: THE AUTOBIOGRAPHY OF A BLACK MILITANT AND THE LIFE AND DEATH OF SNCC

Cleveland Sellers with Robert Terrell

SNCC field-worker Cleveland Sellers was all of nineteen when he arrived in Mississippi in June 1964 to serve as assistant project director for Marshall County. His autobiography recounts his initial shock at the poverty and lack of opportunity Mississippi blacks faced—Sellers was himself from a small South Carolina town—and his respect for Ivanhoe Donohue, the project director. Marshall was a comparatively "safe" place, he remembered, even as he described the extreme danger he and his coworkers faced every day.

He also described the "long list of rules and regulations" Donohue had drawn up for volunteers and staff. Donohue laid special stress on the unacceptability of "affairs between blacks and whites. . . . In a very blunt and forceful manner, he told white females that they were to avoid all romantic entanglements with local black males." Concern over potential interracial sexual encounters was widespread among COFO staff. Their most immediate concern was how local whites would seize upon any such affair to denounce the whole Summer Project. Local blacks were likely to be equally disapproving, some felt. And, in any case, local blacks would see such conduct as foolhardy. Even so, as Vincent Harding pointed out (see Sally Belfrage's "Basic Training"), some African American field-workers would seek sexual favors from white volunteers as "proof" of their commitment to the cause. And, given that more than a thousand people, most of them in their early twenties, were participating in the project, some sexual liaisons were inevitable no matter what precautions leaders like Donohue took.

THE LONG HOT SUMMER

It was the longest nightmare I have ever had: three months. June, July and August of 1964. I was nineteen years old, a man-child immersed in the seething core of the "long, hot summer." These grim statistics relate only a small portion of the horror: one thousand arrests, thirty-five shooting incidents, thirty homes and other buildings bombed; thirty-five churches burned, eighty beatings and at least six persons murdered. Although most of us managed to leave Mississippi, none of us escaped without terrible scars. It happened eight years ago, but the scars are still there, deep inside, where I suspect they will remain for the rest of our lives.

It began in earnest for me when I returned from Meridian to Holly Springs, Mississippi, which was to be our home base for the summer. A small group of people ran out of the office at 100 Rust Avenue when we drove up. They were summer volunteers, our coworkers. Most of them had just arrived from the Oxford orientation sessions. Their sad, searching eyes asked questions that would not be answered for many weeks: "Where are they? What happened to Chaney, Goodman and Schwerner?"

Ivanhoe was the Project director. Although he was of medium stature, standing about five ten and weighing no more than 175 pounds, he had tremendous presence and was a natural leader. He had been working with SNCC for more than two years and knew the South well. He'd made his first trip South in 1962 while a student at Michigan State in response to a SNCC appeal for food and clothing for a group of starving sharecroppers in Leflore, Mississippi. Ivanhoe and his companion Ben Taylor, a fellow student from Michigan State, had been arrested in Clarksdale and charged with the possession of dangerous narcotics. The "narcotics" were aspirin and vitamins.

The two of them remained in jail for eleven days under fifteen thousand dollars' bond until nationwide protests brought their release. Despite the threats of Clarksdale's police, who confiscated the truck-load of supplies they had been transporting and warned them not to be caught in Mississippi again, Ivanhoe made twelve more trips from Michigan to Leflore, laden each time with badly needed food and supplies.

We had a long staff meeting on our first night in Holly Springs. Ivanhoe presided. Everyone sat quietly while he explained the long list of rules and regulations he had drawn up. Everyone was to be on his job by eight-thirty each morning; no one was to make any trip into the city or county without leaving his time of departure and expected return on the check-out list in the office; no one was to be out after dark unless he was on official business; all shades were to be pulled as soon as the sun went down, and no one was to make a target of himself by casting a shadow on a shade; local whites and the police were to be avoided whenever possible and never unnecessarily provoked.

Ivanhoe was particularly emphatic about affairs between blacks and whites. He told us that he did not intend to have any interracial relationships between staff members. In a very blunt and forceful manner, he told the white females that they were to avoid all romantic entanglements with local black males.

"Interracial relationships will provide local whites with the initiative they need to come in here and kill all of us. Even if the whites don't find out about them, the people will, and we won't be able to do anything afterwards to convince them that our primary interest here is political.

"Our entire effort will be negated if we lose the support and respect of the people. I don't intend for that to happen. Anyone who violates any of these rules will have to pack his bag and get his ass out of town. We're here to work. The time for bullshitting is past."

Pausing, Ivanhoe looked around the room from face to face. He wanted to make certain that everyone understood. We did.

The remainder of the evening was spent discussing COFO and the scope of the Summer Project. Although a number of organizations were supporting the Project, SNCC was the prime mover. SNCC people were coordinating four of the five Project areas—CORE was coordinating the fifth. SNCC was supplying 95 percent of the money for operating expenses and facilities throughout the state. Although Aaron Henry was president of COFO, Bob Moses was the Project director.

"The Summer Project has three major objectives," Ivanhoe explained, "registering voters, operating Freedom Schools and organizing Mississippi Freedom Democratic Party (MFDP) precincts. I intend for us to have the best goddamn project in the state. We're going to register more voters than anyone else, have the most efficient Freedom Schools and the best MFDP precincts!"

Before the meeting concluded, someone passed around a copy of a COFO publication titled "The General Condition of the Mississippi Negro." Despite my previous exposure to poverty and deprivation, I found it very disturbing.

The publication revealed that 66 percent of all Mississippi's blacks were living in "dilapidated or deteriorating" housing; that about one-third more blacks than whites died each year; that the chances of a black baby's dying in his first year were twice those of a white child; that one-half of the state's black schools had no equipment whatsoever; that more than 90 percent of the public libraries denied admission to blacks; that the state unemployment rate for blacks was twice that of whites and that the annual income rate for blacks was 71 percent less than that of whites.

"It really is going to be a long, hot summer," I muttered to no one in particular before tossing the pamphlet down and heading for bed.

I suspected from the way he conducted our first meeting that Ivanhoe was going to be a tough taskmaster. My suspicions were confirmed a couple of days later when Hardy Frye was arrested. Hardy, who had been assigned to register voters in the downtown area, was new and Ivanhoe told me to keep an eye on him.

I'd been watching Hardy for about a half hour when the chief of police walked up to him. "You're under arrest," the chief growled in a loud voice.

"Under arrest for what?" Hardy roared in an equally loud voice.

They were on the main street, which was moderately crowded with black and white shoppers. Their loud exchange caught the attention of everyone on the block. There must have been seventy people watching to see what would happen. This was the first confrontation between any of our staff members and local police officials. Everyone seemed to sense that it would have an important effect on the remainder of the summer.

"What the hell am I under arrest for? I ain't done a goddamn thing," Hardy insisted.

About five seven, Hardy was putting on a good show. Despite the fact that the police chief was several inches taller and probably fifty pounds heavier, Hardy wasn't backing down. He had been raised in Alabama and understood the symbolic importance of his confrontation with the chief.

The chief, who had obviously expected a less belligerent response, got confused. "You're under arrest for uh, uh, uhh, blocking traffic."

"Okay," said Hardy. "If I'm under arrest, let's go!"

With that, Hardy raised his hands high over his head and started walking toward the jail. The chief, who had reportedly killed several blacks, was further confused. Hardy was striding dramatically down the street as if on the way to the guillotine. He had a defiant smile playing at the corners of his mouth. The chief stumbled behind him, trying to catch up.

"Put your hands down, nigra!" he growled self-consciously.

When I got back to the office and told Ivanhoe what had happened, he jumped up from his desk and said, "Let's go!" Within an hour he had paid Hardy's fine and had him back in the office.

"You okay, Hardy?" asked Ivanhoe.

"Yeah, I'm okay. They didn't do anything but threaten me."

"Well, go back out there and get back to work," Ivanhoe commanded.

It was Hardy's turn to be confused. "Get back out there?"

"Yes, get back out there. There were a lot of people watching when you got arrested. We can't let them think that we are afraid. You know that. Go right back to the spot where you were when you were arrested and continue to try to register people. Act as if nothing had happened."

"You're the boss," grunted Hardy, who was already on his way out the door. Although the police watched him closely, they did not rearrest him.

Ivanhoe's handling of the situation established two things: his position as the unquestioned leader of the Project and respect for our staff from the blacks of Holly Springs. If Ivanhoe had handled the situation any differently, if he had been softhearted and allowed Hardy to take the remainder of the day off, we probably would have had many more problems than we did during the rest of the summer.

Although I was the assistant Project director, I did not get to spend much time in the office. I was assigned to coordinate voter registration, Freedom Schools and MFDP organizing in Marshall County. The hardest part of my job was organizing Freedom Days. Every two or three weeks we would schedule a Freedom Day and try to get all the people we had contacted to come into town and try to register. Because numerous people had been killed on Freedom Days in other parts of the state, we had to work extra hard to keep the people from losing their nerve.

As each Freedom Day approached, I would move out of the crowded Holly Springs office and into the county so that I could be closer to the people. Working from sunrise long into the hot, humid nights, I had to keep reassuring the people that all hell was not going to break loose if they tried to register.

"You can do it! You can do it! I'll be with you every step of the way," I repeated again and again.

The Freedom Schools played a large part in the success of the Freedom Days. The children who came to the schools, many of whom were twelve and thirteen and still couldn't read or write, understood the meaning of freedom. All the lessons in the schools were tied to the need for blacks to stand up and demand the freedom that was rightfully theirs. The children would return home from the schools and badger their reluctant parents into going to town and registering for freedom.

By midsummer the periodic Freedom Days had evolved into something more than just "registration" days when blacks asked for the opportunity to get their names on the voter rolls. The people saw them as opportunities to stand before their peers, white and black, and declare that freedom was something they intended to have. There is nothing so awe-inspiring as a middle-aged sharecropper trudging up the steps to the voter registrar's office clad in brogans, denim overalls and a freshly starched white shirt—his only one. I grew to love the Freedom Days. More than anything else, they provided the motivation that kept me going.

One of our most difficult tasks was getting people to attend the MFDP precinct meetings. Everyone knew that the three missing men were associated in some way with the party. They also knew that all those who attended the precinct meetings were letting themselves in for the same fate as the missing men. Although most people would not openly support the MFDP, we received invaluable assistance from local black ministers. They allowed us to address their congregations after Sunday morning worship service and urge their members to attend the meetings. By my third week on the job, I could deliver a pretty good sermon—in support of voter registration and the MFDP.

Although Marshall was supposed to be one of the most liberal counties in Mississippi, we had numerous run-ins with law-enforcement officials. I remember two in particular: an event that I call The Chase, and the death of Wayne Yancey.

The Chase took place late one Friday night. Three carloads of us were on our way back to Holly Springs after a big MFDP rally when we noticed that we were being followed by a police car. I was driving the lead car, a 1962 Volvo.

"Maybe we won't have to make a run for it. He doesn't seem to be interested in harassing us," I said to Ralph Featherstone, who was sitting in the front seat with me.

"I hope you're right," he muttered.

The police car followed us until we were in the middle of Oxford, Mississippi, before flagging down the two cars following me. I drove on for about four blocks before pulling to the side of the road to see if the other cars were going to be allowed to continue. When it became obvious that they were going to be detained, I swung the Volvo around in a wide U-turn and headed back.

By the time I got back and pulled in behind the two cars, the Marshall County sheriff and several other police cars had arrived. The sheriff, a short man who looked like a Bantam rooster, immediately turned the situation into a dangerous game.

While a fast-growing crowd of whites looked on, he called us from the cars one by one and attempted to humiliate us. The police officers looked on, chuckling and smiling.

"What yo' name, boy?"

"Cleveland Sellers."

"Where you from?"

"Denmark, South Carolina."

"What's a South Carolina nigra doing over heah in Mississippi? Ain't you South Carolina nigras got enough trouble without comin' over heah to Mississippi tryin' ta stir up our nigras?"

Although his remarks angered me, I remained impassive. I knew that he wanted me to give him an excuse to attack. It took everything in me to keep from spitting in his face and cursing him. His little eyes were shining and his lips were wet. He was really enjoying himself. So was the crowd around us. There were about 250 of them and they were cheering and howling like spectators at a bullfight.

"What's the matta, nigra? Cain't chew talk? Ever' time I turn on the television I sees one of you SNCC nigras talkin' 'bout how bad us white Mississippians is. What chew got ta say now?"

"I don't have anything to say," I replied in a dry voice, which was as devoid of emotion as I could make it.

"Git yo' slack ass back in tha cah! If'n I ketch you ovah heah ah-gin, um gonna puhsonally see to it that you leave in a pine box! Now git!"

Then turning to the other officers, the sheriff said, "He got a white girl in the back of that cah. Take him back and git huh ovah heah."

He was talking about Kathy Kunstler, whose father—William Kunstler—was one of the lawyers working with COFO. "Don't let him get to you," I whispered to her as she clambered from the car. Although the night air was cool, I noticed small beads of perspiration on her forehead.

The sheriff began by questioning her about her birthplace, occupation and residence. He was speaking in a loud voice so that everyone in the tightly packed crowd could hear. Very quickly, he descended to the level of all too many white minds in Mississippi.

"Which one of them coons is you fuckin'?" The crowd roared its approval of the question.

"Slut, I know you fuckin' them niggers. Why else would you be down heah? Which one is it? If you tell me the truth, I'll let you go. Which one is it?"

Although she was clearly frightened, Kathy did not break. Remaining calm, she spoke when it was appropriate and otherwise remained silent.

The crowd, which contained several tobacco-chewing drunks, was so engrossed in the exchange between Kathy and the sheriff that the rest of us were completely forgotten. That was good, because it provided us the opportunity to pass notes from car to car.

There was a federal courthouse across the street and we decided to make a run for its steps if the crowd attacked. There were several empty pop bottles in our car and we passed them to the occupants of the other cars. They were our only means of defense. Fortunately, we did not have to use them. The sheriff decided to let us go.

"Take your white whores and get the hell out of Oxford!" he yelled. "If'n I ketch any one of you heah again, um gonna see to it that you git a quick trip to hell!" He then told one of his deputies to escort us to the edge of town.

Just before the deputy headed back for the center of town, we noticed that we were being followed. Featherstone stuck his head out the window as we turned a corner. There were seventeen cars behind us.

"Oh shit," I muttered under my breath. Just at that moment the deputy sped past us, headed in the opposite direction. There was a big smile on his face.

"Our only chance is to run for it," said Featherstone.

He didn't have to repeat himself. Within seconds, we were speeding down the dark highway at 105 miles per hour. I was driving the last car and wasn't at all certain if the little Volvo could keep up with the big Plymouth Furies that Ivanhoe and Hardy were driving in front of me.

Featherstone stuck his head out the window again as we sped into a long, sloping curve. "There are twenty-one now," he said.

Before I had time to dwell on the significance of his report, we were faced with a new peril. Roadblock dead ahead. Ivanhoe, who was driving the lead car, responded immediately. The roadblock was set up in the right lane only. The left lane was open so that oncoming traffic could get through. Swerving into the left lane, Ivanhoe gunned past the startled little group of white men gathered to the right of the road. Before they could respond, Hardy and I did the same.

The only thing that saved us that night was luck. We drove the thirty miles from Oxford to Holly Springs as if we were Grand Prix racers. Our pursuers slowed down for bridges, sharp curves and small towns. We didn't. Hitting 105, we roared through the two small towns along the way with our horns blaring and our gas pedals on the floor.

Charlie Scales and Wayne Yancey were not as lucky. Wayne was killed one Sunday afternoon in mid-July in a two-car collision. We were sitting in the office trying to catch up on paper work when news of the accident arrived: "You folks better get down to the hospital. Two of your boys had a head-on wreck out on the highway and one of 'em is dead!"

When we arrived at the hospital, Wayne Yancey's body was lying in the rear of the big hearse that had been used as an ambulance. Although the accident had occurred more than an hour before, no doctor had examined him. His blood was seeping through the floor of the hearse and had formed a large dark puddle on the ground.

"Goddammit, what the hell is going on here?" Ivanhoe yelled to one of the white police officers standing nonchalantly in front of the hearse.

"You cain't move the body," drawled one of the officers. "Mayor's orders."

We rushed to the rear of the hearse, which was owned by Mr. Brittenum, the town's lone black mortician. One of Wayne's feet was hanging from one of the doors. It was obvious that his ankle had been broken. We moved closer and looked through the rear window. His face was badly mangled. And his body was bruised and torn by several deep cuts. Blood was everywhere.

I was immediately reminded of the magazine pictures of Emmett Till's corpse. Fighting to control my rage, I backed slowly away from the hearse.

"His head went through the windshield," I heard someone explain to a group of curious onlookers.

I didn't have time to mourn Wayne's death at that moment. We had another problem. Charlie Scales, who had been driving the car in which Wayne was riding, was still alive. Kathy Dahl, who had been with us at the office when the news arrived, was inside the hospital attending him. The white doctors and nurses at the hospital refused to help her. They said they were too busy.

Kathy, who was frantically trying to stem the bleeding of Charlie's wounds, came out briefly and told us that he was going to die unless he got additional assistance. Because we couldn't take a chance on sending him to another Mississippi hospital where he would certainly be refused assistance, we got Mr. Brittenum to agree to transport him to John Gaston Hospital in Memphis. We were preparing to enter the hospital and remove Charlie when we were informed that he was under arrest—for the murder of Wayne Yancey.

"They're trying to kill him, too," bellowed Hardy. In a blind rage, Hardy, Ivanhoe and I rushed the doors of the hospital. We didn't have a chance. There were almost twenty police officers in front of the doors. Ivanhoe sent for a lawyer, who managed after begging, threatening and pleading, to get the mayor to allow Mr. Brittenum to transport Charlie to the hospital in Memphis. If it had not been for Kathy, who remained with Charlie in the rear of the hearse, he probably would have died then.

Immediately after the hearse left for Memphis, Hardy and Bob Fullilove and I were dispatched to the service station where Charlie and Wayne's car, in which the two men had been riding, was being held. We *had* to recover the MFDP membership forms in the car before they were confiscated by the police. We also wanted to inspect the car for signs of foul play.

The car, a brand-new 1964 Ford, was a total loss. It looked as if it had been hit by an explosion. Glass and blood were everywhere.

The force of the collision had smashed the steering column back against the backrest of the front seat. We found one of Wayne's shoes on the floor in the rear.

We had just finished collecting the registration forms and examining the car when two white men came out of the service station and approached us. "Y'all friends of them two who was riding in this cah?" I shook my head affirmatively.

"Too bad you'all weren't in it wit' 'em!"

"Take that bullshit and ram it up your mother's ass," I yelled at the men, who were apparently mechanics. The three of us were advancing toward them, ready to lock nuts, when one of them placed a hand in a rear pocket. We stopped and backed slowly toward our car.

Jumping into the car, we quickly rolled up the windows.

"Let's get out of here," I yelled to Bob, who was sitting in the driver's seat. The white man, his hand still in his pocket, was still advancing toward us. "Let's go!" I yelled as the man began to remove his hand. I was certain that he had a gun. He had a badge instead.

"I'm a police officer. You're under arrest," he said to me.

"Fuck him! Let's go!" I yelled to Bob. But Bob froze. I was arrested for insulting a police officer and resisting arrest. SNCC paid my five-thousand-dollar bond just in time for me to get out of jail and attend Wayne's funeral.

Although we tried, we never did find out just how the collision had occurred. There was nothing at the scene we could use to determine what had happened. We questioned the black man who was driving the car Wayne and Charlie collided with, but he couldn't tell us much.

"I was knocked unconscious immediately," he said. "All I remember is that when my car came over the hill, there was this other car coming straight for me, in my lane."

Charlie couldn't tell us much either. He only remembered one thing. "I was thrown from the car and when I came to there was a white man standing over me. He bent over and said, 'Just lie still and be quiet or you'll get the same thing as your buddy!'"

Wayne's death had a tremendous effect on us. After getting crazy drunk and brooding for a week or so, we tried to pull ourselves together and "keep on keepin' on," but it was impossible. The weeks of tension and strain, coupled with Wayne's brutal death, could not be ignored.

Hate and viciousness seemed to be everywhere. We realized that the only thing keeping us from sharing Wayne's fate was dumb luck. Death could come at any time in any form: a bullet between the shoulder blades, a fire bomb in the night, a pistol whipping, a lynching. I had never experienced such tension and near-paralyzing fear.

The horror of it all was magnified when the FBI found the decomposed bodies of Mickey, James and Andrew. I don't remember what I was doing when the news arrived. It doesn't really matter. What I do remember is the excruciating pain it caused in my stomach. The pain, which remained for several days and nights, plagued my mind until it was impossible for me to rest or to forget what had been done to those three innocent men.

Wrapped in ice and plastic bags to protect them from the intense heat, the three bodies were taken to the University of Mississippi Medical Center in Jackson. Mickey and Andrew had been shot through the head once each with a .38 caliber bullet. James Chaney had been shot three times and, according to one of the examining pathologists, brutally beaten.

"In my twenty-five years as a pathologist, I have never witnessed bones so severely shattered," said Dr. David Spain of New York after examining Chaney's body at his mother's request.

The bodies were found beneath an earthen dam on a farm three miles from Philadelphia. The farm belonged to a white trucker, Olen Burrage, who claimed that he did not know how the bodies had gotten beneath the dam. Herman Tucker, who had been paid $1,430 by Mr. Burrage to build the dam over the site early in the summer, pleaded ignorance.

"I don't know nothing about it," he said, "don't care nothing about it and don't want to discuss it."

Rita Schwerner, who was working for CORE in Washington when the bodies were found, uttered a terse comment when newsmen inquired about her feelings: "Three good men were killed—three good men who could have done a great deal for their country."

When asked if she thought something positive might come from the triple assassination, Mrs. Schwerner gave the only answer any of us could: "That is up to the people of the United States."

BASIC TRAINING

Sally Belfrage

Belfrage spent the summer in Greenwood, one of the few large towns in the northwest portion of the Mississippi Delta. In charge of that part of the state for COFO was Stokely Carmichael who would subsequently become the head of SNCC and lead it in the direction of Black Power. So Belfrage's account is significant as a portrait, by a sympathetic white, of Carmichael before he concluded that blacks could not effectively cooperate with whites.

In the excerpts reprinted here Belfrage, like Cleveland Sellers, described the detailed "rules and regulations" volunteers and staff had to follow. She also reflected upon a question that white volunteers could not avoid: Why had they come to Mississippi? This question was raised first during the training in Ohio by the staff there. Then the press asked: Why would a young, affluent college student risk life and limb to live and work in Mississippi? Next black field-workers asked. When they did, Belfrage realized, it was as much out of resentment as curiosity. And, finally, the volunteers asked the question of themselves: Were they simply trying to do something to help? Were they looking for adventure? Was it guilt—guilt over their own privileges and advantages? As with the question Moses raised about his own responsibility for the safety of the volunteers, the question did not have a simple or straightforward answer. And, like the question of responsibility, it would not go away. In asking it so candidly, Belfrage provided the outlines of an explanation for the split soon to develop within the Civil Rights movement over the issue of Black Power.

. . . The Project Director for the Second District was Stokely Carmichael. A West Indian by birth—as are two other top SNCC staff members, Ivanhoe Donaldson and Courtland Cox—Stokely, an articulate graduate of the Bronx High School of Science and Howard University, was twenty-two, tall, lithe, with a black Indian's face capable of an evil white grin. He flashed it often at the volunteers assembled in the library that night for their first meeting together. They spread around, thirty of them, on benches, boxes, and floor, or arranged themselves on window sills to catch the "breeze," while Stokely sat on a table top swinging his legs and trying to master

Source: Sally Belfrage, "Basic Training" from *Freedom Summer.* (first published in 1965 by The Viking Press, Inc. for University Press of Virginia printing 1990). Copyright © 1965 by Sally Belfrage. Reprinted by permission of the Irene Skolnick Literary Agency.

the names of the new arrivals—an effort he soon abandoned, calling everybody "Sweets."

He had just returned from Philadelphia, where a lot of the leadership had been summoned after the disappearance. "All the whites are out on the corners with their guns," he reported. "I'll bet seventy percent of them know what happened to the boys. But if one of them says anything, he's as good as dead. Sheriff Rainey of Neshoba County got elected on his record as nigger-killer. It's certain about two; some say the number's nearer eight." Stokely's grin, oddly out of key, gave him a reckless quality of immortality in the face of insuperable dangers but the words indicated a mortal's sense of what they were. "The only reason *I* went to Philadelphia was because The Man (the white man, Mr. Charlie) gave us a twenty-four-hour armed guard. After all, I'm my mother's only second child."

He went over our various jobs, the group listening to him as intently as schoolchildren before an exam. They were a handsome, strangely assorted team. Girls in sopping summer dresses and boys with stubbly chins had a general casualness of appearance that was hardly endearing to the white community, balanced by others whose scrubbed, bright-eyed, straight-toothed, indefatigable freshness could survive any possible change in diet, climate, or attempt at self-Bohemianization.

Freedom School teachers, Stokely was saying, should guard against developing the usual teacher-student relationship: there would be a great deal of learning on both sides. The community center people would have the job of finding a community center: the building where we now were had been originally refurbished for that purpose, but the ground floor was needed to house the SNCC national office and space upstairs had to go to Greenwood Project people. The voter registration workers, most of whom had come the week before, were already organized and covering the town to get as many local Negroes as possible down to the courthouse to attempt to register. In a parallel effort they were signing people up in the Freedom Democratic Party. The whites would be working only in town: they were too easily visible on the plantations, whose "owners have a legal right to shoot you if they catch you trespassing." It had been clear on the trip to Greenwood that there was no access to most sharecroppers' houses without trespassing, as they were placed at some distance from the road, with a long flat view.

The plantations would be covered by less conspicuous Negro workers. "SNCC policy is to work the areas where there is violence. Never get scared by violence"—because if such pressures worked, they could be applied everywhere, and the movement would be lost. "Any time they shoot one of us, ten of us go back next time. Then if they shoot ten, we take a hundred."

The unreality of this sort of talk was diluted by the expectations we had developed in Ohio, but it was still disconcerting to be casually told, not that there would be violence, but that we shouldn't fear it. The silence in the room was covered only by the whir of the fan. I tried to look around at the books on the shelves, wondering how to begin organizing them. Stokely went on methodically to list the "taboos."

The first item was religion. "I know many of you aren't religious, but you've got to understand what it means to the people here. Don't go getting into arguments about it with them; you'll only lose them. None of them has ever heard of atheism. The church is the only place that the Negroes can call their own. They would rather have a church than a house, or a Cadillac for the minister than shoes for their own children. We are doing the Lord's work. Don't forget that. The movement developed largely out of the churches, and if God can start a movement, hooray for God." We were to attend Sunday services, an effective way of meeting and influencing people; there would be an opportunity to speak and make announcements. Different churches would be assigned each week.

Then the matter of clothes. Local people were unaccustomed to girls in pants, especially male pants. No male pants.

Drinking. Mississippi is a dry state, which means there is a bootlegger per corner. The police get paid off, of course: the usual rate is a hundred dollars a month and a free bottle each, and there are even laws within laws specifying when "liquor stores," illegal in the first place, may not be open at all. Alcohol is taxed by the state authorities who prohibit it. ("It may be against God's law to drink it," one legislator has said, "but it ain't against God's law to tax it") However, on the basis of theory, if not practice, the authorities would be looking to pick up civil rights workers on drinking charges. If arrested for drunken driving, you can be held for eight hours before being given access to a lawyer. "Anything can happen in eight hours. . . ." Stokely paused, giving us time to imagine what could. "The project is not going to take any responsibility for this, no bail, nothing, across the board. If you're arrested for being drunk, you're on your own. But besides that, if the community sees you drunk in the streets they'll want nothing to do with you." No drinking.

Interracial dating. "There is always the problem of the male going in and taking the female of the other race." Negro women were the historical victims of white men on a spree, and the community had understandable feelings on the subject. "As far as white girls with Negro boys—of course none of that on the other side of town. I don't know what our people's attitude will be. We'll have to wait and see."

No profanity. Besides offending the community, it is a Mississippi crime.

We were warned about speaking on the phone: local vigilantes were in on all the conversations. Soon COFO would be installing two-way radio systems throughout the state; though these were no more private, they might save lives, particularly on the road. When the national SNCC office moved in downstairs, two WATS lines would be installed, one national, one state. (The Wide Area Telephone Service enables a subscriber to make unlimited calls anywhere in the specified area for a large flat rate.) Codes had been established for different towns and counties in the state to avoid pin-pointing those conversing, and others for use in cases of immediate danger.

Finally, again, *never leave a jail at night.* Lawrence Guyot, a SNCC field secretary, was quoted as having told a policeman about to release him: "If you don't rearrest me, I'm going to punch you in the mouth." Jail is safer than the mob.

Stokely checked out those with cars, assigning passengers. "Night begins at five," he said, which meant the period of utmost danger began then, when whites went home from work. (*Travel at night should be avoided unless absolutely necessary.*) The volunteers planned where to meet each other next morning and left. Some would be sleeping in the library as guards. Carol Kornfield, a tiny pretty girl with glasses on her nose and a pigtail to her waist, retired to "the little office"—a three-desk affair with our files, records, and phones—to type up the day's voter registration results and answer the crank calls, which came in by the dozen every hour. (Stu House, our temporary communications man, had just dealt with one, a man announcing: "There's another nigger dead tonight." "Oh, yes," Stu said neutrally. "Yeah, one committed suicide by jumpin' into the Yazoo River tonight." "Is that right?" said Stu; "well, it couldn't have been one of ours, or he'd have walked on the water." Slam.) Dick Frey, who had worked in Greenwood for a year, stalked around taking care of everything. An undernourished student from Pennsylvania, he seemed to subsist entirely on nervous dedication, as he seldom visibly ate or slept. Two or three others found typewriters on which to reassure their parents, sleeping bags unrolled on the floor, and the library was as empty as it would ever be. . . .

Lucius, Samuel, the Amoses, and Mary Lane were free already in the important sense—"freed even from the need to hate," as Vincent Harding had put it in Ohio. They disarmed the enemy with their gift of sight beyond surfaces. But "the enemy" was not a category; their love was color-blind and reserved for what was important. Mrs. Hamer was free. She represented a challenge that few could understand: how it was possible to arrive at a place past suffering, to a concern for her torturers as deep as that for her friends. Such people were rare. All of them began by refusing to hate or despise themselves.

"It has never been proven that Negroes are not inferior to whites," said a Negro doctor. "There isn't a colored man in Mississippi I'd vote for over Governor Johnson."

"Wasn't it a Negro," Lorna Smith asked him, "who developed blood plasma in the Second World War?"

"He just developed it," the doctor said. "White men started it." The doctor refused to sign a freedom registration form.

Another man who was well educated in Mississippi terms—a graduate of a local Negro college—signed the form, though later admitted he believed it hopeless. "After all," he said, "didn't Noah curse Ham—'a servant of servants shall he be unto his brethren'—and wasn't Ham the father of the Negro race?"

A third man who had lived half his life away from the atmosphere that produced these attitudes had learned theoretically that black and white were only colors, and had returned to his native Delta to try to make equality work, for himself as much as for others. His intelligence was warped and frustrated from lack of training, lack of self-respect; a semi-literate Bohemian, he was constantly forced, through confrontations with white volunteers, to see the inadequacy of his weapons to fight or tools to build as well as they. It drove him to blind spells of arbitrariness, silence, aggression; one moment he took off on a flight of meaningless pomposity, the next he was unable to function at all.

Similar reactions were displayed by others in the movement who resented the hundreds of smart, sharp, articulate white students coming down and taking over. Not only were they taking over, they were doing pretty well—they led at meetings, knew something about organization, set up schools and political programs, and in discussion were often *right*. Some of the local SNCC workers faded into the background, away from this onslaught of insensitive Northern energy, becoming sullen from guilt to the extent they felt unjustified in their sullenness. Before the summer they had been a small tight group, bonded together in trust and friendship and in deep understanding of their cause, since they *were* their cause. Now the nation's press was hailing the bravery of the young white army gone to save the Negroes of Mississippi, failing at every point to credit the grass roots. This was aggravated by some volunteers convinced that they personally were working out a set of historic principles, of which they felt they had a special view. "The people who come here and think you can do it like in the thirties"—someone described them—"they're hallucinated. You could write O'Neill plays about their efforts."

The movement, despite any white illusions and black resentments was and is an indigenous one, before, during, and after the summer. Black and white had to fight together in the movement, but the fight was as much against its own internal racism as the outer world's. The only difference was that the movement was in the middle of the mess, acting on it immediately, while the rest of America preferred to ignore it.

In describing the then Chairman of SNCC, with whom he was sharing a Mississippi jail cell, Bob Moses wrote in 1961 that "[Charles] McDew . . . has taken on the deep hates and deep loves which America, and the world, reserve for those who dare to stand in a strong sun and cast a sharp shadow." This could as well describe many SNCC Negroes, whose deep hates and loves were often translated into simple whites and blacks. They were automatically suspicious of us, the white volunteers; throughout the summer they put us to the test, and few, if any, could pass. Implicit in all the songs, tears, speeches, work, laughter, was the knowledge secure in both them and us that ultimately we could return to a white refuge. The struggle was their life sentence, implanted in their pigment, and ours for only so long as we cared to identify with them. They resented us, and this was as difficult for some volunteers to assimilate as it was understandable: the volunteers wanted gratitude, and couldn't understand why there was instead a tendency to use them simply as the most accessible objects for Negro anger.

This was manifested most often in exercises of status, subtle condescensions which acted to diminish any self-important, bloated white prides. It humbled, if not humiliated, one to realize that *finally, they will never accept me.* And this raised the question: Why, then am I here? If they're not grateful for my help, if we are supposed to be struggling for brotherhood and can't even find it among ourselves, why am I here?

This was each one's private battle, rarely discussed. To do so would have meant admissions, giving words to certain uncomfortable doubts. Over and over in Ohio they had told us that we were all the victims of the very prejudice we fought. How could this be so? We were forced to examine ourselves meticulously for symptoms of the disease. Yet those who exonerated themselves could see no contradiction in their innocence and their parallel desire for gratitude. Why gratitude? The battle was as much ours as theirs, and to expect thanks was somewhere to feel superior to that battle. But we didn't *have* to come, did we? We could have stayed at home and gone to the beach, or earned the money we so badly needed for next semester at old Northern White. And here we are: We Came. Among all the millions who could have realized their responsibility to this revolution, we alone came. Few Northern Negroes even came. We came. Don't we earn some recognition, if not praise? *I want to be your friend, you black idiot*, was the contradiction evident everywhere.

SNCC is not populated with Toms who would wish to be white. They are not the ones who fill closets with bleaches and straighteners, who lead compromise existences between reality and illusion. They accept their color and are engaged in working out its destiny. To bend to us was to corrupt the purity of their goal. To understand us meant to become like us, and the situation was too tenuous for the risk—though the temptations to be a white's intimate, whatever the principle involved, must sometimes be strong.

Once I heard a white man say to James Baldwin, "I am Mister Charlie. I feel victimized by some of the things you write in your books. I feel personal guilt for your condition. But it's not my fault. What can I do?" Baldwin answered, "That you are guilty and I am bitter is the state of things. It may not be your fault. But it's not *my* fault. It's not enough to feel guilty. Change things."

How does one bear this responsibility? Was it guilt, after all, which lay behind the thousand motivations a thousand volunteers produced for the television cameras? Was that the answer the reporters sought? It was not the one they were ever given. Is that why they kept asking?

"THEIR DREAM IS NOT TO BE NERVOUS"

Lucia Guest

Lucia Guest was one of several white southerners to join the project. "I had travelled in Mississippi before," she wrote, "and I knew the landscape. . . . But this time I was going to Mississippi as 'one of them freedom riders.'" On the bus to Oxford to begin her week of training, she confided in a fellow passenger, "a Mississippi Negro" man, "'I will be everything the white Mississippian dislikes, a white, Southern woman, involved in civil rights activities, and they will not be glad to see me coming." White Mississippians, she knew, would regard her as a traitor to both race and region. Her fellow passenger, echoing Bob Moses about the sentiment of ordinary black people in the state, assured her: "We welcome you."

Guest's account of her summer in Ruleville is valuable on several counts. One is where she published it. *Madamoiselle*, then as now, normally paid little

Source: "Their Dream Is Not to Be Nervous," by Lucia Guest, from *Mademoiselle*, November 1964.

heed to politics or social issues. Instead it ran stories on exercise, diet, clothes, and dating along with romantic fiction. Its decision to run a story about the Mississippi Freedom Project demonstrates how successful Moses and his cohorts were in attracting national attention. Her account also provides detail about how Freedom Schools worked and includes several fascinating and moving examples of student writing. Guest also exemplifies the perseverance and the courage volunteers brought to the project.

Describe Mississippi. The task seems to be an adult refinement, a sort of parody for today, of the school room challenge: *Spell Mississippi.* To understand Mississippi one must see it for oneself. Yet the better one knows its compartmentalized elements, the harder it is to convey them to others. Perhaps Bob Moses, the overalled 28-year-old director and guiding spirit of the Mississippi Summer Project, sums it up best when he says: "Mississippi is unreal when you are not there, and the rest of the country is unreal when you are."

I am myself a Southerner, white, born in North Carolina, schooled in Florida and Virginia, now taking courses at U. of N. C. Last summer, to the disbelief of my Southern associates, I decided to join 900 so-called "Northern beatniks" (more accurately, civil rights volunteers, most of them students from the North), who went to Mississippi as part of the Summer Project, sponsored by the Council of Federated Organizations. (COFO is made up predominantly of workers from the Student Non-Violent Coordinating Committee, but also includes CORE, NAACP, and the National Council of Churches.) Northern or Southern, most of us were, it was true, strangers to Mississippi, both to the sunbaked Negro sharecropper, whose life we hoped to affect through freedom schools, voter registration and community-center activities, and the die-hard white Southerner whose literature pro-claimed in bitter rationalization: "The Negro is physically, mentally, morally, racially, and eternally the white man's inferior." . . .

At our orientation session, at Western College for Women in Oxford, Ohio, we had one week to prepare both for the specific jobs we were to do, and the dangers we might face in doing them. Removed from the scene of our work, it was the element of danger that stood out during training. Bruce Hansen, chairman of orientation, warned us: "Everyone needs to face up to the risk of being killed, beaten, or imprisoned." His words became a reality with the announcement that three civil rights workers were missing.

The news lent a grim intensity to our classes with professional SNCC workers in which we learned the rudiments of nonviolent techniques— one elementary rule: wearing thick blue-jean jackets to help take the punch out of a beating. Through group "role playing" sessions, both men and women were taught such things as how to go into a crouch position if attacked by an angry mob, and how to think on their feet, to be able to take whatever happened to them without abandoning the policy of non-violence, which delivers its impact in an emotional, intellectual, and spiritual way. We learned by manners and ways of speaking, to appeal to the mind and conscience of our opponent. Yet no one at Oxford was in a position to lay down detailed rules; sensitivity in relations with people constituted our only true source of correct behavior. And each move we made would be a challenge to our creative faculties.

This was also true—as the summer progressed, even more so—in our day-to-day work in the Mississippi Negro communities. My particular job was teaching in a freedom school, 41 of which were set up throughout the state, staffed with more than 175 teachers (some 50 of whom were professional). According to Staughton Lynd, 34, assistant professor at Yale and co-ordinator of the summer schools, their purpose was: "To give the students (Mississippi Negroes) an integrated experience, hopefully to impart some academic content, but more importantly to further their interest in such things as politics, the student movement, their particular situation in the world around them."

. . . To help prepare us for Mississippi, COFO provided us with a reading list that included such works as: *Souls of Black Folk*, by W. E. B. DuBois, *Mind of the South*, by W. J. Cash. *The Other America*, by Michael Harrington. We were also given fact sheets on Mississippi, suggested lesson plans, tentative schedules for classes—all largely speculative, for we did not know what kind of reception we would get once we reached Mississippi. However, as we left we were reassured that we might be the better teachers for our inexperience because we would not be dependent on the basic methods and equipment used in most schools. To accomplish our goals we would have only our own resources to draw on.

I had traveled in Mississippi before, and I knew the landscape. Newly plowed land with cotton plants a foot high, stretching out on one side of the highway, cotton trailers and cotton gins in the distance . . . a cluster of soybean tanks. I had even been in Yazoo County and seen the mysterious kudzu vine that covers the trees like hot wax making strange formations on a candle.

But this time I was going to Mississippi as "one of them freedom riders." I had expressed my apprehension to a Mississippi Negro whom I met on a bus en route to Oxford. "I am going on the Mississippi Summer Project." I told him. "I will be everything the white Mississippian dislikes—a white, Southern woman, involved in civil rights activities, and they will not be glad to see me coming."

My fellow passenger, a day worker in the cotton field, in the Delta, smiled and said, "We welcome you." He then went on to tell me about the difficulty of being a Negro in Mississippi, the problems caused by drought—no food, no cotton to chop—the danger of being fired from jobs (chopping cotton for ten hours for three dollars in the burning sun of the Delta) for getting involved in the civil rights movement.

"Why don't you just move away from Mississippi?" I asked, momentarily forgetting my purpose.

He replied slowly and thoughtfully, "When a man leaves his home, where is he? He is nowhere. When Mississippi gets straightened out, it'll be a good place to live."

A week later, packed with many facts, many ideas, many hopes, and apprehensions, we sang as we rode a chartered bus down into the Delta (from Oxford). I was with a group going to Drew, Shaw, and Ruleville. Voter-registration people—the infantry of the summer project—were already there. We sang spirited, jubilant freedom songs—"We Must Be Free," "Keep Your Eyes on the Prize,"—as a release for our rising emotions; when, at one stop, we were not served at a restaurant, we kept on singing, although our stomachs were empty. We left our chartered bus at Memphis and rode a public bus into Ruleville, where we were deposited at the edge of the highway.

Ruleville, population 2,400, is a cotton-producing plantation town in the heart of the Delta, located in the northern half of Sunflower County. As we debarked, curious Negro citizens brought us water in canning jars, newsmen greeted us with "Why did you come?" Among those we recognized from our training session was Mrs. Fannie Lou Hamer (Freedom Democratic Party candidate for Congress, running against Jamey Whitten, 1964). A few minutes after we arrived a police truck, with a fawn-colored German shepherd dog crouching in the back, drove by. It was followed by the county sheriff in a black Ford with a tall aerial. This was Mississippi—all of its elements.

COFO had arranged for groups of two and three of us to stay with Negro families who risked their lives by keeping us. But, as Mrs. Bates, our landlady said, "I believe everybody should do his part."

Mrs. Bates, a Negro widow, had one of the largest houses in the Ruleville Negro community, a white clapboard, three-room house (one room was closed off) with running water. Kirsty Powell—an Australian citizen and teacher, Lynn Hulse—a '64 graduate of the University of Washington, and I paid Mrs. Bates a small amount of money for room and board. She was glad to have the money, which meant food for her, and glad to have us as company. Her husband, a cotton picker, had died three months earlier, and lonely impoverished months stretched ahead of her. Like many others in Ruleville, she had one shoulder higher than the other—caused by carrying the long, heavy cotton sack since she had been old enough to work, at the age of eight.

We had a steady diet of flour biscuits, black-eyed peas, corn bread, ham hocks, pork, and grits—most of it cooked with flour to make it go further. For bathing we used a two-foot galvanized tub placed in the kitchen. To fill it we carried water from the faucet in a smaller bucket, enough to make about two inches of water. In the first weeks we bathed before dark. We did not want to have to empty the water off the back porch because any hostile segregationist, standing in the truck patch (vegetable garden) outside, need not have been an expert marksman to shoot us. For the same reason we always drew the shades at night.

During the first weeks we were especially nervous because everything was quite new; the very fact that we had to take security measures stimulated our fear, the three civil rights workers were still missing, and a week before we arrived, the Williams Chapel had been fire-bombed (though only slightly damaged).

Nights were dark, and, we felt, dangerous for us as well as for Mrs. Bates. Before the sun went down we sat on the porch in old wooden rockers, legs apart because of the heat, swatting mosquitoes and talking. On Wednesdays and Fridays we did go out at night to attend mass meetings held by the Ruleville Citizens Committee, in Williams Chapel, a four-minute walk away. These meetings promoted voter registration, and attracted such guest speakers as John Lewis, chairman of SNCC, entertainers like the Eastgate folk singers, and four Congressmen who came one evening to speak about their participation in the passing of the Civil Rights Bill.

On our first night in Ruleville, children rode past on their bicycles and walked by in groups to see us. Neighbors came over to chat. They were curious about us, for the Summer Project culminated two years of efforts by SNCC to organize a challenge to the town's overburdening white supremacy. Later in the summer, white families sped up and down the gravel road in front of our house, faces pressed against the windows of their air-conditioned cars.

For most of the young people in Ruleville the arrival of the volunteers was a wonderful and exciting time. Our meeting place was a community center, for which COFO had rented two rooms of a four-room house. The other rooms were occupied by two women, who sometimes gave us coffee as we set about our morning's work.

The community center, as we found it, had no bookshelves, so—as a start—we tore down the door of the outhouse and made some. There was no table, so we unhinged another door and nailed four wooden legs on it. To make a blackboard, we took the headboard of a baby's crib (which we found in the attic of the house), sprayed it with green paint, and used the plaited yarn of a doll's hair for an eraser. One of our first jobs was to make a library from 5,000 books (donated by Northern college students) which COFO had sent to selected communities. Our books included everything from *The Three Bears* to a marriage manual. The result of our sorting and arranging, done with the help of the people of Ruleville, was a library more complete than that of the local Negro high school.

The first morning, our activity attracted many children. They dug into the supplies that lay in satchels on the ground, along with carefully organized heaps of books. Several girls and boys painted bricks—green, purple, blue, yellow. Others romped on the mattresses we had previously moved out of the newly created Ruleville library. A little boy sat on the steps tracing a lion out of a picture book with green Magic Marker. Inside the "history and science" room, I found five green lions, all "by Walter Hicks," thumbtacked on the wall.

Presently, a gusty wind blew across the yard, and before the 30 volunteers (including teachers, researchers, voter-registration people, community-center people) and the Ruleville youths could agree upon a method of protecting the books, rain fell. The children screamed and howled gleefully. The rain very nearly ruined the books, yet it provided entertainment for the children who are not allowed to run through the hose—because of the cost of water.

Children in Ruleville do not have a summer vacation. They either go to school or pick cotton. In March they get out of school in order to pull the weeds that grow between the cotton rows (commonly called "chopping cotton"). They go to school for the months of July and August. But in September they are out picking cotton again, resuming school in October. During the summer months, the heat makes it unbearable for them to stay in school past one o'clock. Freedom school began for them at two o'clock, and we were surprised to find that it attracted an average of 70 children a day.

In the morning, which began officially at eight, the six of us who were teachers took turns instructing a group of 20 Negro women—and one man—in the basic elements of Negro history. In the afternoons when the children came, we divided into smaller classes. We compiled material from books, magazine articles, and outlines that COFO had given us, on such subjects as Negro history and the rights of citizens. One reference source, which we rewrote to suit the local reading level, was an article from *Ebony* listing the ten most dramatic events in Negro history. These were: 1. First Negroes land at Jamestown; 2. Boston

Massacre; 3. Nat Turner Revolt: 1831: 4. Civil War (my fifth, sixth, and seventh graders had never heard about the Civil War!); 5. Emancipation Proclamation; 6. First Negro in Congress; 7. Atlanta Compromise; 8. 1954 Supreme Court Decision; 9. Montgomery Boycott; 10. Little Rock.

One of our problems was that the people of Ruleville had no cultural frame of reference. We found it difficult ourselves to know what was going on outside of Ruleville. The only papers we could get were the *Delta Democrat-Times*, and the Memphis *Press-Scimitar.*

For this reason, the most interesting and successful of my classes involved "role-play," and the use of maps, pictures, and motion. I would pretend I was the face of a world map. Using my hands, I would point to my head and ask my class of 10-year-olds what part of the world it was: they would respond: the North Pole. Similarly, my toes were Antarctica, the Eastern and Western hemispheres were on either side of me, et cetera. In order to demonstrate the four kinds of government, the students would "role-play." A boy representing municipal government lay flat on the ground; county government sat; state government knelt; Federal government stood straight and tall. This conveyed an idea of the relationship of size, power, and responsibility between the four government structures.

As they re-enacted scenes from Negro history, the students absorbed the drama and impact of events; "role playing" created an interest in finding out the facts. In one scene we acted out slaves coming to America: one student was the captain of a ship, four students were white deckhands, and the balance of the class sat crowded together pretending they were chained down, singing freedom songs—"Before I'll be a slave, I'll be buried in my grave;"—as the deckhands pretended to hit them. Then I would tell them, in outline, about the slave trade in America.

Each time I mentioned a new word, like Egypt or the Taj Mahal, I wrote it down on the blackboard, which I took with me to the outdoor classes. Gradually, students began to ask questions such as: "Why did they bury Egyptians in pyramids?" "Was it right that a man at a gasoline station told me not to drink out of his water fountain?"

One method the teachers found particularly effective in putting over a subject was to let the students express the sense of a book they had read—either by drawing a picture of it or by copying at random those sentences that would best express its theme.

One afternoon while I was getting my ten-year-olds to do this with the story of the Montgomery Bus Boycott, three young white men came up to where we were sitting on the steps of an unpainted church.

They were members of ATAC (Association for Tenth Amendment Conservatives), a local group which was formed to try to talk us out of what we were doing. They were clean and well scrubbed in appearance and wore freshly pressed suits, and were extremely polite. Next to them I felt unkempt—a state hard to avoid without hot water, bathtubs, places to go to get a haircut. And I realized they probably judge the Negroes the same way they would judge me, without realizing that untidiness can be a result of poverty rather than indifference.

"Have you had good attendance?" a spokesman for the group wanted to know.

I replied that the class had grown from four to twelve in a week.

Rather than elaborate further on the successes of my class to the three intruders, I asked Bruce, one of my students, to read what he had copied out of a comic book about Martin Luther King and the Montgomery Bus Boycott. He had taken phrases from different pages and arranged them in this order:

MARTIN LUTHER KING by Bruce

Rosa Parks

now take rosa parks. she really had courage, sat there in the bus that night and just quietly said no when the bus driver told her to give her seat to a white man, for the last time . . . are you getting up . . . or aren't you. if a man can see his home bombed and not fight back—except with love then there is hope for all of us.

They could not say much more after that and so they turned on their heels and left. Class continued.

Students began on their own initiative to solicit other young people to come to Freedom School. They enjoyed the idea of being an active part of something, even though they sometimes got such responses as: "The freedom school will get you in trouble," or "The boss man will run me off the place."

Unfortunately, school supplies were limited because of their cost. I had brought with me pencils, legal pads, poster paints, scissors, stencils. But for my typing class in the afternoons, I had to collect typewriters from my fellow volunteers every morning. I placed the typewriters along the edge of the porch. The students sat with their legs squashed against the wooden base of the porch. After a rain, mosquitoes gathered in the gulley at their feet, and flew up in droves. All through the class, the students typed and swatted, typed and swatted with admirable endurance.

Many of the adults who had chopped and picked cotton much of their lives were unused to the feel of a pencil in their hands. When they tried to write, letters such as C or O, would come out jagged instead of smooth and round. One almost had the feeling they were carving the letters out of wood. "Treat us like children," they told me, "cause we very slow." They became nervous under pressure. This is one of the reasons they dread the ordeal of registering to vote; it means confronting "the red-faced law officer" whom they see as "plenty mad."

Only one adult man attended any of our classes. To determine his reading and writing abilities, I asked him to write a theme about his early days in Ruleville. He hesitated, not knowing what "theme" meant, and so I suggested instead that he write a letter. "My friend, My dear friend," he wrote. "I was born in Copiah County. I have haid sum good days and haid sum bad days." As the summer progressed I felt a profundity in his statement. I came to have a deeper understanding of the intimidation the people in Ruleville have undergone.

Some of them, particularly those Negroes contacted by the voter-registration volunteers, had become deadened or lifeless by their fear. But most of the younger people were bursting with vitality and imbued with determination, illustrated by one of the popular freedom songs: "I ain't gonna let nobody turn me round, turn me round, turn me round."

One little girl was very excited when a correspondence began (arranged by the Australian, Kirsty Powell) between herself and an Australian girl. She wrote:

> Dear Margaret,
> How are you today fine I hope. Kirsty told me you haven't never seen a Negro. Well we are different from you all. Some of our faces are brown and some are almost black. And we have to go to the field and chop and pick cotton. Can you just think how cotton look it is a tall stalk with a brown stick with green leaves on it and when it bloom it look like a pink flower then it become a cotton bowl it is light green and have a little sharp end on it and inside it is a heavy lomp of cotton. And then it open up to be big and fluffy white cotton and I going to send you one of my pictures about August 29, 1964. And will you send me one of yours. Oh, I forgot to tell you we do not have Freedom in Mississippi but the white folks do. Most of them is rich. We don't have jobs and our mother and father hardly can't go register and vote who they want to be president or government. I am 11 years old and don't forget to send me your picture. I will send you mind I will send you a picture of cotton.
>
> Yours truly Bettie

During one of the morning classes, Mrs. Fannie Lou Hamer told us that 30 boxes of clothing, sent from the North, had arrived. Since 1962, clothes had been sent down (not with any dependable regularity) from the North, as a result of movement activities. The clothes were a bribe of sorts, for only those families who had been down to Indianola, the county seat, to register to vote would be eligible for them. This seemed cruel, yet those who participated in voter registration were more likely to need the clothes; they often lost their jobs—once they got involved in the movement. Mrs. Hamer told the women: "It's time for everybody to show that he wants to do something for himself. And this is the way, through the power of the ballot, to change the system so we don't work nine to ten hours a day."

. . . in Ruleville, toward the end of summer, the dominant mood was one of pessimism. The cotton crop would be nonexistent this year; what tasks there were could be done by weed killers and cotton-picking machines. (Mississippi is mechanizing as fast as it can.) There was talk—never acted upon—from one young SNCC worker that if the Negroes abandoned nonviolence and fought back physically they might then feel like men; even if they were defeated, they would have made a stand and would go down in history.

. . . During the entire summer we had not even made dent in the white community of Ruleville. The two communities were still two separate and distinct entities. There was not one newly registered voter in Sunflower County when I left at the end of August, despite all the efforts during the summer of the voter-registration volunteers.

But, through the regenerative power of hard work, we had gained new strength and the mood of concern we had brought with us in the beginning had been shaped into a mood of commitment and drive.

. . . As for our part of the project, the freedom schools will continue in Ruleville two nights a week, evenings being the only time available when adults and young people are not picking cotton or are in school.

Although we freedom school teachers were not directly involved in the over-all political problems in Mississippi, as were the voter-registration workers, we were able, through compositions written by the women in the morning, to feel the weight of the system on the Negroes and their hope for change. Here is one of the compositions:

I HAVE A DREAM

I have a dream that one day the people in the State of Mississippi
Will Make a great change, that Negro people Will be treated like
human, Not by the Color of their Skin. One day We sit down together
and talk things Over and Not be Nervous.

"MEDICAL MISSION TO MISSISSIPPI"

V. McKinley Wiles

V. McKinley Wiles was an African American surgeon who, with his wife, volunteered to spend several weeks in Mississippi as part of the Medical Committee for Human Rights. The MCHR, formed at the urgent request of COFO, was to provide emergency care and medical advice to volunteers and COFO field-workers, in the first instance, and to assess the long-term medical needs of black Mississippians in the second. As with the other volunteers, Wiles and his wife had to adhere to a strict set of guidelines.

They no sooner arrived in Mississippi than Wiles found himself involved in the autopsy of Michael (Mickey) Schwerner, whose body, along with those of James Chaney and Andrew Goodwin, had just been discovered. This was the second autopsy, he pointed out. It was needed, not because there was any medical mystery to be solved, but because the white doctors at the University of Mississippi Medical Center refused to give *murder* as the cause of death. Surely, these physicians thought, the whole Mississippi Project was a Communist plot. Wiles, an experienced surgeon, described himself as "quite shaken and stunned" by this "evasion" of the plain truth.

Much else happened in the weeks he and his wife spent in the state to leave them both "stunned." It also left them determined.

. . . The Medical Committee for Human Rights was formed at the urgent request from the Council of Federated Organizations in June, 1964, to recruit physicians, nurses, dentists and other health workers who believe in the aims of the civil rights Movement and wish to take an active supporting role. These doctors and nurses were all volunteers, serving without remuneration, many of them paying their own transportation and serving one to three weeks in Mississippi. My wife, who is a nurse-educator, and I applied so that to us this important struggle would not be "a thing apart" but a real part of our lives. This was a serious decision and I requested the prayers of my church for the success of our tour.

I was assigned to lead a group of twelve from Newark airport to Jackson, Mississippi. We were briefed at MCHR headquarters on security. Instructions were to report by phone, back to New York headquarters upon arrival in Jackson, where we were to be met by

Source: "Medical Mission to Mississippi," by V. McKinley Wiles, *Freedomways*, Spring 1965, pp. 314–317.

representatives of the Jackson office. Accommodations had been made for us at the Sun'n Sand Motel which had complied with the civil rights law. Our baggage was sent to our room, but before we could unpack or see the room, I rushed off to accompany Dr. Aaron Wells to the University of Mississippi Medical Center where he participated in the second autopsy of Michael Schwerner, one of the civil rights workers who was so brutally murdered.

Frankly I was quite shaken and stunned by the evasion of medical scientists to admit that the cause of death was *murder*. Also from those to whom I spoke, it was always that the "Communists" were behind a "plot" to discredit and smear the *fair name of Mississippi*. This line of "reasoning" exposes a most sensitive area of attack to civil rights public relations experts. Since the Second World War we have seen how critical world opinion has generated Federal action because of embarrassment over the race question. For this reason everything and every act of this vicious system of disfranchisement should be fed to the national and international mirror for reflection.

On return to the motel, a crowd of young white toughs were milling around the entrance and as we approached, shouted quite clearly, "Here they come! There will be some nigger blood spilled tonight," looking squarely and hatefully at us. It was unsafe to stay there so we were put up at the home of a Negro dentist overnight. MCHR had set up four area headquarters in Mississippi; at Clarksdale, Greenwood, Jackson and Hattiesburg. I was assigned to the Hattiesburg office with two dedicated nurses, one white, (Mrs. Leona Nash, a teacher in Williston, N.Y.) and my wife. From Hattiesburg we visited and contacted Laurel, Biloxi, Gulfport, and Moss Point on the Gulf.

We were assigned a leased air-conditioned car with Mississippi license to lessen attention. Then we were rehearsed on strict security precautions as follows:

1. Obey all Mississippi traffic laws, driving at least 5 miles slower than the regulation speed to avoid encounters.
2. Fill gas tank before setting out. Never stop on highways.
3. Get detailed directions how to reach your destination.
4. Use your air-conditioner. Always drive with windows closed and doors locked.
5. Register with the F.B.I.
6. If you get lost, never ask a white man directions and never ask a Negro who is at work for a white man, else he may be pressured to reveal our presence. Find the Negro neighborhood before inquiring.
7. Remove the dome light if driving at night so as not to attract attention should the doors be opened.

8. Call destination before leaving so that any unusual delay in arrival may be investigated.
9. On safe arrival, call back to office of origin to verify same.
10. If arrested call COFO immediately. Assert rights quietly. Plead "not guilty." Ask for postponement for time to get a lawyer. Carry bail money or have it available if arrested.

All these seemed more like wartime, battle-front regulations than the U.S.A., until you know Mississippi!

The function of each team was to identify urgent health problems among civil rights workers, including those beaten or jailed. We were to be consultants in health, sickness and injury to the workers and to solicit, on a professional and humanitarian level, the cooperation of the local physicians in providing care for them. We escorted workers to local doctors. We paid for services and supplies which was re-imbursed by MCHR. It was hoped that our "mere presence" would influence local white doctors to recall the Hippocratic Oath. The local Negro doctors were the backbone of the medical care program, offering assistance wherever requested. Both doctors and nurses gave emergency assistance. Efforts were made to establish relationships with the local health agencies, to assist in enlisting the Negro community to take advantage of their services. Group talks were made at Freedom Schools, on personal health, sanitation, venereal diseases and sex. Among adults, family planning and sex education were discussed. The eagerness for learning was evident at every session.

Surveys were begun regarding the public health programs relating to child care, prenatal and postnatal care, immunization services, and free venereal disease therapy not familiar to the Negro community either because of apathy or negligence of the power structure.

At each center we equipped first aid supplies boxes with vitamins, salt tablets, iron, aspirin, insect repellent, bandages, dressings, laxative, cough mixture, thermometer, alcohol, and peroxide.

After prayer we drove from Jackson to Hattiesburg, a distance of ninety miles. My white nurse crouched in the back seat, anxious not to attract attention. *In all my travels in Africa, never had I known fear; but, in Mississippi it was here in depth.* The emphasis was on the denial of civil rights. We received daily bulletins of beatings, arrests, jailings, and the burning of churches. Two people could be arrested for "unlawful assembly." One woman worker from New York was arrested for vagrancy and jailed until released on bond. The Negro community stayed quietly indoors whenever the police patrol cruised. Many homes of Negroes are bonded to release those arrested. But the spirit of resistance and determination to be free is admirable and worthy of the support of all of us.

HEARINGS BEFORE THE UNITED STATES COMMISSION ON CIVIL RIGHTS, VOLUME I: VOTING

The Mississippi Project succeeded in riveting the national media's attention on the state. In the process it demonstrated that the Civil Rights Act of 1964, however important it would prove, was not sufficient to change conditions in Mississippi. That, as Bob Moses had observed in his speech at Stanford in April of 1964, would require the break-up of the all-white "regular" Democratic Party in the state. And that, in turn, would require taking away the power of local registrars over voting.

Charles Cheney Humpstone, a staff attorney for the commission, testified about the practices in Issaquena County where, between July 1961 and February 1965, all-white applicants became registered voters while all but nine (out of more than 100) African Americans had their applications denied. Further, he documented that, of the 138 successful white applicants, many received coaching. Fifteen of the applications, for example, contained the same word-for-word explanation of section 35 of the state constitution. Fourteen of these fifteen also answered the question on the duties of citizenship in identical words. He concluded:

> White persons not qualified to register, under Mississippi statutory requirements, were also nevertheless permitted to take the registration test and to register. Twelve applicants were permitted to register although their own statements showed that they did not meet the requirement of residence in Mississippi for 2 years prior to the next ensuing election.

What was needed, COFO and other civil rights organizations would argue, was a federal voting rights act under which federal courts could supervise registration.

The hearings held by the U.S. Commission on Civil Rights in Jackson in February 1965 played an important role in gathering support for a voting rights bill. They also provide compelling testimony about the struggles civil rights activists and ordinary citizens encountered in the preceding summer and years. Almost as important as this testimony was that of Mississippi Governor Paul B. Johnson, Jackson Mayor Allen C. Thompson, and Humphreys County Registrar Guthrie Hays Hood. These white voices convinced much of the rest of the country that white Mississippians would never address the problem unless forced by court order.

Source: Hearings before the United States Commision on Civil Rights, Volume I: Voting (hearings held in Jackson, Mississippi, February 16–20, 1965).

STATEMENT OF HON. PAUL B. JOHNSON, GOVERNOR OF THE STATE OF MISSISSIPPI

. . . I am delighted to be here this morning before this Commission, and I have a statement that I would like to read because I would like for this statement to be a part of the record, Dr. Hannah.

My statement is entitled "Mississippi, the State of Law and Order."

The Civil Rights Act of 1964 as passed by the Congress is the law of the land, and Mississippi knows it.

Most Mississippians do not like the new law. They are convinced that its passage was unwise and unnecessary. Some of them will challenge its constitutionality in the courts, as is their right. But resistance will be confined to such accepted legal processes. Law and order will be maintained in Mississippi by Mississippians.

Violence against any person or any group will not—I repeat, will not be tolerated. Criminal acts will be punished with all law violators being dealt with equally.

In stating these policies, I am joined and supported by the statewide association of local law enforcement officials. Other leaders and statewide organizations representing business, professional, industrial, and religious groups have urged our people to make the necessary adjustments to the Civil Rights Act in a calm, intelligent manner, regardless of personal convictions.

I wish to assure all Americans that Mississippi will continue to be the most law-abiding State in the Nation.

The Federal Bureau of Investigation's 1964 report of crime in the United States established Mississippi as the State with the lowest crime rate in the Nation. In the past, at the present time, and in the future the streets, the alleys, the byways, sidewalks, playgrounds, the recreational areas, and schoolyards and corridors, and all other public areas of Mississippi, are completely safe for all persons by day and by night. I believe this to be a record without equal in any other State of the Nation.

The unfavorable and in many instances the false image of Mississippi that has been created by the few in our State who have committed unpardonable criminal acts has been exploited by unfriendly national news media. Most thoughtful persons will concede that Mississippi is facing enough problems and difficulties without having to endure longer the excessive criticism and artificially created characterization to which the State and its citizens have been subjected.

What we need from our fellow Americans is good will, encouragement, understanding, and assistance. Having accepted the will of the Nation's majority, Mississippi now asks those who have criticized our former position and actions to get off of our back and to get on our side.

With your help, I predict that from this turbulent time will be born expanding opportunities for the disadvantaged people, white as well as nonwhite, of our potentially wealthy or rich State, increasing productivity through which we can earn a standard of living closer to the national average, a better balanced and more rapidly growing local economy through which we can shoulder a more proportionate share of the national load, and a full integration of Mississippi into the wealthy, growing, urban industrial society which in the present day is America. . . .

STATEMENT OF HON. ALLEN C. THOMPSON, MAYOR OF THE CITY OF JACKSON, MISS.

Jackson is a city where law and order prevails. Main thing, we have one of the best police departments in the world. It is large, it is powerful, it is trained.

We have received a great deal of criticism—I have 5 minutes. I'm watching the time very carefully, and don't worry.

We were criticized in the press, television, magazines: "What do you mean having such a powerful force? What do you mean?" One large city, the city council criticized us. The next day they had a terrible riot and for weeks they had to work and do everything they could to put it down. What did they do? They added more policemen; they added more riot training; they added more equipment. They attempted to do just what we were trying to do, to protect the rights, the civil rights of our people.

We do not have any harassment on the streets, in the homes; and when there is, we have people here who will testify that I personally said that we would catch them, it doesn't matter whoever it is. And we will, as long as I live, continue to investigate, and we will find the people who have perpetrated these crimes against anybody in this city.

Now, when the civil rights law became effective, we were among the first to let it be known that we were going to obey the law. I do not know whether you know it or not, but I fought this civil rights law probably more than any other mayor in the United States. I went all over the country talking about it. I went to Washington talking about it. Frankly, I think it is a terrible piece of legislation, but Congress passed it, and as long as it is on the books, we are going to obey the law.

Now, the thing that worries me, though—and I want to get this point over—is not so much the civil rights law, but the pressure groups who are going to say the civil rights law does not go far enough. "If you do not do this, if you do not do that," which is beyond the civil rights law, "we are going to march, we are going to demonstrate, we are going to intimidate, we are going to threaten, we are going to bring violence by nonviolence, we are going to tear up your city unless you do everything that we say."

We are going to abide by the civil rights law. Now we have gone through some turbulent times. I have just a few minutes to wind this up. I'm not worried. I know that the rest of the Nation, when they realize and see the facts, are going to know that we are a part of America. In fact, we are going to demand that we be considered as a part of this country. We are going to earn the respect.

But now here is what does worry me—and I mention this for your information as to what has happened, what is happening today and what is going to happen in the next few months. First, one of the hardest things we have ever had to endure was the invasion of the COFOs last summer. Although, of course, there were a few sincere members, the most were here either as troublemakers or as completely innocent or ignorant of the difference between right and wrong, with no ability to bring any good to the community. They were not accepted, or practically completely ignored by the good people of this city.

One of the greatest tributes I can give to our people, white and colored, is the fact that we went through this potential explosive time without any real trouble. It was worse than the suffering that Job had to put up with in the old days. . . .

Finally, I am worried about some of our fine, wonderful, colored people in Jackson who obey the laws of the city, work at jobs every day, are interested in their families and churches—when there was a bombing at one of the professors' houses, I went out there and everybody said, "That's fine." And then all of a sudden something else came along and a pressure was started.

Now listen, they are subject to threats and intimidation by so-called leaders of pressure groups who won't let them put up Christmas trees during Christmas time, who make them boycott, who refuse to let them have $2,500 which I personally raised the other day for a colored youth center, and numerous other things. Now that is what I'm worried about.

But now listen: No matter what is said, the citizens of Jackson, both white and colored, Dr. Hannah and gentlemen and lady of the Commission, are guaranteed equal protection under the law in Jackson, and in Mississippi.

This is a city where it is up to the individual to decide for himself how far he will go. This depends on what use he makes of the splendid educational facilities he has in this city. It depends upon his ability, depends upon his intelligence, his courtesy, his commonsense, and upon the assumption of responsibility to his family, to his fellow man, and to his community.

TESTIMONY OF MRS. JEREMIAH (UNITA ZELMA) BLACKWELL, ISSAQUENA COUNTY, MISS.

MR. TAYLOR: Mrs. Blackwell, will you state your full name and address for the record?

MRS. BLACKWELL: My name is Unita Zelma Blackwell, General Delivery, Mayersville, Miss.

MR. TAYLOR: How long have you lived in Issaquena County?

MRS. BLACKWELL: Three years and over.

MR. TAYLOR: And where did you live before that?

MRS. BLACKWELL: I lived in Helena, Ark.

MR: TAYLOR: Is there currently an effort to get Negroes in Issaquena County to vote?

MRS. BLACKWELL: It is now. It has been since June of 1964.

MR. TAYLOR: Could you tell us a little bit about it and your part in it?

MRS. BLACKWELL: Well, I am now a COFO worker, and we are getting people to go down to the courthouse to register to vote. They are afraid, but they goes now, because, you know, since COFO came in there and explained to the peoples that they had a right to register, to go down to try to register to vote, and people are going out now to, you know—they's afraid to go and get cut off their welfare and get thrown off the farms and everything else, but they're standing up because we are talking to them and explaining everything.

MR. TAYLOR: Do you know of any Negroes who were registered to vote in the county prior to the summer of 1964?

MRS. BLACKWELL: No, because they didn't even want to talk about it. They used to talk about it and they just said "You know the white folks, they don't want us over to the courthouse, and you just can't do that."

MR. TAYLOR: Can you give us an estimate of just how many Negroes attempted to register since the drive began?

MRS. BLACKWELL: About 150 attempts.

MR. TAYLOR: Did you try to keep some records of this?

MRS. BLACKWELL: Well, up until the time now, we're just too busy going from house to house and talking to people. People are just going now every once in a while on their own now.

MR. TAYLOR: Do you know of any Negroes who have passed?

MRS. BLACKWELL: Yes, I do.

MR. TAYLOR: About how many?

MRS. BLACKWELL: Well, about nine or ten.

MR. TAYLOR: Have any of the applicants for registration had better than a sixth grade education?

MRS. BLACKWELL: Yes.

MR. TAYLOR: Have there been any high school or college students?

MRS. BLACKWELL: There has been; teachers.

MR. TAYLOR: Have they passed?

MRS. BLACKWELL: Well, I know of a teacher; she went twice, and then she passed the last time she went. And I know a college student, and he didn't pass, and I know another college student, and she didn't pass. And that's the way it has been.

MR. TAYLOR: How far did you go in school?

MRS. BLACKWELL: I went through the eighth grade.

MR. TAYLOR: Have you attempted to register?

MRS. BLACKWELL: I have. Three times.

MR. TAYLOR: Well, tell us about your first attempt.

MRS. BLACKWELL: Well, the first time I went over, my husband and I—well, the first time, it started the day before then; the COFO workers came in, and we had a mass meeting, and they says, "Well, who would volunteer to go over to the courthouse and try to register to vote." And we had people—to start off, we had three or four go that day and three or four go the next day, and the first day there was a group that went, and we were in the group that went the next day. And my husband and I went in, and she says, "What do you want?" and we said, "We came in to try to register." And she says, "Well, can't all of you—one at a time." And so we just went out.

And she told me to sit down, and I sit down at a little table, and she gave me this slip of paper—because I had never saw one before—and I looked at it and took my time, and I filled it out, and she stood there hanging over the bannister. And then she gave me a book, pointed out a section for me to copy, and I copied it and tried to interpret it like it said. And then the next it says about the citizenship—obligations of a citizen—and I put that down.

And then I asked her when it got down there what oath, general oath, minister's oath, I said "What oath reckon I should take?" She said "I can't help you. You have to do it yourself."

MR. TAYLOR: She gave you a copy—she gave you a section of the Mississippi constitution to interpret?

MRS. BLACKWELL: That's right. The first time I went in was 182.

MR. TAYLOR: Do you have a copy of your application form?

MRS. BLACKWELL: That's right, I do.

MR. TAYLOR: Could you read that section that she gave you to interpret?

MRS. BLACKWELL: (reading):

The power to tax corporations and their property shall never be surrendered or abridged by any contract or grant to which the State or any political subdivision thereof may be a party, except that the legislature may grant exemption from taxation in the encouragement of manufactures and other new enterprises of public utility extending for a period of not exceeding 5 years, the time of such exemptions to commence from date of charter, if to a corporation; and if to an individual enterprise, then from the commencement of work; but when the legislature grants such exemptions for a period of 5 years or less, it shall be done by general laws, which shall distinctly enumerate the classes of manufactures and other new enterprises of public utility entitled to such exemptions, and shall prescribe the mode and manner in which the right to such exemptions shall be determined.

MR. TAYLOR: Thank you. Did you go back to find out whether you had passed the test?

MRS. BLACKWELL: She said come back in 30 days.

MR. TAYLOR: Did you pass?

MRS. BLACKWELL: No, I didn't. And I asked when could I take the test again and she said about 2 weeks.

MR. TAYLOR: Did you go back again a second time?

MRS. BLACKWELL: I did go back.

MR. TAYLOR: Do you know what section of the constitution you were given to interpret the second time?

MRS. BLACKWELL: Yes, I do. 111.

MR. TAYLOR. That is the section dealing with the judicial sale of land. Did you attempt to interpret——

MRS. BLACKWELL: No. I had wrote out affidavits showing that I had had over a 6th grade, you know, schooling, and I gave it to her and explains that— and she says "Well, that's all right; you'll have to do it anyway." And so I just didn't fill it out. I just wrote it and signed my name and came out.

MR. TAYLOR: Did you go back a third time?

MRS. BLACKWELL: I did.

MR. TAYLOR: And what section did you get on the third time?

MRS. BLACKWELL: Ninety-seven.

MR. TAYLOR: Did you pass?

MRS. BLACKWELL: I did. And this time she helped, because of all you know, so much had been going on and everything; all the civil rights and Justice Department, everybody running in. And she was all upset. And I went in and asked for a precinct map to find out what precinct I live in because I was paying my poll tax and one of these days I may pass, but you have to pay, you know, 2 years, and so I went in there and I says "Could you give me a precinct map, Mrs. Vandevender," and she says, "Well, Unita, I just don't have one and we don't know—we don't have anything but land maps, and that's all I can give you," and I said, "Well, since I'm here, I'll take the registration test."

And I filled it out and I had section 97 and I wrote it down and looked it over and I picked some of the words out of, you know, what I had wrote down; put that in there and turned it over. And I misspelled "length" and I said "Oh, my Lord." And so then I filled out the rest of it and when I got through I handed it to her, and I said "Well, I misspelled this, and well, I didn't date the top," and she said "Oh, that's all right, it's all right, it's all right." And then she ran and got the book and, you know, she was just tired of looking at me.

MR. TAYLOR: Did you understand section 97?

MRS. BLACKWELL: Well, I don't know. Because I just picked out, you know, what—half of what was in there. . . .

MR. TAYLOR: Do you think things are changing now in Issaquena County?

MRS. BLACKWELL: Well, I hope so. But, you know—well, the people now are still afraid, and they still, you know—they just don't know what to do, because now they say the checks is going to get cut off. Because there's not no work or nothing in the wintertime, and they slowly but surely they're going down to the courthouse and trying to register to vote.

Of course they're not passing, but they're going.

MR. TAYLOR: Do you intend to vote now that you are registered?

MRS. BLACKWELL: I do intend to vote. . . .

COMMISSIONER HESBURGH: Mrs. Blackwell, do you anticipate having any difficulty because of coming here today and making this testimony?

MRS. BLACKWELL: Well, I don't know, because it has got to the place, you know—well, the other day we was coming out—we had been to Mr. Jackson house, and was talking to him about coming to a parent's meeting, and some white guys came up in a truck and blocked us and got out and told us all kinds of nasty things, "Get out of here and don't come back." This was a Wednesday, and the Sunday before then, and the same truck, they run a lot of school kids out because they was down talking to people, and had a shot gun out and flashing it, you know, and saying "I could have killed you way back yonder in the woods," and all this kind of stuff. And you just get to the place you know it's going to happen but you've just got to stand up and got to do something.

COMMISSIONER HESBURGH. Thank you very much. . . .

TESTIMONY OF MR. AND MRS, CLARENCE HALL, JR., ISSAQUENA COUNTY, MISS.

CHAIRMAN HANNAH: How long were you in the armed services?

MR. HALL: I was in the armed services 5 years 4 months.

CHAIRMAN HANNAH: In the Army?

MR. HALL: In the Army.

CHAIRMAN HANNAH: I gather you were overseas?

MR. HALL: I were overseas 3 years.

CHAIRMAN HANNAH: Where did you serve overseas?

MR. HALL: European theatre of operations.

CHAIRMAN HANNAH: You had no problems in the armed services?

MR. HALL: I did not.

CHAIRMAN HANNAH: Do you have children in school?

MR. HALL: I had one in school, but he is not in school today.

CHAIRMAN HANNAH: Will he be in school tomorrow or next week?

MR. HALL: He will not unless the condition is changed.

CHAIRMAN HANNAH: Why will he not be in school?

MR. HALL: Because our—they taken our—at least the kids—their button to school, which is COFO, they're student nonviolent. And the principal put them on a bus and sent them all home. And now you have to sign for the right for your kids to go to school.

You didn't sign them in school, and I don't think you should have to sign to send them back to school.

Also we sent a committee to talk to the school board, the superintendent of education; and he refused to talk with them. He told them—we told them that we wanted—the parents wanted to meet the board of education and explain to them and get their decision on why the kids had to pull off their button to go back in the school, and other problems which we are having at the school we want to tell them.

And the school board, school board of education, refused to meet the parents. They turned it down: "No, we can't meet you."

CHAIRMAN HANNAH: Is it a son or daughter that you have in school?

MR. HALL: A son.

CHAIRMAN HANNAH: How old is the boy?

MR. HALL: Eight years old.

CHAIRMAN HANNAH: And he was sent home because of some button he was wearing? Is that what I understand you to say?

MR. HALL: He wasn't sent home because of the button he was wearing, but the other people's children in the neighborhood was sent home, and we are trying to get to meeting with the school board to clear up all the problem. And we decided, after they sent one of them home, to take all of them out of the school until we could meet the board and get the board to talk to us personally.

CHAIRMAN HANNAH: Does the school board control all the schools in the two counties?

MR. HALL: It do that.

CHAIRMAN HANNAH: Are there any Negroes on the school board?

MR. HALL: That's one of the points: No Negroes on the school board. We want to get some on the school board.

Chairman HANNAH: How large is the school that your son attends?

MR. HALL: His elementary school, I think it's about 500 or 600 kids there, which is real small; they're crowded; 60 I think would be to one teacher, which I think the minimum is about 25 and the maximum about 30, if I'm not mistaken. But we understand they have from 30 to 40 and sometimes 60 in a room to one teacher. And these are some of the problems we would like to get straightened out.

CHAIRMAN HANNAH: What grade is your son in?

MR. HALL: Third grade.

CHAIRMAN HANNAH: Do you know exactly how many students are in the one room with your son?

MRS. HALL: Thirty-four.

MR. HALL: My wife says 34.

The reason I don't know directly, because I was elected on the PTA at the Letter-Menzer School, and the principal—we met about 3 or 4 time and we discussed some problem about our desegregating the school and about what was happening under the new civil rights bill and how it would affect us. And he told me flat that he wasn't going to have no civil rights lesson in school, and I asked him whether the superintendent of education told him to do it, and he told me no; he just turned a fit and I said from that day on he wasn't going to have any more PTA meeting in the school. We don't have any PTA meeting in the high school or in the elementary school.

When the principal say no, the school board go along with the principal; the superintendent of education tell the principal what to do and he is backed up by the school board.

CHAIRMAN HANNAH: Are there any other questions?

MR. TAYLOR: No further questions.

CHAIRMAN HANNAH: You are excused. Thank you very much. (Witnesses excused.)

TESTIMONY OF MARY THOMAS, HUMPHREYS COUNTY, MISS.

MR. TAYLOR: Mrs. Thomas, would you give your full name, your address, and your occupation?

MRS. THOMAS: My name is Mary Thomas. I live at Belzoni, Miss., 279A, Hadden Street.

MR. TAYLOR: What is your occupation?

MRS. THOMAS: Merchant in a grocery store.

MR. TAYLOR: How much education have you had?

MRS. THOMAS: I finished high school.

MR. TAYLOR: Have you had any contact or dealings with civil rights workers recently?

MRS. THOMAS: Yes, I have.

MR. TAYLOR: Have you ever attempted to register to vote?

MRS. THOMAS: Yes, I have.

MR. TAYLOR: When was that?

MRS. THOMAS: I went down to register to vote about the first of September in 1964.

MR. TAYLOR: Did you go alone at that time?

MRS. THOMAS: No. I went with two ladies and two COFO workers.

MR. TAYLOR: Can you tell us what happened, Mrs. Thomas, when you got to the registrar's office?

MRS. THOMAS: Well, when we got to the registrar's office, we walked in and one of the COFO workers stepped in behind, and the chancery clerk looked up and saw he was in the room and he demanded that he leave the room, and so he did.

And then he asked us what did we want, and I stepped to the desk and told him that I came down to register to vote. And he asked me my name, my address, how old I was, and how long had I lived in Mississippi. And I told him.

MR. TAYLOR: And then what happened?

MRS. THOMAS: Then he said why did we come down; why did we let those boys bring us down. We didn't say anything. He said, "Well, why didn't you come alone?" We still didn't say anything.

So then he opened the desk and got the blank and a card with the 66th amendment of Mississippi, and he told me to come on around the desk and go in there and have a seat.

And then when he had finished with the other lady, she got in, he said, "Well, haven't we all been good to you all?" He said, "We've always given you commodity, and any time you say you wanted money or needed money, we would give it to you." So we didn't say anything.

Then I decided I would read my blank and start filling in my questions. And he sat at the end of the table and steadily picked on the table until we were finished.

MR. TAYLOR: What happened after you finished?

MRS. THOMAS: Well, after we finished we passed our blanks in and he told us that he would have to run our name in the Banner for 2 weeks and then he would let us know if we passed.

And just as we were leaving his office, someone snapped our picture. I don't know just who it was, because it was a number of people standing in the hall.

MR. TAYLOR: Were these people who were standing in the hall wearing uniforms?

MRS. THOMAS: Well, some of them; and some were in plain clothes.

MR. TAYLOR: Did anything happen to you, Mrs. Thomas, when you got home?

MRS. THOMAS: Yes. I guess about 15 minutes after I arrived home from the courthouse, the deputy sheriff came in and told me he had a warrant for my arrest.

MR. TAYLOR: Did he say what he was arresting you for?

MRS. THOMAS: Yes. He said he had a warrant for my arrest for selling beer without a license.

MR. TAYLOR: Did you have a license to sell beer?

MRS. THOMAS: Yes. I had the city license, the State permit, and the Federal stamp. And I live within the city limit, and I had been operating for about 8 years or longer, and I had never bought a county license. So I didn't know about county license, so that's what I was fined for: County license.

MR. TAYLOR: Did the sheriff know that you had been involved with civil rights workers before your arrest?

MRS. THOMAS: Yes, I would say he did.

MR. TAYLOR: How did he know that?

MRS. THOMAS: Well, he came down one night the youngsters were out front. There had been some disturbance outdoors. I don't know what it was because I was inside working. And so somehow or another they got confused and they got right out on the ground there and was singing some freedom songs. And so the police kept passing and they didn't change, they just kept singing. And then later on the sheriff came in and two police. The sheriff came first and then a police with the dog, and another one came in alone.

The sheriff asked me did I sell beer; I told him yes, sir. He said "Well, I could have you put in jail or I could make you pay $250."

And I said, "For what?"

And he said for selling—he said "Just for selling beer."

And I asked him, well, what kind of license, really, that I didn't have. Well, he never did tell me what kind. He just said without a license.

MR. TAYLOR: What happened to you after you were arrested?

MRS. THOMAS: Well, after I was arrested, the deputy carried me on down and he opened the cell door and I stepped in, and he turned the key on the door. He told me "Your bond is $1,000 if you want to get out."

MR. TAYLOR: Did someone raise your bond for you?

MRS. THOMAS: Well, yes. The next day I got out about 2:00—something after 2:00.

MR. TAYLOR: And what happened after you were released from jail?

MRS. THOMAS: Well, after I was released from jail, they held court that following Monday, and I was fined $365.71 and suspended from selling beer for 1 year.

MR. TAYLOR: Have you since gotten your license to sell beer?

MRS. THOMAS: Yes. I got my license Friday.

MR. TAYLOR: This past Friday?

MRS. THOMAS: This past Friday, in February.

MR. TAYLOR: Thank you.

CHAIRMAN HANNAH: Father Hesburgh?

COMMISSIONER HESBURGH: Did you ever get word whether or not you were registered, Mrs. Thomas?

MRS. THOMAS: Well, no, I didn't. Everyone else went down and they didn't pass. So I didn't want to be intimidated any more, so I just assumed I didn't pass, because I didn't want to be seen any more to have anything else to happen.

COMMISSIONER HESBURGH: You didn't have any official word from them, from the registrar, as to whether you passed or failed?

MRS. THOMAS: No.

COMMISSIONER HESBURGH: Just no word whatever?

MRS. THOMAS: No word whatsoever.

COMMISSIONER HESBURGH: Do you intend to go back and try to register again?

MRS. THOMAS: I will, probably, later on.

COMMISSIONER HESBURGH: Did you have anybody defend you when you went in for this so-called trial?

MRS. THOMAS: Yes. It was a COFO lawyer. I don't remember his name.

COMMISSIONER HESBURGH: And you said you were fined $375, was it?

MRS. THOMAS: $365.71.

COMMISSIONER HESBURGH: No one had said anything about this county beer license before?

MRS. THOMAS: Well, no. I had received a card stating that I was late for some license, but I didn't understand it. It didn't say for what license. And in August, my permit and my Federal stamp all was due around that time, and I had sent them off, but they hadn't got back. And so I just thought maybe that was it.

COMMISSIONER HESBURGH: How much does a county beer license cost?

MRS. THOMAS: $15.

COMMISSIONER HESBURGH: One last question: Why do you want to vote, Mrs. Thomas?

MRS. THOMAS: Well, I want to vote to be a citizen. I am a taxpayer. And I want to be a citizen. I just don't feel right paying taxes, can't get any representatives. I have no voice.

COMMISSIONER HESBURGH: You have paid taxes all the time you have been making money?

MRS. THOMAS: Yes, sir; each month.

COMMISSIONER HESBURGH: Are you a widow, Mrs. Thomas?

MRS. THOMAS: Yes, sir.

COMMISSIONER HESBURGH: And you support yourself?

MRS. THOMAS: Yes, sir.

COMMISSIONER HESBURGH: Did you find it difficult paying this $375 fine?

MRS. THOMAS: I could not have paid it myself.

COMMISSIONER HESBURGH: You had to get help to pay it?

MRS. THOMAS: Yes, sir.

COMMISSIONER HESBURGH: Thank you. Mrs. Thomas. . . .

VICE CHAIRMAN PATTERSON: Mrs. Thomas, you say you have lived in Mississippi all your life. But you didn't try to register to vote until 1964; is that right?

MRS. THOMAS: That's right.

VICE CHAIRMAN PATTERSON: What moved you to try to register to vote in 1964?

MRS. THOMAS: Well, I had begun to understand business a little more and I was in business alone and I was straining paying my taxes. And then I wasn't a citizen. I didn't have no voice. So that made me want to go register.

VICE CHAIRMAN PATTERSON: Did anyone encourage you to go and register?

MRS. THOMAS: Well, yes. The COFO workers asked me if I would go down. So I agreed that I would go.

VICE CHAIRMAN PATTERSON: We have heard from a preceding witness that many Negro citizens of Humphreys County are afraid to register. Weren't you afraid?

MRS. THOMAS: Well, I should have been, but I guess I had just reached a stage that it didn't matter.

I was afraid in a way. In a way I wasn't. Because I wanted so much to be able to register and vote. . . .

CHAIRMAN HANNAH: Father Hesburgh.

COMMISSIONER HESBURGH: Mrs. Thomas, who took care of your children when you were put in jail all night?

EXHIBIT NO. 4

WARRANT FOR THE ARREST OF MRS. MARY THOMAS, HUMPHREYS
COUNTY, MISS., DATED SEPT. 4, 1964

General Warrant

STATE OF MISSISSIPPI

COUNTY OF HUMPHREYS

TO ANY LAWFUL OFFICER OF HUMPHREYS COUNTY — GREETING:

WE COMMAND YOU TO TAKE forthwith the body of _Mary Thomas_

and bring _her_ before the undersigned Justice of the Peace of _1_ District to

answer a charge of _Selling Beer Without a License_

Witness my hand, this the _4th_ day of _Sept_ 19 _6_

Justice of the Peace

FACSIMILE OF RETURN ON WARRANT

I have this day executed the within writ by arresting the within named

MARY THOMAS

and placing him in the county jail.
This 4th day of September 1964.

JOHN D. PURVIS, *Sheriff,*
By (S) J. L. HUFFSTICKLER.

MRS. THOMAS: Well, I just left them there. I tried to train them. My mother was there. She lives with me. But she was sick and I left them there. So a girl that helped me sometimes, she, knowing that I was gone, she came in.

COMMISSIONER HESBURGH: Did you have time to make any arrangements before being taken off to jail?

MRS. THOMAS: No. I didn't.

COMMISSIONER HESBURGH: Did the sheriff know you have a family at home?

MRS. THOMAS: Yes.

COMMISSIONER HESBURGH: Thanks.

CHAIRMAN HANNAH: One more question: You think that the reason that you were arrested was because you had tried to register to vote?

MRS. THOMAS: I do.

CHAIRMAN HANNAH: And you were arrested within 15 minutes after you returned from the courthouse?

MRS. THOMAS: That's right.

CHAIRMAN HANNAH: Any further questions?

Thank you very much, Mrs. Thomas. You are excused.

TESTIMONY OF GUTHRIE HAYES HOOD, CIRCUIT CLERK AND REGISTRAR, HUMPHREYS COUNTY, MISS.

MR. TAYLOR: Mr. Hood, would you please state your full name, residence, and occupation?

MR. HOOD: Guthrie Hayes Hood, 156 Central Street, Belzoni, Miss.

MR. TAYLOR: And you are the——

MR. HOOD: I am circuit clerk and the registrar of Humphreys County.

MR. TAYLOR: How long have you served as registrar?

MR. HOOD: Since 1960. . . .

MR. TAYLOR: How many Negroes have applied to register during your term of office? About how many?

MR. HOOD: During my term of office? About 16.

MR. TAYLOR: About 16?

MR. HOOD: Yes, sir.

MR. TAYLOR: How many of these have succeeded in registering, Mr. Hood?

MR. HOOD: None have passed the test.

MR. TAYLOR: Has any Negro made any request for a copy of his application?

MR. HOOD: Only one has made a request for a copy of his application.

MR. TAYLOR: Did you furnish the copy?

MR. HOOD: I told him to bring me a written request and the State law allows me $1.50 for a certified copy, and I would be glad to furnish it to him.

MR. TAYLOR: If he paid $1.50?

MR. HOOD: Yes, sir.

MR. TAYLOR: Were you aware at the time that on various occasions police have photographed Negroes outside the door of your office after they applied to register?

MR. HOOD: No, sir; I could not answer that because I was trying to run my own office.

MR. TAYLOR: You do not know whether——

MR. HOOD: No, no, no. . . .

Commisioner FREEMAN: Mr. Hood, how long have you lived in Mississippi?

MR. HOOD: All my life.

COMMISSIONER FREEMAN: Were you educated in the schools in Mississippi?

MR. HOOD: I was.

COMMISSIONER FREEMAN: How much education do you have?

MR. HOOD: Well, I don't see where that enters into this at all.

COMMISSIONER FREEMAN: Did you complete elementary school?

MR. HOOD: Yes, sir.

COMMISSIONER FREEMAN: Did you complete high school?

MR. HOOD: I finished 11th grade.

COMMISSIONER FREEMAN: You then have completed 11 years of school?

MR. HOOD: Yes.

COMMISSIONER FREEMAN: Have you taken tests to interpret the Mississippi constitution?

MR. HOOD: Myself?

COMMISSIONER FREEMAN: Yes; you.

MR. HOOD: No.

COMMISSIONER FREEMAN: You have never tried to interpret it?

MR. HOOD: No; I can interpret it.

COMMISSIONER FREEMAN: Will you explain for us how you select the questions that are given to persons who make application?

MR. HOOD: The State law prescribes the questions on the application blanks.

COMMISSIONER FREEMAN: Will you explain for us how you select the sections?

MR. HOOD: The section?

COMMISSIONER FREEMAN: That you give——

MR. HOOD: I have my section of the constitution typed on a 3 by 5 card. Whoever comes in gets the next section. If you would come in, if it is 100, you get 100. The next person will get 101.

COMMISSIONER FREEMAN: Is that the way you have administered the tests for the last 4 years?

MR. HOOD: That's right. Ever since I've been in there.

COMMISSIONER FREEMAN: How many sections of the constitution of the State of Mississippi are there?

MR. HOOD: If I remember correctly, there is 285.

COMMISSIONER FREEMAN: 285. Which would mean that you would start at section 1 and the next person would get section 2?

MR. HOOD: Yes.

COMMISSIONER FREEMAN: And on through the first 285?

MR. HOOD: Right on down. I put the—like if you get 100, that would go over to the back.

COMMISSIONER FREEMAN: Well, then, if only 16 Negroes have made application to take the test, then no one of them should have the same section; is that correct?

MR. HOOD::   That's right.

COMMISSIONER FREEMAN: And have they all been given different sections?

MR. HOOD: To the best of my ability, yes, sir.

COMMISSIONER FREEMAN: Have you ever made any distinction between a hard section and what is called an easy section, or do you believe that one section is easier than the other?

MR. HOOD: Well, I couldn't say that one section is easier than the other, but I don't make any distinction. I try to give them all as they come in there.

COMMISSIONER FREEMAN: Have you selected the sections fairly?

MR. HOOD: To the best of my ability. I—just like I told you that I selected them: They're all typed and they're all in the box.

COMMISSIONER FREEMAN: And they're all in ascending order, beginning with section 1?

MR. HOOD: Right. If some of my clerks don't go in there and mix them up, they're right in rotation. Yes.

COMMISSIONER FREEMAN: But the instructions are that the first person gets the first section, the next person gets section 2?

MR. HOOD: It is the next section.

MR. BRIDGES: It is in rotation. It is set up from 1 to 285.

COMMISSIONER FREEMAN: Thank you.

MR. HOOD: Whoever comes in, I give them the next section. That one get 100, the next person get 101.

CHAIRMAN HANNAH: Dean Griswold?

COMMISSIONER GRISWOLD: Mr. Hood—

MR. HOOD: Yes, sir.

COMMISSIONER GRISWOLD: I hand you a copy of section 182 of the Mississippi constitution.

Would you please make a reasonable interpretation of section 182 for the Commission? (Pause.)

MR. HOOD: You say 182?

COMMISSIONER GRISWOLD: Yes.

MR. HOOD: I'm sorry, sir. I've been reading 183.

(Pause.)

MR. HOOD: Well, it means that the power to tax corporations, their property, shall never be surrendered or abridged by any contract. And——

COMMISSIONER GRISWOLD: I didn't ask you to read it, Mr. Hood. I asked you to interpret it.

MR. BRIDGES: (Aside to Mr. Hood.)

COMMISSIONER GRISWOLD: Mr. Chairman, I think it should be the witness' interpretation; not his counsel's.

MR. BRIDGES: If you please, gentlemen, the conference between the witness and his attorney had nothing to do with the question. It was a question whether he was to answer it or not.

MR. HOOD: Which I will not.

MR. BRIDGES: Which he will not.

COMMISSIONER GRISWOLD: You decline to interpret section 182?

MR. HOOD: On pressure being put on me before a Committee like this.

COMMISSIONER GRISWOLD: On the ground it may incriminate you?

MR. HOOD: That's right.

COMMISSIONER GRISWOLD: You decline to interpret section 182 on the ground that to do so would incriminate you? Because if that is your ground, of course it is a valid one.

MR. HOOD: That's right.

CHAIRMAN HANNAH: Any further questions? Dean Griswold, do you have any further questions?

COMMISSIONER GRISWOLD: No.

I find it a little hard to see how citizens of Mississippi are expected to interpret the section if the registrar is unable to do so and he is the person who grades the interpretation which is made by a citizen of Mississippi.

I find his refusal to interpret it rather surprising.

4

Atlantic City

As Bob Moses told his Stanford audience in April 1964, COFO realized that it was necessary to break the power of Mississippi's Democratic Party if segregation were to be overcome. The state party, despite its complete domination of the electoral process for almost a century, was in fact vulnerable, he argued. This was because the state party had consistently defied the rules of the national Democratic Party. Starting in 1948, when South Carolina Governor Strom Thurmond led a walkout from the national convention over the party's adoption of a civil rights plank in its platform, Mississippi Democrats had refused to support the party's presidential nominees. In 1960, true to form, the state party refused to support the Kennedy-Johnson ticket and instead urged white Mississippians to support a slate of unpledged electors. Then, as in 1948, their hope was that the election would be so close that the state's unpledged electors in the Electoral College would hold the balance of power. As in 1948, the hope proved unfounded. But, in a close race, the state party clearly posed a danger to the national party's ticket.

It was this pattern of defiance Moses planned to exploit. COFO would organize a new, integrated Freedom Democratic Party (MFDP) pledged to support the national ticket. It would elect delegates to the national convention in Atlantic City and there challenge the seating of the "regular" state delegation before the Credentials Committee. To make this plan work, Moses and his colleagues would need support from state parties in the North. And so COFO lobbied sympathetic Democrats to sponsor resolutions at their state conventions calling upon the national party to refuse to seat the regular Mississippi delegation. Several important state parties did just that. Below are the texts of the resolutions adopted by Minnesota, New York, and Wisconsin Democrats in the summer of 1964.

MINNESOTA STATE DEMOCRATIC FARMER-LABOR CONVENTION

Whereas:

1. The traditional Democratic Party of Mississippi is a totally segregated party which does not permit hundreds of thousands of Negro citizens in Mississippi to vote or otherwise participate in its affairs.
2. The traditional Democratic Party of Mississippi did not support the 1960 platform or candidates of the National Democratic Party and now proclaims that it is not a part of the National Democratic Party.
3. A Freedom Democratic Party is being established in Mississippi which is open to all citizens regardless of race and is committed to support the national platform and candidates.
4. The Freedom Democratic Party is seeking to seat its delegates to the 1964 Democratic National Convention in place of the delegates from the traditional Democratic Party of Mississippi.
5. Minnesota welcomes this opportunity to demonstrate its devotion to justice and equal rights for all citizens regardless of race, creed, color, or national origin.

Therefore, be it resolved that this Convention instructs the Minnesota delegation to the forthcoming Democratic National Convention:

1. To take all appropriate action to prevent the seating of the delegates from the traditional Democratic Party of Mississippi.
2. To consider the request to seat the delegates of the Freedom Democratic Party with sympathy and in the light of all the facts that will be presented to the Credentials Committee of the Democratic National Convention.
3. To follow the same policy if the credentials of any other State delegation are challenged on the grounds on which the Mississippi delegation will be challenged.

Be it further resolved that copies of this resolution shall be sent to the members of the Democratic National Committee, its Chairman, and to the Chairman of each State Democratic Party.

(This resolution was passed unanimously by the Democratic Farmer-Labor Party, meeting in convention June 27, 1964, at the St. Paul Hotel, St. Paul, Minnesota.)

NEW YORK STATE DEMOCRATIC COMMITTEE

As Democrats and as members of the National Democratic Party, we believe that the national convention, the governing body of the Democratic Party, should consist only of delegates devoted to the principles and objectives of the Party and who are duly elected by members of the Party.

Whereas, the present Democratic Party of some states publicly stated that they are independent of the National Democratic Party and that they do not support the policies and platform of the National Democratic Party or the Party itself; and that they oppose the principles, candidates, and objectives of the National Party; and,

Whereas, the present Democratic Party in certain states has systematically prevented Democrats, who happen to be Negroes, from voting in the Party primaries and from electing delegates to the Democratic National Convention and, therefore, has no properly elected delegates,

Therefore, be it resolved, that the Credentials Committee of the New York State Delegation at the Democratic National Convention shall exercise every effort to make certain that only those delegates who are pledged to the principles, and objectives of the National Democratic Party as expressed in the Party platform be seated as representing their state Party.

(This resolution was passed by the New York State Democratic Committee on June 15, 1964.)

WISCONSIN STATE DEMOCRATIC CONVENTION

Whereas, the Democratic Party of Wisconsin is firmly committed to the principle of one-man one-vote; and

Whereas, the Democratic party of this state is committed thru its platforms and its candidates to actively strive for legislation that will ensure equality under the law for all citizens; and,

Whereas, in certain states such as Mississippi delegates are selected by a non-representative white minority; and,

Whereas the official Democratic Party in certain states has not supported the national ticket or the national platform particularly in regard to civil rights;

Therefore, be it resolved that the Wisconsin delegation to the Democratic National Convention be urged to oppose the accrediting of those state delegations that are not loyal to the basic civil rights principles of the Democratic national platform; and be it further resolved that the Wisconsin delegation to the Democratic National Convention be urged to support the accreditation of the "Freedom Delegation" as an expression of our support for the principle of one-man one-vote, and to encourage those who are working for voter registration of a disenfranchised minority.

(This resolution was passed unanimously by voice vote at the Wisconsin State Democratic Convention, Milwaukee, Wisconsin, June 20, 1964.)

COFO PAMPHLET (UNTITLED) DETAILING PRO-GOLDWATER POSITIONS OF "REGULAR" MISSISSIPPI DEMOCRATS

As the slow work of organizing the Mississippi Freedom Democratic Party proceeded, "regular" Democrats played into COFO's hand by proclaiming their intention to support Republican Barry Goldwater, a "true conservative," who had voted against the Civil Rights Act of 1964. COFO made sure that Democrats elsewhere learned of this latest gesture of defiance for national party rules. Below are excerpts from a COFO pamphlet sent to its supporters in other states.

The following quotations give some idea of the current thinking of some of the major political figures in Mississippi, as well as some of the presidential electors. The system of unpledged electors may well be paving the way toward a "Democrats for Goldwater" movement:

JACKSON MAYOR ALLEN THOMPSON (QUOTED IN THE *JACKSON CLARION-LEDGER,* JULY 17, 1964)

Jackson Mayor Allen Thompson Thursday voted his approval of Republican presidential nominee Barry Goldwater, but affirmed continuing support of Alabama Gov. George Wallace. Thompson . . . said

Mississippi "has a golden opportunity with Goldwater, because he is a man who thinks like we do."

The mayor said he felt Goldwater could carry Mississippi "and possibly one or two other states without the support of Wallace," but "if Wallace decides to give everything he's got to Goldwater the South will have a chance in November. We'll have a chance to have somebody not afraid of pressure groups."

Thompson said he felt Goldwater was unafraid of "pressure groups or liberals" because he told the Negro vote "we don't want you, or care about you."

The South, Thompson said, will be "wooed" by the Democrats this summer. There will be quite a change in the attitudes of the Democratic Party, he said. "You talk about a hot summer—it's going to be a long hot summer for the National Democratic Party."

Presidential Elector Frank E. Shanahan, State Rep. from Warren County, said he had offered to aid in a "Democrats for Goldwater" movement if it promoted the Arizona Conservative in his presidential bid and not just the Republican Party. "You've got a lot of local (Democratic) office holders in Mississippi who are going to vote for Goldwater," Shanahan said, and contended many would join a "Democrats for Goldwater" organization if the National Republican Party would promote such a group (*Jackson Daily News*, July 17, 1964).

State Legislators Hayden Campbell and Russell Davis from Hinds County announced their support for Barry Goldwater, Republican presidential candidate, saying that Goldwater was the last hope for conservative government. Campbell said, "We, in America, have just witnessed the founding of a new political party. . . . We have seen the birth of a new party in San Francisco. It is now the Conservative Party. . . . [We] in the South cannot be a part of splitting the Conservative vote and giving the election to Lyndon Johnson. It is a time for all true conservative Southerners to come out openly in every way and support the leader of our new national party. . . ."

WASHINGTON POST EDITORIAL CRITICIZING COFO

By early summer, it was clear that COFO's plan to challenge the seating of Mississippi's "regular" Democrats was gathering enough support to produce a very bitter struggle in the Credentials Committee. This was not how

Source: *Washington Post* editorial criticizing COFO, June 24, 1964. Reprinted by permission of the *Washington Post*.

President Lyndon Johnson envisioned the convention proceeding. He wanted to secure a mandate for his Great Society. He wanted the focus to be on how he had picked up the mantle of John Kennedy and had led the party and the country forward. The keynote was to be unity, not a bruising battle over the Mississippi delegation.

Johnson made no public remarks about COFO or the Mississippi Freedom Democratic Party, but a *Washington Post* editorial likely captured his views. Moses and his fellow activists, the *Post* argued, were wrong to attempt to force the administration's hand. The passage of the Civil Rights Act of 1964 that summer was proof that the administration and the Congress were doing everything they should. COFO should not endanger its idealistic volunteers. It should not provoke further white resistance.

THE *WASHINGTON POST,* JUNE 24, 1964, ON THE FREEDOM SUMMER

The young project workers will be acting in the most lawful way and for the worthiest of purposes. They are entitled to the protection of the law. The primary duty to provide that protection rests with the peace officers of Mississippi. If violence comes, it will not be done by the students but by the racists they encounter. . . .

But having said this, one must add that the young civil rights workers . . . have an obligation to consider deeply all the likely fruits of their action. The possibility of violence, despite best efforts of responsible Mississippians, remains enormous and indeed, as now seems terribly probable, has already begun. The young project workers cannot claim they do not foresee the response their presence may provoke. . . . Some of the adult organizers not only expect mayhem but also see as one purpose of the operation— perhaps the major purpose—the compelling of Federal intervention in force, by marshalls or troops, to quench the expected violence.

. . . Moreover, and more important, both the adult organizers and the young participants . . . must know that in fixing on these means to carry on this fight in this way and in this time and place, they are not necessarily acting in response to a national consensus nor embracing a tactic that has been determined by democratic choice, as right and necessary. Nor can they assume that it is proper, wise or justifiable to force Federal action as they propose. We cannot feel that the Federal Government now shows itself so apathetic, stupid, hypocritical or cowardly that it must be constrained to act by the threat of piling martyrs' corpses on its doorstep. The President, the Department of Justice and its Civil Rights Division and even the Congress, on the eve of enacting America's most encompassing civil rights law, have not demonstrated such feebleness of purpose and such pusillanimity that their course of action must now be mortgaged to the decisions of a thousand collegians and a handful of ruthlessly righteous organization leaders.

PRESIDENT JOHNSON SUGGESTS A DEAL: THE CREDENTIALS COMMITTEE'S BATTLE—TEXT OF FANNIE LOU HAMER'S TESTIMONY

Moses' hopes and the *Post's* concerns were both realized as the summer's work in Mississippi proceeded. The disappearance of the three volunteers, Goodwyn, Cheney, and Schwerner, immediately focused national media attention on Mississippi. Every night Americans turned on their televisions to see crowds of abusive whites seeking to block African Americans as they tried to exercise their right to vote. They saw the earnest faces of black children flocking to the Freedom Schools. They heard COFO supporters singing "We Shall Overcome." The campaign captured, and captivated, the national imagination. This, plus the growing support among state parties for the MFDP's challenge, forced President Johnson's hand.

Hoping to head off a Credentials battle, he offered a deal. Under its terms, the MFDP would get two "at large" seats in the Convention and the party would adopt a rule barring any "lily white" delegation in future conventions. For the 1964 convention, the "regular" Mississippi delegation would remain the official state representatives and would cast Mississippi's votes.

To Johnson this seemed more than fair. The MDFP would gain official recognition, albeit not as the official Democratic Party in Mississippi. The "regulars" would be banned from future conventions, thus opening the way for the MDFP to become the nucleus of a new state party. This, to Johnson's way of thinking, gave the MDFP the substance of its major demands. The seating of the regular delegation was not an attempt to placate white Mississippians. Johnson had no illusions about carrying the state in the fall. It was an attempt to placate other southern Democrats.

Historians have treated Johnson's offer harshly. Their sympathies are with the MDFP. Yet, Johnson did think his offer was one the MDFP could and should accept. He had spent his life making political deals. No one side got everything it wanted. That was the way politics worked. It was not the way politics worked in Mississippi, however. There, the all-white Democratic

Source: Testimony of Fanny Lou Hamer before the Credentials Committee, July 22, 1964.

establishment had gotten everything it wanted. There, compromise was a dirty word. The MDFP delegates had not practiced a politics of wheeling and dealing or of compromise. They had risked their lives to secure rights guaranteed them by the Constitution. By any rule of justice, what they wanted was fair. Further, they saw no reason to conciliate white southerners. Years of struggle had instead taught them the necessity of confrontation.

Unsurprisingly they decided to confront President Johnson. They brought their challenge to the Credentials Committee. The television networks decided to carry the hearings live. MFDP delegate Fannie Lou Hamer transfixed that national audience. Below is the text of her remarks.

FANNY LOU HAMER, "TESTIMONY," JULY 22, 1964

Mr. Chairman, and the Credentials Committee, my name is Mrs. Fanny Lou Hamer, and I live at 626 East Lafayette Street, Ruleville, Mississippi, Sunflower Country, the home of Senator James O. Eastland, and Senator Stennis.

It was the 31st of August in 1962 that 18 of us traveled 26 miles to the country courthouse in Indianola to try to register to try to become first-class citizens.

We was met in Indianola by Mississippi men, Highway Patrolmens and they only allowed two of us in to take the literacy test at the time. After we had taken this test and started back to Ruleville, we was held up by the City Police and the State Highway Patrolmen and carried back to Indianola where the bus driver was charged that day with driving a bus the wrong color.

After we paid the fine among us, we continued on to Ruleville, and Reverend Jeff Sunny carried me four miles in the rural area where I had worked as a timekeeper and sharecropper for 18 years. I was met there by my children, who told me that the plantation owner was angry because I had gone down to try to register.

After they told me, my husband came, and said that the plantation owner was raising cain because I had tried to register, and before he quit talking the plantation owner came, and said, "Fanny Lou, do you know—did Pap tell you what I said?"

And I said, "yes, sir."

He said, "I mean that," he said, "If you don't go down and withdraw your registration, you will have to leave," . . . "Then if you go down and withdraw," he said, "You will—you might have to go because we are not ready for that in Mississippi."

And I addressed him and told him and said, "I didn't try to register for you. I tried to register for myself."

I had to leave that same night.

On the 10th of September 1962, 16 bullets was fired into the home of Mr. and Mrs. Robert Tucker for me. That same night two girls were shot in Ruleville, Mississippi. Also Mr. Joe McDonald's house was shot in.

And in June the 9th, 1963, I had attended a voter registration workshop, was returning back to Mississippi. Ten of us was traveling by the Continental Trailway bus. When we got to Winona, Mississippi, which is in Montgomery County, four of the people got off to use the washroom, and two of the people—to use the restaurant—two of the people wanted to use the washroom.

The four people that had gone in to use the restaurant was ordered out. During this time I was on the bus. But when I looked through the window and saw they had rushed out I got off the bus to see what had happened, and one of the ladies said, "It was a State Highway Patrolman and a Chief of Police ordered us out."

I got back on the bus and one of the persons had used the washroom got back on the bus, too.

As soon as I was seated on the bus, I saw when they began to get the four people in a highway patrolman's car, I stepped off of the bus to see what was happening and somebody screamed from the car that the four workers was in and said, "Get that one there," and when I went to get in the car, when the man told me I was under arrest, he kicked me.

I was carried to the county jail, and put in the booking room. They left some of the people in the booking room and began to place us in cells. I was placed in a cell with a young woman called Miss Ivesta Simpson. After I was placed in the cell I began to hear the sound of kicks and horrible screams, and I could hear somebody say, "Can you say, yes, sir, nigger? Can you say yes, sir?"

And they would say other horrible names.

She would say, "Yes, I can say yes, sir."

"So say it."

She says, " I don't know you well enough."

They beat her, I don't know how long, and after a while she began to pray, and asked God to have mercy on those people.

And it wasn't too long before three white men came to my cell. One of these men was a State Highway Patrolman and he asked me where I was from, and I told him Ruleville, he said, "We are going to check this."

And they left my cell and it wasn't too long before they came back. He said, "You are from Ruleville all right," and he used a curse word, and he said, "We are going to make you wish you was dead."

I was carried out of that cell into another cell where they had two Negro prisoners. The State Highway Patrolmen ordered the first Negro to take the blackjack.

The first Negro prisoner ordered me, by orders from the State Highway Patrolman for me, to lay down on a bunk bed on my face, and I laid on my face.

The first Negro prisoner began to beat, and I was beat by the first Negro until he was exhausted, and I was holding my hands behind me at that time on my left side because I suffered from polio when I was six years old.

After the first Negro had beat until he was exhausted the State Highway Patrolman ordered the second Negro to take the blackjack.

The second Negro began to beat and I began to work my feet, and the State Highway Patrolman ordered the first Negro who had beat me to sit upon my feet to keep me from working my feet. I began to scream and one white man got up and began to beat my head and told me to hush.

One white man—since my dress had worked up high, walked over and pulled my dress down and he pulled my dress back, back up.

I was in jail when Medgar Evers was murdered.

All of this is on account of us wanting to register, to become first-class citizens, and if the freedom Democratic Party is not seated now, I question America, is this America, the land of the free and the home of the brave where we have to sleep with our telephones off of the hooks because our lives be threatened daily because we want to live as decent human beings, in America?

Thank You.

PRESIDENT JOHNSON PREEMPTS THE HEARINGS

The national television audience did not hear the last portion of Mrs. Hamer's testimony live. President Johnson called a press conference. Television networks obligingly cut away from the hearing. But the power of her words, coming at the end of a summer of sacrifice in Mississippi, threatened to overturn the president's control of his own convention. He renewed his offer to the MFDP, this time sending future Vice President Hubert Humphrey. Senator Humphrey, while mayor of Minneapolis, had introduced the civil rights resolution in the 1948 convention which had provoked Strom Thurmond's walkout. He had since then proved a staunch advocate of civil rights. Surely, the MFDP would listen to him. Or, if not, the president was prepared to pressure their supporters. The United Auto Workers Union had supplied financial help to COFO. Its president, Walter Reuther, urged the dissidents to accept the president's offer. So did a number of others who had contributed to the movement.

Moses and his colleagues were outraged. Once again the white power structure had betrayed them.

Epilogue

Moses' plan, outlined in his April 24 speech at Stanford, succeeded brilliantly. A thousand volunteers, most of them white students from affluent backgrounds, had flooded the state and had generated unprecedented national attention. That, in turn, had led to irresistible demands for change in Mississippi and the rest of the South. Council of Federated Organizations (COFO) could justly claim much of the credit for the Voting Rights Act of 1965, a measure that transformed politics in Mississippi and everywhere else in the South. Under its terms, federal courts could appoint registrars in areas where blacks had experienced difficulty in registering. Soon large areas of the South, including all of Mississippi, had federal registrars. No longer could white registrars keep blacks from exercising their right to vote. With black voters came black officeholders, including black sheriffs. The "way of life" so dear to white Mississippians changed forever.

Part of that change was the birth of a new, integrated state Democratic party, a direct legacy of the MFDP. White Mississippians unwilling to support such a party overcame the voting habits of generations and learned to vote Republican. Trent Lott, for example, chose to run for the House of Representatives in 1972 as a Republican, even though he had been the legislative assistant of the longtime Democratic incumbent who was retiring. But, while Mississippi Republicans like Lott might vote against affirmative action or against making Dr. Martin Luther King's birthday a national holiday or toast Strom Thrumond on his birthday with the wish that he had been elected president in 1948, they entertained no illusions that the state would ever return to segregation. The "whites-only" primary was a thing of the past. Celebrations of Thurmond's 1948 campaign were excercises in nostalgia, very expensive exercises in Lott's case as he had to resign as Senate Majority Leader.

Victory, however, tasted like defeat to many COFO field-workers. They had ended segregation in "the most southern place on earth." They had crushed the party of Theodore Bilbo and Ross Barnett. They had pushed Lyndon Johnson out of the spotlight at his own national convention. Yet these architects of a nonviolent social revolution abandoned the strategies that had worked so brilliantly, convinced that it was not possible to "work within the system."

Equally important was the fact that the very people who demonstrated to the country at large that whites and blacks could cooperate in voter registration, in freedom schools, in free clinics, and in a dozen other activities concluded that blacks and whites could not, indeed should not, work together. Student Nonviolent Coordinating Committee (SNCC), despite Bob Moses' protestations, adopted "Black Power" as its new agenda. So did the Congress of Racial Equality (CORE).

Why turn away from the strategies that had worked so well? One way of pondering this question involves taking another look at Moses' Stanford speech. After four years in Mississippi, years of arrests and beatings and of narrowly escaping death, Moses and other SNCC and CORE field-workers were prepared to give the "system" a last chance. They would once again put their lives on the line. They would continue to endure the taunts and the threats. They would put in the long days and longer nights. They would do it for virtually no pay. President Johnson might well have smiled at the irony of COFO staffers giving him and the system one last chance. His presidency was the best thing that had ever happened for the cause of civil rights, he might have said. He had already done more than any of his predecessors since Lincoln. And he was prepared to do still more. Who, after all, was Bob Moses to give him a last chance? This was the question raised in the *Post* editorial. The Civil Rights Act of 1964 was a watershed. Further, it was proof that the system was working.

If Johnson were the consummate insider, the politician who knew every string to pull, Moses was the consummate outsider. He did not wheel and deal. He persuaded people by strength of character and force of logic. Unlike the president, he did not seek attention. He did not seek to claim credit for anything achieved under his leadership. He invariably credited the people of Mississippi and his coworkers.

Moses was like the president in one crucial respect, however. He understood something about power. He understood how to mobilize a small army of volunteers, how to organize them, how to get national attention, how to bring pressure to bear on the key weaknesses in the Mississippi power structure. He understood how to bring pressure on Johnson himself. And he was every bit as determined as the president. The irony was that both men wanted to advance the cause of civil rights. Both wanted an end to the "Old South." Neither could have succeeded without the other. Johnson needed the thousands of volunteers, black and white, whose struggles dramatized the necessity of civil rights legislation. And the movement needed Johnson, the wily politician who could put together the bipartisan coalition to defeat a filibuster by southern Democrats. But neither Johnson nor the activists in the field could fully appreciate their interdependence at the time. Hence the disastrous confrontation in Atlantic City.

An even more painful irony was the repudiation of black and white cooperation by key participants in the movement. At Stanford Moses had outlined the problem. Most of his fellow field-workers did not want whites coming into the state. The volunteers would try to take over. They would assume they knew what was best, even though they had no practical experience. They would be arrogant and condescending. And the media would give them all the credit for whatever good came out of the summer. All of this could well be so, Moses had responded. But they *needed* white volunteers. They needed to fix the attention of the nation on Mississippi. The media would follow the activities of the whites. *That* was the idea. Further, there was a core principle at stake.

SNCC, CORE, and COFO—all were working to create a multiracial society. If they were going to succeed, they would have to succeed within their own ranks. The summer project had to be multiracial. It had to show that blacks and whites could cooperate, even though there would inevitably be friction. This argument, and the fact that ordinary black Mississippians welcomed the idea of white volunteers, carried the day. But only the day. The dissenters went along, since such was Moses' prestige. But many remained unpersuaded.

The events of the summer proved the efficacy of multiracial efforts. But the psychic costs, as several of the accounts here reveal, were high. Whites did act as though they knew best. They did condescend. Blacks sometimes acted as though only they were truly committed to the struggle. They often made it clear they resented white volunteers. Both groups, that is, proved all too human. The question became: Which lesson should one draw? Was it Moses', namely that, whatever the frictions and problems, interracial cooperation was both vital and possible? Or was it that whites always sought to dominate, that blacks had to make civil rights a question of black liberation from whites?

Complicating the efforts to draw the proper lessons from experience were two factors that made it virtually impossible for the field-workers and the volunteers to gain a clear perspective on what they had actually achieved. One was their youth. SNCC workers were mostly in their twenties. If anything, the volunteers were even younger. The other, and more telling factor was that working in

Mississippi was like living in a war zone. There was constant danger, constant fear. The toll of living in such conditions was enormous. It is no wonder that people embroiled in such a struggle were in no condition to step back mentally and survey the broader perspective of what they had accomplished. They were simply too caught up in the moment, and the moment was simply too traumatic.

In 1966 Stokely Carmichael, the incoming president of SNCC and one of five project directors during the Freedom Summer, attempted to sort all of this out in a position paper, "The Basis of Black Power," excerpted below. Carmichael conceded that whites "had an important role in the movement. In the case of Mississippi, their role was very key in that they helped give blacks the right to organize. . . . "But, Carmichael continued, "that role is now over, and it should be." In spelling out the reasons why he and others in SNCC thought this was so, he gave voice to the same objections raised against Moses in the winter of 1963–64.

Moses (a name not mentioned in "The Basis of Black Power") clearly had been right about Mississippi. His plan had worked. But that did not mean that those who had objected had been wrong. They had had the right idea, Carmichael asserted. Whites would inevitably dominate any organization in which they participated. In taking this stand, advocates of Black Power undercut the moral dimension of the Civil Rights movement. It was, as Martin Luther King, Jr. tirelessly maintained, a moral crusade, a call to Americans to live up to their own ideals of equal rights and equal opportunity. Black Power transformed the movement into a campaign for black liberation. In the process, African Americans became another interest group, like senior citizens.

King repudiated Black Power. But the movement split, and many white activists turned to the emerging antiwar and women's liberation movements as outlets for their idealism. SNCC, unable to raise money and drawn into endless ideological arguments with both mainstream organizations like the NAACP and other radical groups like the Black Panthers, became ineffectual. Its glory days of organizing were suddenly behind it. CORE too slipped quickly into ineffectualness.

Carmichael's is the last voice in this book, an unintentionally tragic voice. Yet he cannot have the last word. This is a story of triumph as well as tragedy. A small army of heroic idealists and believers in the possibility of genuine interracial cooperation wrought wonders. With little in the way of resources beyond courage, resilience, and intelligence, they forever destroyed Theodore Bilbo's principality of "peckerwoods." They ended whites-only politics in Mississippi, in the South, and in the nation.

SNCC POSITION PAPER: "THE BASIS OF BLACK POWER"

The myth that the Negro is somehow incapable of liberating himself, is lazy, etc., came out of the American experience. In the books that children read, whites are always "good" (good symbols are white), blacks are "evil" or seen as savages in movies, their language is referred to as a "dialect," and black people in this country are supposedly descended from savages.

Any white person who comes into the movement has these concepts in his mind about black people, if only subconsciously. He cannot escape them because the whole society has geared his subconscious in that direction.

Miss America coming from Mississippi has a chance to represent all of America, but a black person from either Mississippi or New York will never represent America. Thus the white people coming into the movement cannot relate to the black experience, cannot relate to the word "black," cannot relate to the "nitty gritty," cannot relate to the experience that brought such a word into existence, cannot relate to chitterlings, hog's head cheese, pig feet, ham hocks, and cannot relate to slavery, because these things are not a part of their experience. They also cannot relate to the black religious experience, nor to the black church, unless, of course, this church has taken on white manifestations.

WHITE POWER

Negroes in this country have never been allowed to organize themselves because of white interference. As a result of this, the stereotype has been reinforced that blacks cannot organize themselves. The white psychology that blacks have to be watched, also reinforces this stereotype. Blacks, in fact, feel intimidated by the presence of whites, because of their knowledge of the power that whites have over their lives. One white person can come into a meeting of black people and change the complexion of that meeting. . . . People would immediately start talking about "brotherhood," "love," etc.; race would not be discussed.

If people must express themselves freely, there has to be a climate in which they can do this. If blacks feel intimidated by whites, then they are not liable to vent the rage that they feel about whites in the

Source: Student Nonviolent Coordinating Committee Position Paper: The Basis of Black Power (1966).

presence of whites—especially not the black people whom we are trying to organize, i.e., the broad masses of black people. A climate has to
be created whereby blacks can express themselves. The reasons that
whites must be excluded is not that one is antiwhite, but because the
effects that one is trying to achieve cannot succeed because whites
have an intimidating effect. Ofttimes, the intimidating effect is in
direct proportion to the amount of degradation that black people have
suffered at the hands of white people.

ROLES OF WHITES AND BLACKS

It must be offered that white people who desire change in this country
should go where that problem (racism) is most manifest. The problem
is not in the black community. The white people should go into white
communities where the whites have created power for the express
purpose of denying blacks human dignity and self-determination.
Whites who come into the black community with ideas of change
seem to want to absolve the power structure of its responsibility for
what it is doing, and saying that change can only come through black
unity, which is the worst kind of paternalism. This is not to say that
whites have not had an important role in the movement. In the case
of Mississippi, their role was very key in that they helped give blacks
the right to organize, but that role is now over, and it should be.

People now have the right to picket, the right to give out leaflets,
the right to vote, the right to demonstrate, the right to print.

These things which revolve around the right to organize have been
accomplished mainly because of the entrance of white people into Mississippi, in the summer of 1964. Since these goals have now been
accomplished, whites' role in the movement has now ended. What does
it mean if black people, once having the right to organize, are not allowed
to organize themselves? It means that blacks' ideas about inferiority are
being reinforced. Shouldn't people be able to organize themselves?
Blacks should be given this right. Further, white participation means in
the eyes of the black community that whites are the "brains" behind the
movement, and that blacks cannot function without whites. This only
serves to perpetuate existing attitudes within the existing society, i.e.,
blacks are "dumb," "unable to take care of business," etc. Whites are
"smart," the "brains" behind the whole thing. . . .

In the beginning of the movement, we had fallen into a trap
whereby we thought that our problems revolved around the right to
eat at certain lunch counters or the right to vote, or to organize our
communities. We have seen, however, that the problem is much
deeper. The problem of this country, as we had seen it, concerned all

blacks and all whites and therefore if decisions were left to the young people, then solutions would be arrived at. But this negates the history of black people and whites. We have dealt stringently with the problem of "Uncle Tom," but we have not yet gotten around to Simon Legree. We must ask ourselves, who is the real villain—Uncle Tom or Simon Legree? Everybody knows Uncle Tom, but who knows Simon Legree? So what we have now in SNCC is a closed society, a clique. Black people cannot relate to SNCC because of its unrealistic, non-racial atmosphere; denying their experience of America as a racist society. In contrast, the Southern Christian Leadership Conference of Martin Luther King, Jr., has a staff that at least maintains a black facade. The front office is virtually all black, but nobody accuses SCLC of being racist.

If we are to proceed toward true liberation, we must cut ourselves off from white people. We must form our own institutions, credit unions, co-ops, political parties, write our own histories. . . .

These facts do not mean that whites cannot help. They can participate on a voluntary basis. We can contract work out to them, but in no way can they participate on a policy-making level.

BLACK SELF-DETERMINATION

The charge may be made that we are "racists," but whites who are sensitive to our problems will realize that we must determine our own destiny.

In an attempt to find a solution to our dilemma, we propose that our organization (SNCC) should be black-staffed, black-controlled, and black-financed. We do not want to fall into a similar dilemma that other civil rights organizations have fallen into. If we continue to rely upon white financial support we will find ourselves entwined in the tentacles of the white power complex that controls this country. It is also important that a black organization (devoid of cultism) be projected to our people so that it can be demonstrated that such organizations are viable. . . .

Too long have we allowed white people to interpret the importance and meaning of the cultural aspects of our society. We have allowed them to tell us what was good about our Afro-American music, art, and literature. How many black critics do we have on the "jazz" scene? How can a white person who is not part of the black psyche (except in the oppressor's role) interpret the meaning of the blues to us who are manifestations of the songs themselves?

It must be pointed out that on whatever level of contact blacks and whites come together, that meeting or confrontation is not on the level of the blacks but always on the level of the whites. This only means that our everyday contact with whites is a reinforcement of the myth of white supremacy. Whites are the ones who must try to raise themselves to our humanistic level. We are not, after all, the ones who are responsible for a genocidal war in Vietnam; we are not the ones who are responsible for neocolonialism in Africa and Latin America; we are not the ones who held a people in animalistic bondage over 400 years. We reject the American dream as defined by white people and must work to construct an American reality defined by Afro-Americans. . . .

Index